A THEORY OF UNDERSTANDING

Clearly written, this book makes a very useful contribution on an important issue; whilst the general issue of explanation has been widely discussed, Chart's approach is fresh and developed in a creative way.

Professor Peter Lipton, Department of History & Philosophy of Science, University of Cambridge, UK

A Theory of Understanding provides a philosophical and psychologically grounded account of understanding. The philosophical tradition has been largely concerned with explanation, seeking to provide characteristics by which an explanation can be distinguished from other types of utterances. Chart argues that this is the wrong approach and proposes that anything which improves understanding should be regarded as an explanation. His approach requires a theory of understanding; Chart proposes a new theory claiming that we understand something when we can predict what it will do under a wide range of possible conditions, and that explanations are statements that improve our understanding.

The theory presented sees understanding as a matter of the possession of mental models, which provide the ability to simulate things and situations. The structure of these mental models is described, and suggestions as to the way they might work, and the sorts of utterances that could improve these models, are presented. Experimental evidence drawn from the cognitive science literature shows that this substantive psychological theory is an accurate description of the mind.

Setting out a new theory of understanding that draws on both the philosophical and cognitive science traditions, this book presents important insights for philosophers of science and mind, epistemology, and cognitive science.

David Chart is a researcher in the philosophy of science and medicine at King's College, London, UK.

ASHGATE NEW CRITICAL THINKING IN PHILOSOPHY

The *Ashgate New Critical Thinking in Philosophy* series aims to bring high quality research monograph publishing back into focus for authors, the international library market, and student, academic and research readers. Headed by an international editorial advisory board of acclaimed scholars from across the philosophical spectrum, this new monograph series presents cutting-edge research from established as well as exciting new authors in the field; spans the breadth of philosophy and related disciplinary and interdisciplinary perspectives; and takes contemporary philosophical research into new directions and debate.

A Theory of Understanding

Philosophical and psychological perspectives

DAVID CHART
King's College London

Ashgate

Aldershot • Burlington USA • Singapore • Sydney

Published by
Ashgate Publishing Ltd
Gower House
Croft Road
Aldershot
Hants GU11 3HR
England

Ashgate Publishing Company
131 Main Street
Burlington, VT 05401-5600 USA

Ashgate website: http://www.ashgate.com

British Library Cataloguing in Publication Data
Chart, David
    A theory of understanding : philosophical and psychological
    perspectives. - (Ashgate new critical thinking in
    philosophy)
    1.Comprehension - Philosophy 2.Explanation 3.Learning,
    Psychology of
    I.Title
    121

Library of Congress Control Number: 00-134437

ISBN 0 7546 1400 X

Printed and bound by Athenaeum Press, Ltd.,
Gateshead, Tyne & Wear.

Contents

Preface

This book aims to set out the basic ideas behind a new research project in the philosophy of science and cognitive psychology. The central claim is that much of our thinking depends on a certain kind of mental model. I believe that these models have applications in many (although not all) parts of philosophy of science, but that their influence is particularly clear in the philosophy of explanation.

My main aim is to explain my concept of mental models, and to distinguish it from other, similar accounts. The second aim is to argue that we can account for the observed features of explanations in terms of mental models, in a way that no competing account can manage. The explanation of explanation depends on the account of mental models, but it is also the main evidence for the theory that I present in this book.

This work is almost entirely constructive. The first chapter is devoted to arguing that there are reasons to be dissatisfied with all the currently available philosophical accounts of explanation, but not to providing a conclusive refutation of any of them. Rather, I argue in the sixth chapter that my account can handle the problem cases without any contortions or epicycles, and that it is therefore a better theory than its competitors. Most of the intervening space is devoted to constructing and explaining my theory, so that Chapter 6 makes sense to the reader.

As I am a philosopher by training and inclination, I have concentrated on the philosophical issues raised by the account. However, issues in other disciplines are very relevant to my project, and I have tried to take them into account. I argue that some computational implementation of my theory is possible, although I do not spend time detailing any particular realisation. Similarly, while I consider some results from cognitive psychology, I do not pretend to have done a comprehensive literature review, nor to have done any original research in that area. I do hope, however, that my results will be of interest to people working in those fields.

Acknowledgements

This book has been a number of years in the making, and discussions with many people have contributed to it.

I should particularly like to thank Peter Lipton, who supervised the PhD dissertation on which this book is founded. His guidance and comments were invaluable, and his willingness to talk about repeated drafts was exemplary.

I would also like to thank the following people for their assistance at various stages: Daniela Bailer-Jones, Louis Caruana, Rachel Cooper, Anandi Hattiangadi, Katherine Hawley, Sam Inglis, Joel Katzav, Martin Kusch, Keiko Saito, Tana Silverland, Neema Sofaer, and Rie Tsutsumi. I apologise to anyone I have forgotten.

I would also like to thank Daniela Bailer-Jones for permission to refer to her unpublished PhD dissertation.

Finally, I would like to thank Sarah Lloyd and Pauline Beavers at Ashgate for helping me through the mysteries of preparing Camera Ready Copy.

For my family

Introduction

Explanations are a vital part of daily life. We often give and receive them, explaining the results of elections, the changes in the weather, or our own behaviour to one another. In the scholarly enterprise they are even more important. While the researcher who discovers important facts will be respected, the scientist who explains them may be in line for a Nobel prize. Those features of the world that we cannot explain are a major focus of research, even if we know a great deal about them.

It is thus not surprising that philosophers have been greatly concerned with the nature of explanation. If we understood what we had to produce in order to explain something, we would understand a lot more about human thought and the process of scholarship. Of course, we need to understand explanation to be sure that the philosophical account we offer really does explain the matter of explanation. The difficulties raised by this self-reference have led many philosophers to try to cut explanation up.

One popular sub-section has been scientific explanation: the sort of explanation used by scientists *qua* scientist. Several accounts have been given, relying on logical deduction, or statistical relevance, or causal links. None of these have proved to be fully satisfactory within science, and all are highly implausible in the wider world.

I believe that the reason for this failure has been a misplaced focus. Instead of concentrating on explanation, we should consider understanding. Once we have an account of understanding it is fairly easy to give an account of explanation: roughly, an explanation is something that increases understanding. Of course, this requires us to give an account of understanding that does not rely on the concept of explanation in any way at all.

What, then, is understanding? It is easiest to get a handle on this by thinking about what is missing when we *don't* understand something. Suppose that I have been using a computer for quite some time, but I don't understand it. I know to press one button, type in my user id and password, then select one of the options. This allows me to read my email. However, I still don't understand the process. This, clearly, means that I don't know *why* I must do these things. That approach is unlikely to get us anywhere, though.

I also don't know what would happen if I did something differently, how to recover if something goes wrong, or what else the computer might do. One or more of the stages through which I go might be completely unnecessary. I am completely unable to say what the computer would do, were I to do something different, or what I should do in order to make it do something different.

I think that this is the heart of understanding. We understand something when we know how it will behave under a wide range of circumstances, when we know which shortcuts can be taken, and which processes are vital. When we understand something fully, we can, in principle, use it to its full effect, and cope with unexpected contingencies. This idea can be explicated without any reference to notions of explanation, or knowing why, and thus provides a firm basis for a theory of understanding.

I think that this idea is best explicated in terms of mental models. These are mental constructs a lot like physical models. If I build a model of an aeroplane, for use in a wind tunnel, I will make sure that the model has the relevant properties of the real thing, so that its behaviour will be relevantly similar to that of the real thing. Mental models work in the same way. Clearly, they do not have mass in the same way as real objects do, but they have some property that corresponds to mass, and that allows the models to simulate the way that massive objects behave.

By building many mental models of the things that we might encounter, we open up the possibility of understanding situations that we have never previously encountered. If we understand, have models of, all the things involved in the situation, then we can, at least in principle, simply put all the pieces together and see what happens, and what would happen.

Given this account of understanding, an account of explanation can be easily built upon it. The account that results turns out to match our actual explanatory practices very closely, better than any of the other accounts that have been given, and also explains why explanations can be such varied things, while still all being called 'explanations'.

This, of course, is merely an introductory sketch of my theory. The rest of this book is devoted to explaining it, in the hope that, by the end, the reader will truly understand understanding. The book only works as a whole, and should be read as such. The first chapter argues that there are good reasons for taking the approach that I do take, but has nothing to say about the approach itself: if you are willing to take it on faith that there are reasons for working this way, this chapter can be skipped without loss.

The second, third, and fourth chapters describe the theory, and defend it against some objections. However, their purpose is primarily expository, and the theory is not fully defended in these sections. The fifth and sixth chapters provide the defence, the fifth from an empirical, the sixth from a philosophical point of view, but they will be incomprehensible unless the earlier chapters are read first. The seventh chapter considers some of the implications of the theory for metaphysics, and thus assumes that you both understand the theory and believe that it might, at least, be right.

Attempts to understand understanding tend to become self-referential. The book has been written to enable the reader to build a good mental model of my theory: if you feel that this has granted you understanding, that is, in itself, further evidence for it.

Chapter 1

Explanation: A Poor Foundation

In the first chapter of this book, I will use three important terms of art. A candidate explanation is anything that is being offered as, perhaps, an explanation. It need not even be verbal, and certainly could be any sort of utterance. These are the things that a theory of explanation will attempt to classify. Potential explanations are candidate explanations that pass the theory's tests: they could be explanatory. Ideally, the only additional requirement is that the potential explanation be true, but this requires that the conditions on potential explanations, together with truth, are sufficient for something to be an actual explanation. Actual explanations, finally, are just what they sound like: candidate explanations which are actually explanatory. I will argue that neither the form nor the content of candidate explanations can provide necessary or sufficient conditions on whether they are potential explanations. Along the way I will consider, and reject as inadequate, various theories of explanation. The final considerations, on the insufficiency of content, will suggest that a theory of understanding might allow us to get around the severe problems, and provide a theory of explanation by derivation.

In this chapter, I will move quickly: the territory is mostly familiar from the literature, and my purpose is merely to highlight those problems for various accounts which point at the solution I favour. My aim is to show that there are no necessary or sufficient conditions on the concept of explanation, and to suggest that the concept of an explanation is not even a family-resemblance concept. Rather, explanations are drawn together by their common purpose — the explanations themselves may look nothing like one another.

A second reason for moving quickly is that these arguments are concerned with clearing the ground for my thesis, not with doing any constructive work. There is a large literature on the subject of explanation, and it is important that I show why I do not think that it is a good basis from which to develop a theory of understanding. Accordingly, this section is important, but it does not form part of the positive argument for my account: should the arguments here fail, the positive arguments will be unaffected. Thus, any reader with absolutely no interest in the philosophical debates over explanation can skip this chapter without missing anything vital.

The Insufficiency of Form

The Hempelian Covering-Law Model

The Hempelian Covering-Law model of explanation was the earliest modern model,[1] and it has had a great influence on the field ever since its presentation. Hempel concentrated on the form of explanations, claiming that possession of a certain form was necessary and sufficient for being a potential explanation. If the potential explanation was also true, then it was also an actual explanation.

There are in fact two important Covering-Law models: the Deductive-Nomological[2] for deterministic explanations, and the Inductive-Statistical,[3] providing for the probabilistic explanation of certain events. Deductive-Nomological explanation is the basic type,[4] and best illustrates the problems with this model that are relevant to my project, so I will concentrate on this type.

A Deductive-Nomological explanation is an argument, with the explanandum[5] as its conclusion. The argument must be deductively valid, and essentially involve a law-like premise. As Hempel says:

> A D-N explanation will have to contain, in its explanans, some general laws that are *required* for the deduction of the explanandum, i.e. whose deletion would make the argument invalid.[6]

If these conditions are fulfilled, then the argument is a potential explanation. If, in addition, the premises are all true, the argument is an actual explanation .

Hempel recognises that the form in which an explanation is given will vary depending on pragmatic factors. However, he believes that it is both necessary and sufficient that there be a covering law form of the candidate explanation if it is to be a real potential explanation. He says:

> [A] nonpragmatic concept of scientific explanation — a concept which is abstracted, as it were, from the pragmatic one, and which does not require relativization with respect to questioning individuals any more than does the

---

[1]   First set out in Hempel and Oppenheim 1948.

[2]   Hempel 1965b, §2. (Deductive-Statistical explanations are really a kind of Deductive-Nomological explanation.)

[3]   Hempel 1965b, §§3.3–3.6.

[4]   Hempel and Oppenheim 1948 is exclusively concerned with Deductive-Nomological explanations, although it notes that statistical explanations have peculiar problems, and Hempel 1965b starts with Deductive-Nomological explanations.

[5]   The explanandum is the thing to be explained: the explanans is the thing doing the explaining.

[6]   Hempel 1965b, p 338, emphasis Hempel's.

concept of mathematical proof. It is this nonpragmatic conception of explanation which the covering-law models are meant to explicate.[7]

He also recognises that the word 'explanation' is used in other contexts, such as 'an explanation of how to bake a cake'.[8] However, he regards these uses as somewhat peripheral, and not the sort of thing which we generally think of as 'explanation'. Thus, with certain limitations, Hempel claims to have given necessary and sufficient conditions on the form of explanations.

Hempel's model has been widely criticised,[9] and is no longer thought to be satisfactory without, at the least, a great deal of extra work. I will concentrate on one line of criticism, which has it that Hempel's model is too permissive: many candidate explanations pass its tests without being potential explanations. These come in several classes,[10] of which I shall concentrate on one. An example of such a pseudo-explanation is as follows:[11]

No man who takes birth control pills regularly becomes pregnant.
<u>Jim, a man, takes birth control pills regularly.</u>
Jim is not pregnant.

Clearly, the explanandum follows deductively from the explanans. We can assume that Jim, for some reason, does indeed take the pill, so that premise is true. The other premise is essential to the deduction, and it is not only law-like, but a law of nature. Thus, this argument meets all the requirements of the model, and it is true, so it ought to be an explanation. It is not, of course, because the information that Jim takes the pill is completely irrelevant to whether or not he is pregnant. The relation of explanatory relevance seems not to be the same as deductive subsumption under natural law.

This example is not unique, and indeed similar examples can be constructed very easily. For example, all salt dissolves in holy water,[12] where holy water is water that has been blessed in a church service. Therefore, from this law and the specific fact that this salt was placed in

---

7 Hempel 1965b, p 426.

8 Hempel 1965b, pp 412–13.

9 See, e.g. Bromberger 1966 on explanatory asymmetries, Scheffler 1964 on the failure of the prediction/explanation isomorphism thesis, Achinstein 1983 for an argument that Hempel was talking about entirely the wrong things, and Brody 1972, among others, for a criticism similar to the one given below. Salmon 1989 contains a good summary of most criticisms of the model.

10 For a discussion of another class, that of explanatory asymmetries, see van Fraassen 1980, §3. Van Fraassen's claims that these explanatory asymmetries are governed by pragmatic factors.

11 This example is taken, with slight modifications, from Salmon 1989, p 50.

12 This example is credited to Noretta Koertge in Salmon 1989, p 50 fn 18 (p 190).

this holy water, we can deduce that the salt dissolved, but this does not seem to be an explanation. Similarly, all hexed salt (which has had a spell chanted over it by a man with a long white beard and a pointy hat) dissolves in normal water,[13] and yet this law could not be used to explain such dissolution.

Further examples can be constructed as desired, by conjoining some irrelevant fact to the explanatory one in the law. This addition of irrelevant material does not spoil the deductive validity of the argument, but it does seem to spoil the explanatory power of the putative explanation. In this case, it seems that the requirement that an explanation be a deductively valid argument does not, in fact, capture the structure of explanations.

It could be argued that the above examples do not involve real laws, but only 'pseudo-laws'.[14] While I do not think that this criticism is correct, perhaps it would be wise to show that there are examples of the same sort of problem involving indisputably real laws. It is (suppose) a law of nature that all massive bodies attract one another with a force proportional to, among other things, the inverse square of their separation. It follows from this that all massive bodies attract one another with a force proportional to some power of their separation, and yet the former statement does not seem to explain the latter in any way.

Further examples are provided by cases of overdetermination. For example, suppose that someone, at a certain date, has a fatal disease, and that it is a law of nature that all people with that disease die within three weeks. We can therefore deduce that he is dead three weeks later, as indeed he is, but if he was hit by a truck and killed, we cannot explain his death in terms of the fatal disease.

The burden of this class of criticisms is that there is more to explanation than the Deductive-Nomological model tells us. The restrictions that it places on form do not constitute a sufficient condition on explanation. I think that this criticism has implications beyond the Deductive-Nomological model, however. The Deductive-Nomological model was well constructed, and it seems that it tells us as much as we could learn from deductive entailment. That is, since the non-explanatory arguments do entail their conclusions, it seems unlikely that it will be possible to exclude these without appeal to something beyond deductive logic. Since similar arguments also apply to the Inductive-Statistical model (replace hexed salt with hexed uranium, deduce the probability of decay, and then inductively infer that the hexed uranium will almost certainly decay), it seems likely that form alone cannot be sufficient. In the next section I will argue for this more generally.

---

[13]   This example is credited to Henry Kyburg in Salmon 1989, p 50 fn 18 (p 190).

[14]   Although not, I think, without violating Hempel's empiricist principles, and I am not sure that a theory of law that violated those principles would sit easily in the Covering-Law models of explanation, anyway.

In General

In this section, I shall attack the idea that there could be a theory of explanation based on the form of the explanation which would constitute a sufficient condition. I shall work from a definition of 'form' which is as general as possible, in order to make my argument as strong as possible.

The form of an explanation is clearly one of its internal features. No matter how much the external world changes, the explanation will still have the same form. It is thus the case that the explanans is a potential explanation of the explanandum in all possible worlds.[15] If the syntactic model is right, it must be the case that, in all worlds in which the explanans and the explanandum are both true,[16] the explanans explains the explanandum.

However, it seems that we can easily think of examples in which an explanation is true and explanatory in the actual world, but not in various possible worlds, and conversely. Consider the explanation 'He has cancer because he has smoked heavily all his life, and most people who smoke heavily all their lives get cancer'. This is obviously slightly elliptical, on a form-based model, but it seems to be a good explanation in the actual world. Consider, however, a possible world in which possession of a certain gene gives you a 90% chance of developing lung cancer, and requires that you start smoking heavily by puberty, and continue to smoke heavily, or you will die of a stroke within two months. On the other hand, the absence of that gene makes you violently sick on inhaling tobacco smoke. Tobacco smoke itself, however, is causally neutral with respect to cancer. Smoking and possession of the gene are co-extensive, so all the statements are still true, but they no longer seem to be explanatory.

Alternatively, suppose that a falling barometer is always followed by a storm. The explanation 'The barometer fell, and that is always followed by a storm, and the storm occurred' is then true in all such possible worlds. In some such worlds, however, the storm is caused by the falling barometer, and so the explanation is truly explanatory, while in others the two events are effects of a common cause, and the explanation is not truly explanatory.

---

[15] This includes worlds in which the words used to express the explanans in the actual world have different meanings. I do not want to get into the technicalities of drawing the distinction, but I am taking it that the homonymic explanation in such a world is a different explanation, and that the explanation that is the same as that in our world must be expressed in different words. Similar considerations apply if externalist theories of reference are true, and consistent with the concept of 'form' as used here.

[16] Requiring the truth of the explanandum is not redundant, as I am no longer restricting my opponent to deductive entailment. Thus, there may be syntactic relationships that hold between the explanans and the explanandum, but which do not require that the explanandum be true if the explanans is. See, for example, Hempel's *Inductive Statistical* model (Hempel 1965, pp 381–412).

The source of the problem is that we can imagine most linguistic relationships holding on the basis of properties or regularities that have no explanatory import, so that the requirement of the form-based model that the candidate explanation be explanatory in all or none of the possible worlds wherein it is true seems to be too strong. This formulation of the problem also suggests a way in which form based theories could be rescued. The idea that the linguistic relationships could hold by chance implies that there is some other sort of relationship that needs to hold in order for something to be truly explanatory. If this relationship can be expressed in language, then surely we can include it in the explanation, and thus rescue the 'all-possible-worlds' property, since the relationship can no longer hold by chance.

This, however, is an illegitimate manoeuvre. If the explanation requires that a statement of the form 'X is the cause of Y' be true, then the criteria are not, in fact, purely formal. The causal criterion has been smuggled in, and the form of the explanation is no longer terribly relevant. Indeed, to claim that the 'real' explanation must include an explicit statement of the causal relationship, in those words, is highly implausible.

Thus, I have shown in this section that it is not possible to delineate a set of formal conditions on explanation which will be sufficient for something to be an explanation. Any formal conditions must apply to an explanation given in any possible world. It is, however, possible to have the formal conditions satisfied by true statements without the argument being explanatory. The explanatory nature of an argument seems to depend on features of the world other than the truth of the premises. Perhaps, however, Hempel's claim was not really that strong, and he just got carried away by his own rhetoric. Perhaps the formal conditions are only supposed to be necessary. In the next section, I will consider this possibility.

Is there a Necessary Form?

Covering-Law Form

The arguments of the previous section have made it clear that conformity to covering-law form is not sufficient for something to be a potential explanation. In this section, I will consider whether it may be necessary.

In one sense, it is obviously not necessary. Very few people give any explanations in full and explicit covering-law form. However, Hempel argues that this does not matter. He is interested in the underlying logical form. Thus, it is necessary to argue that there are some potential arguments which *cannot* be put into covering-law form.

Consider explanations in areas where we do not know the relevant laws. Many biological explanations are of this type. We are confident that we can explain the existence of the eye in terms of natural selection, but we do not know the laws governing this process in any great detail. We are, however, sure that there are such laws. Hempel could claim that only those explanations which will prove to be of covering-law form when the laws are known are good, no matter what we may think now. This would commit him to the position that it is not necessary for anyone alive today to be able to put an explanation into the necessary form, and, possibly, that it will never be possible. This is a somewhat uncomfortable position: if it need never be done, what do we gain by supposing that it is a necessary condition that a nomological connection exists? Nevertheless, it is not a fatal objection, because there may be good theoretical reasons for keeping the condition.

A better sort of counter-example would be explanations in areas where there are no laws. Consider the explanation of human action. Some philosophers (such as Ginet[17]) have argued that we can explain human actions by giving reasons, but that there are no laws at all governing these actions. Ginet's position does not seem to be wrong by definition, even though it is controversial. He accepts that it is clear that we can explain free action by giving reasons, and argues that these explanations can be true in the absence of any covering-laws.

Given that Hempel must admit that the inclusion of a covering-law is not necessary for the process of actually giving an explanation, as noted above, it is hard to see how arguments from the nature of explanation could give us a good reason to believe that Ginet's position is wrong. We can give explanations even if we don't know whether there is a covering law of the appropriate form, so it would seem that we can give them even if there is no such law. If there are realms within which there simply *are* no laws, then that seems to give no reason why we cannot continue to give explanations in that area.[18]

Thus, we know that actual covering-law form is not necessary, and there are arguments that possible covering-law form cannot be. Given this, I am inclined to say that covering-law form is not necessary at all.

Probabilistic Forms

If we accept that the presence of a covering law in the explanation is not necessary, we may look elsewhere for necessary features of form. One promising area is in the probabilistic relationship between the explanans and explanandum. In this section, I will argue that these features are also not necessary.

The strongest such feature is entailment. It could be suggested that the explanans must entail the explanandum. Note that this is not the same as the covering-law model: the explanans can entail the explanandum without including a covering law, and since we are only seeking a necessary

---

[17] Ginet 1989.

[18] Note that this argument leaves open the possibility that the covering law *is* necessary if the area of the explanation is law-governed. Nevertheless, the covering law is not absolutely necessary for something to be an explanation.

condition we need not worry about attempts to use the explanandum as the explanans.

This, however, seems to be unnecessary. We explain events that we believe to be irreducibly probabilistic. For example, we might claim that an atom is in an excited state because the area is bathed in light of a certain frequency. This seems like a good potential explanation, but the light only makes it probable that the atom will be excited: it is not certain. Some people might argue that we cannot, in fact, explain probabilistic events: we can only explain their probability of occurrence, and that can be entailed by the explanans. The burden of proof, however, is definitely on their side, as it seems that we do explain probabilistic events.

If one accepts that probabilistic events can be explained, one could claim that, when the event to be explained is intrinsically probabilistic, the explanans need only make the explanandum highly probable. This is the position that Hempel took, in his Inductive-Statistical model of explanation.[19] Thus, although we cannot get entailment, we can get something close: the explanandum is 'almost entailed'.[20]

This is also unnecessary, as we can see by considering a variation of the example. Suppose that the atom only has a 40% chance of becoming excited when bathed in the light, although the chance when the light is not on is 10%. The probability of the explanandum is not high, even given the explanans, and yet we would still say that the account was explanatory. If the base probability was zero, we would feel this even more strongly: nobody gets a job if they don't apply, so applying is part of the explanation for why someone does get a job, even if only 1% of those who apply are successful.

It might, then, be claimed that the explanans must raise the probability of the explanandum.[21] The event would have a high probability in many cases, when the explanans raised its probability by a great deal, and in some cases the probability might even be raised to one, giving us entailment. Even when the final probability fails to get above 50%, however, the fact that it has been raised from the base rate underwrites the explanation.

This condition is also not necessary, however.[22] Suppose that I shine light of a certain frequency on some atoms. These atoms have three states, with equal energy gaps between them. The highest and lowest states are quite stable by nature, but the intermediate state is highly unstable. Thus, if an atom in the ground state absorbs a photon (a probabilistic event), it will

---

[19]   Hempel 1965b, §3.3.

[20]   Note that this idea has particular force for someone who, like Hempel, accepts the symmetry thesis, that explanations and predictions have the same structure.

[21]   This is a stage that van Fraassen 1980, Humphreys 1989, and Salmon 1990 all explicitly mention in developing their accounts of explanation, although none of them stop here.

[22]   This is widely recognised in the literature: see all the accounts cited in fn 9.

rise to the intermediate state, and quickly decay back to the ground state. If an atom in the highest state interacts with a photon, it will decay to the intermediate state, by stimulated emission, and then quickly to the ground state. In order to rise to the highest state, the atom must absorb a second photon during the brief time that it is in the intermediate state, or be excited by thermal collisions.

Now let us consider varying the intensity of the light. When it is switched off, some atoms will be raised to the highest state through collisions with other atoms. They will tend to stay in that state, so there will be a certain probability of finding an atom in the highest state, for each atom. If we turn the light on, at a low intensity, then there will be a very small chance of interacting with two photons in quick succession, but a reasonable chance of interacting with one. This will tend to knock atoms out of the highest state, thus reducing the number in that state. Overall, then, this light reduces the probability that any atom will be in the highest state. Some atoms will, nevertheless, absorb two photons in quick succession, and thus be raised to the highest state. The presence of the light source seems to explain the excitation of these atoms, even though it reduces the probability that they will be found in that state. Thus, it seems that an event can be explained by a cause which lowers its probability.

The fall back position from here is that the explanation must change the probability of the event to be explained. This is, essentially, Salmon's Statistical Relevance theory[23] and the core of Humphreys's account.[24] More precisely, a complete explanation cites all the factors that changed the probability of the explanandum from some base state. The example can, however, be modified to tell against this account as well. As the intensity of the light in the previous example is increased, more and more atoms will be found in the highest state. At some intensity, the probability of finding an atom in the highest state will be the same as it is when the light is switched off. The light, in this case, has not changed the probability, but it still explains the state of the atoms.

Thus, the explanans need not raise, lower, or even change the probability of the explanandum. Clearly, then, a direct influence on the probability cannot be a necessary condition on explanations, since none of the forms that a direct influence can take are necessary. Salmon's and Humphreys's accounts will exclude some explanatory factors: those which have no effect on the probability of the outcome.

There is another possibility, discussed by van Fraassen.[25] The explanans need not change the probability of the outcome, but it must favour it over the other members of the contrast class.[26] He considers the following example. Suppose 50% of people smoke, 50% have heart attacks, and 40%

---

[23]   See Salmon 1971.

[24]   Humphreys 1989.

[25]   van Fraassen 1980, pp 148–50.

[26]   I will say more about van Fraassen on contrasts in the next section.

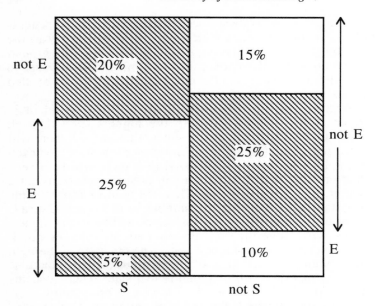

Figure 1 — An artificial probability distribution for heart attacks

exercise. Further, of the people who smoke, 60% exercise, while 40% don't, and conversely among the ones who don't smoke. 50% of smokers have heart attacks, as do 50% of non-smokers, but no non-smoking exercisers do, while one sixth of exercising smokers do. (See figure 1, in which the shaded areas indicate heart attacks.)

Now consider the consequences of this highly artificial probability distribution. While the probability of a heart attack is the same whether you smoke or not, if you exercise, then smoking increases the probability that you will have a heart attack (from zero to one sixth), and if you do not exercise, then smoking will also increase the probability (from 62.5% to 100%). Thus, given the right reference sets, smoking does increase the chance of a heart attack, and so it picks out that member of the contrast class.

This response will not, however, work for the example of the atoms. The probability that an atom is in the highest state is exactly the same whether the light is on or off, and there are no other relevant factors. Turning the light on in no way favours the probability of the highest state over the probability of being in the intermediate or lowest state. Indeed, although the probability that an atom is found in the lowest state will have dropped, the probability that an atom will be found in the intermediate state will have risen. This is because many more atoms are being raised to that state by photon absorption, and knocked down to that state by stimulated emission, than entered it by spontaneous emission or thermal collision in the base state. The probability of the intermediate state could even have been raised above that of the excited state. In this case, the explanandum has the same probability, and it has become less favoured in the field of probabilities: it no longer stands out from the crowd, because it is overtopped by the intermediate state. However, we would still feel that many of the atoms in the highest state were there because they had been excited by the light. Thus, the condition proposed by van Fraassen is not necessary.

It is widely recognised that an explanatory factor need not raise the probability of its explanandum. In this section, I have argued that it also need not alter the probability in any way, nor need it make the (possibly unaltered) probability stand out any more from the probabilities of members of the contrast class. Thus, it seems that no formal constraints on the probability of the explanandum relative to the explanans are necessary.

A final possibility, along very different lines, is suggested by Railton's Deductive-Nomological-Probabilistic model.[27] This is that the explanans must entail the probability of the explanandum. This probability can be anything you please, even exactly the same as it would be in some base state, but the explanans must entail the correct value.

This certainly cannot be a necessary condition on explanations as they are given. It is very rare indeed for an explanation to contain any information allowing the calculation of a probability at all, let alone the correct one. Indeed, in the example developed above, unless the precise intensity of the light is given it is not possible to calculate the probabilities for any of the states, and yet such precision does not seem to be necessary in the explanation. It might be claimed the ideal explanation must contain enough information to allow the deduction of the correct probability, but if this explanation is never, maybe can never be, given, what is the use of the ideal?[28]

It seems, then, that the explanans need have no particular effect on the probability of the explanandum, and need not entail either the explanandum or its probability. This does not quite exhaust the possibilities of necessary form, however, and in the following section I will discuss another one raised by van Fraassen.

van Fraassen and Contrasts

van Fraassen, in *The Scientific Image*,[29] gives the necessary form of explanations as follows:

---

[27] See Railton 1978.

[28] This dismissal is, by itself, too quick. However, in the light of the theory presented later in this book, the whole idea of an 'ideal explanation', in this sense, is deeply misconceived, so I do not wish to spend time on it.

[29] van Fraassen 1980.

[T]he why-question Q expressed by an interrogative in a given context will be determined by three factors:

The topic P_k

The contrast-class $X = \{P_1, ..., P_k, ...\}$

The relevance relation R

[...]

[L]et us inspect the form of words that will express such an answer:

(*) P_k in contrast to (the rest of) X because A.[30]

van Fraassen does not, of course, require that explanations all have exactly that verbal form. He does require that they distinguish the topic from the contrast class by means of the relevance relation. Is this a necessary constraint on the form of explanations?

As a beginning, we can neglect the relevance relation. It is completely undefined, and thus does not restrict the form of the explanations at all. It is, after all, trivially necessary for the explanation to bear *some* relation to the topic: it must explain it. This leaves the existence of the contrast class as the interesting part of the claim. Must there always be a contrast class?

I suspect not. Consider requests for explanation which are not framed in terms of 'why?'. For example, 'how did that get here?'. These are still requests for explanation, as is evinced by the expanded version 'how did that get here? I want an explanation!' as said by a parent to children. In this case, however, it seems that there is no contrast class in mind at all. The questioner does not care about alternative possibilities in which the thing is not there, merely about the actual case, and the actual method by which it became present.

Perhaps the 'how?' questions were never supposed to fall under van Fraassen's analysis: he does, after all, refer to 'why-questions' as such. In that case, however, since the answers to how-questions are, in some cases, explanations, he has certainly failed to give a necessary condition on the form of explanation. Either way, it would seem that there is no necessary condition here, either.

In this section, I have argued that there are no non-trivial necessary conditions on the form of a potential explanation. The explanans must explain the explanandum, but this relationship does not supervene on any other formal features of the explanation. I argued above that there were no sufficient formal conditions, since non-formal factors to do with the way the world works are often relevant. In this section I have argued that there are no necessary conditions, either: the explanans need not contain a law, relate in any particular way to the probability of the explanandum, or deal with a contrast class. Thus, the form cannot help us in our quest for a theory of explanation. What about content?

---

[30]   van Fraassen 1980, pp142-143.

Is there Necessary Content?

In this section, I shall argue that there is no content that is necessary for something to be a potential explanation. It is immediately obvious that no particular content is necessary: we give explanations in very different fields, and the details of the content of an explanation in particle physics will not overlap with the details of the content of an explanation in literary criticism. The interesting claim is that all explanations must contain a certain *type* of content. This type must obviously be unitary: some disjunctive type of content is trivially necessary, as the enumeration of all explanations forms a disjunctive type.

I shall consider three types of explanation: causal, functional, and identity. I shall show that there are no interesting types of content common between these types of explanation, generally by arguing that they rely on different types of content and cannot be reduced to one another, that each type is genuinely explanatory, and that there are no other interesting types of content hiding in the formulation.

One type of content is generally present. Every explanation must have explanatory content. This, however, gets us nowhere, and ultimately I will argue that explanatory content must be defined in terms of its purposes, not its content as such. While this may seem like an obvious point, we will be considering some very abstract types of content, and it will be important to be on guard against the possibility that our definition is just some way of saying 'explanatory content'.

Causal Explanation

Causal theories of explanation are the nearest thing to a consensus in current philosophy of explanation. A quick survey of some literature will demonstrate this:

> Here is my main thesis: *to explain an event is to provide some information about its causal history.*[31]
> The explanation, on this view, is incomplete until the causal components ... have been provided.[32]
> Explanation of why an event happens consists (typically) in an exhibition of salient factors in the part of the causal net formed by lines 'leading up to' that event.[33]

Indeed, in some work this theory is taken for granted, and the effort is expended on illuminating some part of it:

---

[31] Lewis 1986a, p.185, emphasis Lewis's.
[32] Salmon 1984, p 85.
[33] van Fraassen 1980, p 124.

Our task is thus a restricted one. It is to provide an account of the nature of singular causal explanations. [fn: I acknowledge here that there are other kinds of explanation than those which cite causes of the explained phenomenon.][34]

Humphreys' footnote (above) draws attention to one limitation on this theory: it is not supposed to apply to all explanations. If we consider Lewis's theory, as the best-known and possibly the purest, we find that it is explicitly limited to the explanation of singular events. However, the theory is preserved from near-vacuity by the assertion that all such explanations provide information about the causal history, and are explanatory in virtue of that:[35]

[I]s there also any such thing as non-causal explanation of particular events? My main thesis says there is not.[36]

Thus, these theories assert that, for at least some explanations, there is a necessary condition on the content. It must refer to a cause of the explanandum.

Causal theories do not, however, offer a general theory of explanation. Their proponents explicitly state that it is necessary to give information about causal history only if you are explaining a certain type of thing. If there is to be necessary content in explanations in general, it must be something more abstract than 'information about the casual history', something that causal explanations have in common with the other types. In this section I will argue that there cannot be, in general, any such condition. In passing, I will suggest that it is even possible to explain singular events in non-causal terms, but nothing hangs on this. Since causal explanation is admitted to cover only some explanations, only the argument that there is no more abstract category covering all is essential to my case.

Let us, then, consider the content of causal explanations. They are certainly not identity explanations, in any guise. Cause and effect are rigorously treated as distinct existences, and if the two things in an explanation are the same, it is agreed that the explanation cannot be causal.[37]

It also seems certain that they are not functional explanations. Aristotle may have admitted purpose as one of his 'causes', but the contemporary meaning of 'cause' is narrower than Aristotle's. To the best of my knowledge, von Wright[38] has come closest to claiming that causal explanations are functional explanations, with his claim that action

---

[34]   Humphreys 1989, p 99.
[35]   Were it to assert only that *some* explanations of particular events were causal, it is clearly not providing a necessary condition on explanation.
[36]   Lewis 1986a, p 189.
[37]   See Lewis 1986a, p 190.
[38]   von Wright 1971.

explanations are always prior to causal ones. However, even this claim is not that causal explanations are a type of functional explanation, being rather the claim that the idea of cause is dependent on the idea of action. The dependence also seems to be largely epistemological: we cannot know that a cause is involved in a certain situation unless, by our actions, we can manipulate that situation to add or remove the putative cause, and then observe the presence or absence of the effect. Thus, causes are distinct from actions, so no matter how functional the explanation of actions, causal explanations will not be a type of functional explanation. Indeed, it is central to von Wright's thesis that these types of explanation are entirely separate.

So, it seems that it is not possible to reduce causal explanation to identity or functional explanation. Is it possible to argue that causal explanations are not really explanatory? Perhaps, but to do so one would have to take on most of the current philosophical consensus, and a substantial weight of common sense opinion. The only way that I can see such a position being made plausible is if it flowed from a more general theory of explanation or understanding, and no theory with such consequences is currently on offer. Thus, since my intuitions incline me to believe that causal explanations really can explain, and there are no arguments on the other side, I shall take it that they are genuinely explanatory.

The final possibility for unification involves necessary content that is more abstract than 'information about the causal history'. I will argue that there are no candidates for such content, and that, therefore, the other types of explanation must either be reduced to causal explanation, or shown to be unexplanatory, in order to allow the possibility of necessary content.

I do not believe that there is going to be a more abstract category for the simple reason that 'information about the causal history' is already about as abstract as it can get. Recall that Lewis includes negative information under the rubric. Thus, the information that the CIA man who was around when His Excellency dropped dead actually had nothing to do with the death is classed as explanatory.[39] So is the information that the star stopped collapsing because there were no more collapsed states for it to enter: it ran out of state space.[40] The information given, then, need not be positive information about the causal history. Nor need it tell you very much — the example of the CIA man certainly doesn't, and if something was, in fact, uncaused, then that information would probably count as an explanation, as it is information about the causal history.

Also, the information need not be directly about the causal history: that is, the information about the causal history can be conveyed by implication. Suppose that someone asked why Britain entered World War II, and was told 'Well, Churchill only became Prime Minister nine months later'. This

---

[39] Lewis 1986a, p 188.
[40] Lewis 1986a, p 189–90.

is explanatory, on this account, because it provides the information that Churchill was not Prime Minister at the time, and that his handling of that office was, therefore, not part of the causal history of the event.

This makes the requirement look suspiciously like 'any information': after all, the explanation can contain information about the past, present, or future. However, this is not quite true. For example, if someone were to say 'Well, the Soviet flag is red' in response to the question about World War II, that would not count as an explanation. It does not tell you whether this fact was part of the causal history, or excluded another important factor. Indeed, the information given seems to be about part of the universe that has nothing to do with the causal history of the event.

This is, however, tricky. Every object in the universe is affected by the gravitational field of every other object in its backwards light-cone (that is, all space-time points in the universe from which a ray of light could have reached the point in question). Intuitively, these are not all part of the causal history, but had any of them been different, the event would have been different, maybe radically so. An example from chaos theory is that the weather on Earth could be totally changed by the difference due to the gravitational attraction of a proton on Sirius. It will require great care in the account of causation, and of what individuates the relata of causation, to avoid the conclusion that anything in the backwards light cone is part of the causal history, and thus that any information, direct or indirect, about that section of the universe qualifies. Again, I think that the burden of proof lies on the other side. This is ignoring the possibility, raised by certain results in quantum mechanics, that there may be causal links from outside that area. It is fortunate for the causal model that this is sufficiently controversial to lay the burden of proof on those who want to include the other areas, because if they were included, the causal model would reduce to 'give information about the world', which is fairly empty.

Let us, in the absence of good arguments to the contrary, assume that the causal model is going to reduce to 'Give any information about the backwards light cone of the explanandum, directly or indirectly'. There are few categories more abstract than this. 'Any information at all' is one, but the requirement that an explanation must convey information is weaker than the requirement that it must be explanatory. Indeed, this would be the requirement that an explanation *have* content. A possible compromise would be 'information about the actual world'. That is, information purely about unrealised possibilities cannot be explanatory. Unfortunately, any explanation must provide some information about the actual world, namely that in the actual world the explanans explains the explanandum. Thus this condition is also entailed by the triviality that explanations must explain. Further, we may want to explain events in possible worlds, in which case this restriction will exclude some explanations.[41]

---

[41]   I owe this point to Anandi Hattiangadi.

A final possibility might be some development of 'information about the conditions of the event'. The danger here is that the condition will be equivalent to 'explanatory information'. Certainly, any reference to 'the reasons for the event' will tend to imply explanation. Thus, for this to serve, the conditions of an event would have to be specified in a unified way, independent of their explanatory abilities. I cannot see how this would be done, and I am sure that the burden of proof rests with someone who would claim that it is possible.

It seems, then, that causal explanations really explain, that they cannot be reduced to functional or identity explanations, and that there is no plausible candidate for a more abstract but still useful type of content that all causal explanations have in common. If either functional or identity explanations can be shown to be truly explanatory and not reducible to causal explanation, then I will have shown that there is no content that something must have if it is to be an explanation.

Functional Explanation

Functional explanations, of the form 'X exists in order to Y', or 'A does B in order to C', seem, at least on the surface, to be highly distinct from causal explanations. For a start, the explanatory factor generally occurs only after the thing that it explains and, in some cases, it need not occur at all. For example, we can explain a person's actions by saying that he intends to build a perpetual motion machine, but not only has he not built one yet, he will never do so.

It has been argued by some that functional explanations are not really explanatory, and by others that they are actually forms of causal explanation. I will argue that both of these positions are mistaken, and that functional explanations are actually independently valid explanatory forms.

Let us first consider the charge that functional explanations are not truly explanatory. As it was put in a botany textbook:

> Such teleological explanations, crediting the plant with intelligent and purposeful behavior, are easy to formulate but totally inadequate in explaining plant responses. ... If botanists were satisfied with teleological explanations for plant behavior, research aimed at discovery of the actual course of events would cease.[42]

What grounds could there be for such an assertion? Clearly, the claim that functional explanations do not give an account of the causes is insufficient. Such an argument only has force if we accept that there can be no other type of explanation. Further, it is not enough to say that an account of the causes would be more explanatory. Even were this true, it would not

---

[42] Greulach and Adams 1967, *Plants: An Introduction to Modern Botany* 2nd edition (New York: John Wiley & Sons, Inc.) p 261, quoted in Wright 1976, p 9.

prevent the functional explanation from having some explanatory force, and some is enough.

Most importantly, we use functional explanations constantly in everyday life. I include footnotes and a bibliography so that people can look up my references. Fire exits are clearly marked so that people can find their way out in an emergency. Examples can easily be multiplied: if these are not *really* explanations, then everyday usage is radically mistaken. A theory could make such a claim, but it would need very good reasons if it were still to claim that it was a theory of explanation. Again, the burden of proof seems to be on those who would claim that functional explanations do not explain, and there is no obvious way for them to discharge the burden.

The main line of attack on functional explanations is the claim that they are, in fact, special forms of causal explanation. Such an account is seen as vindicating the use of functional explanations in science, but, as I have argued above, it is far from clear that they need such vindication. Nevertheless, the discovery that functional explanations were a type of causal explanation would allow one to require that explanations provided causal information, without running into the problems involved in denying that functional explanations are at all explanatory.

Functional and causal explanations have been most effectively assimilated in terms of etiology. Wright characterises the general pattern as follows:

S does B for the sake of G iff:

(i) B tends to bring about G.

(ii) B occurs because (i.e., is brought about by the fact that) it tends to bring about G.[43]

He also argues, in the development of this formulation, that nothing more specific will do the job. Indeed, when he discusses the application of this formula to functional explanations he says:

So there is a sense in which the functional account is better than either the theological account or the evolutionary one: for it is true on both. Settling the further issue is an independent empirical matter.[44]

This, I think, is the fatal flaw in the model, at least insofar as it is taken to assimilate functional explanations to causal ones. Let us suppose that everything Wright says is correct, and that teleology can be analysed in terms of consequence-etiology. Now, in order for this to assimilate functional to causal explanation, in the terms of this section, this must require that any functional explanation convey information about the causal

---

43   Wright 1976, p 39.
44   Wright 1976, p 105.

history of the thing explained (the existence of the function). Recall the discussion of causal explanation, above. On Lewis's account, it seems, any information about those parts of the universe that could have been part of the causal history of the event counts as information about the causal history. Thus, to argue that functional explanations are not reducible to causal explanations, I must argue that a functional explanation may not give information about the universe preceding the function, even indirectly.

The first part, (i), of the pattern is irrelevant, as G is not part of the causal history of B, for the simple reason that it occurs later than B. Thus, we must concentrate on (ii). This might seem to give some very abstract information about the causal history of B. In particular, some of the causes are sensitive to B's ability to do G, and have brought B about as a result of that ability. This tells us nothing about whether those causes were part of natural selection operating over millions of years, or operations of divine will operating over seconds, or human forethought acting over hours, but, if 'information about the causal history' is to be construed as broadly as Lewis suggests, this does count. It could be argued that it condemns functional explanations to always be very bad explanations, and that this is at variance with common usage, but I will not pursue that line here.

Instead, I will argue that the information provided might be purely about the universe *after* the function arises. Let us suppose that there are final causes in something like Aristotle's sense.[45] The existence of the final cause, which is in the future of the event that it causes, brings it about that the final cause is brought about, and the intermediate steps are brought about because they tend to produce the final cause.

To take a concrete example, consider a modern Aristotelian discussing the growth of the body. The final cause is the particular mature human body, and the DNA structure is as it is in order to bring about that particular mature body. According to the consequence-etiological account, these explanations have the right structure, but they tell you nothing about the causal history of the event. The DNA structure does tend to bring about that mature human body (point (i)), and the final cause (the mature human body) brings the DNA structure about because it tends to produce that mature human body (point (ii)). The mature human body is not, however, part of the causal history of the DNA. The DNA is already present and active in the embryo, at which time the mature human body in question will not exist for another twenty years or so.

It should be noted that the DNA does have a causal history, but that we can tell nothing about it from the information about the final cause. The explanation is completely indifferent between the case in which the DNA appears *ex nihilo* at the moment of conception, and the case in which the DNA is laboriously created in the parents. Thus, we have a functional explanation which fits the consequence-etiological account, but which gives no information about the causal history.

---

[45]   Aristotle, *Physics*, II.3, 194^{b}32–195^{a}3.

There are two obvious ways to respond to this sort of example. The first is to claim that such imaginary examples can tell us nothing of interest about the real world, and the second is to claim that part of the causal history of the plans is in their future, and little of it in their past.

The first objection does have a reasonable point. It might well be the case that, in the actual world, functional explanations always give us information about the causal history of an event, because that is the only place that the consequence-etiology could reside. However, this information is not part of the content of the explanation: it is the content of the explanation taken in conjunction with certain other background beliefs. The situation is parallel to the evolution/creation one. For me, a functional explanation of a natural feature conveys information about its evolutionary history, because I know that it evolved by natural selection. For a committed creationist, the explanation would convey very different information. Wright, as noted above, explicitly claims that the explanation itself is neutral as regards these two options.[46] Accordingly, it is also neutral as regards the possibility of active final causes, time travel, and similar weirdnesses. Thus, the *explanation* need not contain information about the causal history.

The second objection is the more interesting: the functional explanation does give us information about the causal history, but it does not tell us whether that history is in the future or the past. This, however, is not a tenable position. Recall that the causal account had reduced to 'give information about the backward light-cone of the explanandum'. If it must also allow for the possibility that the cause is in the future, then it reduces to 'give information about the actual world', and that is an uninteresting triviality.

This might be taken as indicating that a more restrictive notion of causal history needs to be developed. However, since it must now allow for backwards causation, the task has been made much more difficult. We know from various bilking arguments that our intuitive notion cannot handle backwards causation very well. It is also clear that any account based simply on conditional probabilities will fail, since the probability of a cause, given its effect, is higher than the base probability of the cause, but the effect is not part of the causal history of the cause. Similarly, Lewis's account, which refuses to countenance backtracking counterfactuals, cannot handle this kind of causation. Since none of the most promising contemporary analyses of causation are available, I would suggest that the burden of proof is both extremely heavy and on anyone who claims that a suitable account of causation can be given.

In summary, then, the current weight of evidence strongly suggests that functional explanations are truly explanatory and that they need not convey any information about the causal history of an event. If this is right, it

---

[46]   Indeed, if God is outside time, as orthodox theology holds, then it is not clear that the creationist account gives any information about the causal history.

suggests that there can be non-causal explanations of particular events: there can certainly be functional explanations of such events, and such explanations could be non-causal.

Structural Explanation

A structural, or identity, explanation is one in which the explanans and the explanandum are the same thing. Ruben gives the following introductory characterisation:

> Peter Achinstein has discussed cases of this sort, and I owe much of what follows to him.[47] Achinstein's examples of this type of explanation include: explaining why the pH value of some solution is changing on the grounds that the concentration of hydrogen ions which the solution contains is changing; explaining why ice is water on the grounds that it is H_2O; explaining why some gas sample has temperature t on the grounds that its constituent molecules have a mean kinetic energy m.
>
> In its simplest form, we can sometimes explain why some particular, a, has property P by identifying P with a property, Q, which a also has. In a somewhat less simple form, we can sometimes explain why a is P, by identifying a with the sum of its parts, [b&c&d], and identifying P with some property of the sum, Q, or, sometimes, with a property Q had individually by each member of the sum.[48]

In this case, it is immediately obvious that structural explanation cannot be a kind of causal explanation. Something is not part of its own causal history: it cannot cause itself. Similarly, possession of a property P cannot cause possession of a property Q if P and Q are the same property. It is less obvious that structural explanations are really explanatory.

In the first place, common usage is not (apparently) saturated with explanations of this sort in the way that it is with causal and functional explanations. Second, there is intuitive appeal in the idea that you cannot explain something simply by redescribing it, and this is all that structural explanations do. In this section, I shall argue that structural explanations are more common than we might think, and that the intuition is flawed.[49]

Let us first consider mathematics. We certainly give explanations in mathematics, such as the explanation of the mechanism of PGP encryption, which involves the properties of the prime factors of a number. However, these explanations seem to involve structural explanations. A number simply is the product of its prime factors: it isn't caused by the product. Indeed, since mathematics generally proceeds by logically valid (or, at

---

[47]   In Achinstein 1983 (my footnote).
[48]   Ruben 1990, pp 218–19.
[49]   See Ruben 1990, pp 218–22, for another discussion of these issues.

least, necessarily truth-preserving) deductions, at least when it is done right, it seems that explanations in this field will always involve redescriptions of the explanandum. This leads us into difficult waters in the philosophy of mathematics, however, so I will rest my argument on the simpler cases.

If I need to explain why the highest common factor of 6480 and 25116 is 12, I can do so by pointing out that 6480 is $2^4 \times 3^4 \times 5$, and 25116 is $2^2 \times 3 \times 7 \times 13 \times 23$, and that the highest number in common is $2^2 \times 3$, which is 12. This explanation proceeds entirely in terms of identities, and yet seems to be explanatory. It is true that mathematical explanations are not as common as other sorts, but they do occur in everyday life. Consider the explanation of a bill, where the items on the bill are not in dispute but their total, including VAT, is.

This book forms, by itself, a further example. I am attempting to explain understanding, and I do so by redescribing understanding, asserting that it simply is the possession of mental models. While my theory may be wrong, philosophers and psychologists work this way a lot, and so it is unlikely that I am wrong by definition because my chosen technique is incapable of explaining.

The natural sciences furnish further examples. The operation of the gene was explained with the discovery of DNA, its structure, and the triplet code. These do not, however, cause genes: they are the genes. In particular, the way in which genes code for proteins is not caused by the arrangement of bases, it *is* that arrangement. Similarly, materials scientists explain substances in terms of the arrangement of atoms and bonds within them. The substance is not caused by this arrangement: it *is* the arrangement. A particularly clear example is diamond, which differs from graphite and buckminsterfullerene purely in the arrangement of the carbon atoms making it up. This structure of carbon atoms does not cause diamond, it is diamond, and yet it explains why a particular sample of carbon is diamond, rather than graphite.

Thus, anyone who wishes to deny that structural explanations really explain is going to have to explain away a lot of apparent counter-examples. They are also likely to have problems with their own methodology, working as they most likely will be within philosophy. What, then, about the intuition that you cannot explain something simply by redescribing it?

I think that the intuition is simply wrong. It is true that I do not explain a lightning bolt by redescribing it as Zeus's spear, but I do if I redescribe it as an electrical discharge. Similarly, I explain the political power of a person if I redescribe him as the President of the United States of America, but not if I redescribe him as a millionaire, even though the second redescription may be implied by the first. I cannot, at this stage, say what makes one redescription explanatory while another is not, but the examples should make the point clear, and I will return to the theoretical issues when I have built the theory in terms of which to consider them.

In conclusion, then, it seems that structural explanations genuinely explain, and apparently genuinely explain particular facts, such as the hardness of this diamond, while it is clear that they do not involve information about the causal history of the explanandum.

Conclusions

In this section I have argued that causal, functional, and structural explanations are all perfectly good examples of explanation. Further, it is not possible to reduce all three of them to examples of one kind. Structural explanations are the biggest sticking point here: they are obviously not a kind of causal explanation, and they have nothing to do with function. I also argued that there could be no more abstract content in causal explanations, other than the empty 'explanatory content'. Thus, no type of content is necessary for something to be an explanation.

It might be thought, however, that if something includes information about the causal history, it will be an explanation, and similarly for candidates that include information about functions and structure. This, however, is to consider the possibility that there is content which is sufficient for something to explain, and it is to this issue that I now turn.

The Insufficiency of Content

In this section, I will argue that there can be no conditions on the content of an explanation that are sufficient. This argument relies heavily on Achinstein's *The Nature of Explanation* (1983) throughout, although he uses these arguments to a slightly different end.

Consider John, who oversleeps and, as a result, misses a supervision. John's friend, Janet, phones the supervisor and says 'John overslept'. The supervisor says 'It isn't like you to criticise John.' She says 'That wasn't a criticism, that was an explanation.'

This exchange does not seem unreasonable. However, the content of Janet's statement seems to be constant: it is only the intention with which it is uttered that makes the difference between a criticism and an explanation. Thus, having given content seems to be insufficient for something to be an explanation.

Janet's statement is, however, very brief. Perhaps one with more content would be sufficient for being an explanation. What about 'John missed the supervision because he overslept'? This seems like a very strong formulation: indeed, the presence of 'because' might seem to guarantee that this is an explanation.

Not so, however. This could still be a criticism. Suppose that both supervisees missed the supervision, and the supervisor says 'Beth attended the supervision although she had appendicitis: John missed it because he overslept'. This could well be a criticism of John, and a commendation of Beth (even if followed up with 'I sent Beth away to hospital, of course').

Further, if John suffered from M.E., meaning that he had little or no control of his sleeping patterns, 'John missed the supervision because he overslept' could be offered as a good excuse for his absence.

It might be suggested that, in these cases, the criticism is only a criticism *because* it is also an explanation. If John's oversleeping does not explain his absence from the supervision, then perhaps it cannot be used to criticise him. The criticism is, in effect, that he missed the supervision for this reason, not simply that he overslept. Thus, if the statement does not explain his lateness, the criticism rests on a false presupposition.

I think that there are cases in which it can be convincingly argued that the statement can serve as an explanation or something else, without serving as something else because it is an explanation. In particular, let us consider excuses. Suppose that John oversleeps. When he wakes up, he discovers that his bike has been stolen. He tells the supervisor, as an excuse 'I missed the supervision because my bike was stolen'. John would not offer this as an explanation, as he knows that he would have missed the supervision anyway. The supervisor might also reject it as an explanation: John could have left earlier and walked. The fact that they both reject this as an explanation does not prevent either of them accepting it as an excuse. John thinks it is a bit weak because it wasn't really the point, and the supervisor thinks it is weak because John could have been more enthusiastic.

This argument has shifted the focus from abstract explanations to particular acts that are explanations. However, since we can deny that something like 'John missed the supervision because his bike was stolen' is an explanation, asserting that it is an excuse, this still seems to be a valid point. The content of a statement cannot guarantee that it is an explanation: it cannot provide a sufficient condition. Thus, we cannot consider the proposition alone when devising a theory of explanation.

Achinstein develops an ordered pair view, in which an explanation is the pair of a speech act and an intention to explain. This is, of course, inadequate for our purposes, since the reference to an intention to explain is clearly circular. It does suggest an alternative possibility, however. Suppose that the intention 'to improve understanding' is substituted. This is not obviously circular, and if an independent account of understanding can be given, it would not be circular at all. Thus, an explanation could be a speech act performed with the intention of improving understanding.

Further, these arguments about explanation have no direct bearing on understanding. Consider the analogy with chairs and sitting. It is not possible to provide necessary and sufficient conditions for being a chair, although some loose necessary ones may be possible. A chair is, however, something that allows a person to sit, and it may be possible to give necessary and sufficient conditions on sitting, irrespective of the variability among chairs. Similarly, it may be possible to provide necessary and sufficient conditions on something being understanding. It should then be possible to assess a candidate explanation for whether it has the potential to improve understanding. Finally, we can unproblematically require that something be uttered with the intention of improving understanding if it is to count as an explanation. Understanding, then, seems to be the way to go.

Conclusion

In this chapter I have argued that there are no necessary or sufficient conditions on either the form or the content of explanations. From a consideration of Hempel's covering-law models I argued that there were no sufficient conditions on form, because features of the external world always seemed to get involved. From further consideration of that theory, of probabilistic situations, and of van Fraassen's account, I concluded that there were no necessary conditions either.

I then turned to the consideration of content. I argued that causal, functional, and structural explanations are all perfectly good independent types of explanation, and that they have no interesting type of content in common, so that there is no necessary content. Finally, I considered the nature of explanations as acts to argue that there can be no sufficient condition on content either.

The upshot of these arguments can be viewed as two-fold. First, there is no real notion of a potential explanation. It is not possible to look at something and judge that it could be a good explanation, and that if it is true, it is such an explanation. There are no features of the candidate explanation taken in isolation that could justify such a judgement. This undermines most previous work in the field, which has been concerned with an account of potential explanation, and it also tells against the feeling that some sorts of theory can be rejected *a priori* because, even if true, they would not explain, or that some theories are worth pursuing because they would explain if true. The latter case requires sufficient conditions, while the former relies on necessary ones.

Further, necessary and sufficient conditions on actual explanation cannot be given. This is simply because truth is the only additional constraint available to actual explanations that is not available to potential. Truth can, at best, be a necessary condition on explanation, and so would need to be combined with a sufficient condition to give necessary and sufficient conditions.

The argument that there can be no necessary conditions on explanation, except, perhaps, for truth, suggests that explanation can, at best, be a family resemblance concept, since no explanation will have any one feature in common with all other explanations. I suggested, at the end of the chapter, that explanations could be viewed as things that provide understanding. This consideration of purpose could provide the link between explanations, much as the purpose of providing seating provides the link between chairs.

Chapter 2

Understanding and Simulation

The central claim of this book is as follows: to understand something is to possess a mental model of it, a mental model that allows us to simulate the behaviour of the thing under a wide range of circumstances. The better the simulations a model can produce, the better the model, and the better the model, the better the understanding.

In this chapter, I will argue that simulation and understanding really are this closely linked, and that quality of simulation is the only real criterion we can apply in assessing the quality of understanding. In the following chapters I will describe the mental models by which I believe we carry out these simulations.

What is Understanding?

The theory that I am presenting is supposed to be one of understanding in the sense that is used when we speak of understanding a person,[1] thing, or situation. People often claim that they understand cars, or a certain person, or computers. Even more often, they claim not to understand the same sorts of things. In this section I will argue that, in making such claims, people claim to possess, or lack, the ability to simulate the thing in question. I will first briefly explain what I mean by simulation, before going on to link it to understanding and to argue that they are the same.

Simulation

The ability to simulate is the ability to produce, in and by means of a model, behaviour corresponding to the actual behaviour of the object simulated. In order to make the argument easier to follow, I shall consider a particular example: simulating a computer. I think that this is a typical example, albeit a fairly complex one.

First, it is necessary to consider what the model could be. Suppose that I aim to simulate the behaviour of a Wintel (Windows/Intel) computer. There

---

[1] There is an important current debate in the philosophy of mind between the 'theory' and 'simulation' models of our understanding of other people. Other than our common use of the word 'simulation', there is very little in common between my account and the simulationist position in this debate. In particular, my account proposes a completely different mechanism for simulation.

are several obvious ways to do this. The easiest is to set up an exactly similar machine, and see what it does. This might seem pointless, but if the computer you want to simulate is controlling something important, a battleship, say, and you want to find out what happens when the sensors tell the computer that the ship is being attacked, you have good reasons not to do this with a computer wired up to the ship's guns. However, if the set-up is the same, except that the commands do not actually fire weapons, the model can tell you what would happen.

A slightly harder way is to obtain a program that pretends to be the hardware of a Wintel machine, and run the software on that. (Such programs are available for a number of other types of computer.) This model will be slightly more limited, as it won't be able to simulate hardware problems directly. However, the emulator program could be altered to allow you to pretend that a vital chip had failed.

Harder still would be to write down all the ways in which the computer behaves in a huge book, and follow the consequences with paper and pencil. This would take a very long time, but could simulate the computer.

What, then, must happen in one of these processes for it to count as a simulation? Essentially, if I put the simulation in a situation, then it must move to the same state as the real computer would. Thus, if the isolated computer says that the battleship's computer would fire its guns, then this is a good simulation if, and only if, the battleship would fire its guns. It is, therefore, possible to test a model by putting the thing modelled into some simulated situations, and seeing whether it matches up to the model.

'Same state' has to be interpreted in terms of the implementation of the model. In no case will it be *exactly* the same state, as that would undermine the purpose of simulation. In the first case, all the differences are outside the computer. The model computer can't tell that it isn't really connected to the battleship, and so its states are the same as the internal states of the modelled computer. In the second case, the software states are the same, but the hardware states supporting them are completely different. In the third case, the states of the model are descriptions, not copies, of the states of the computer, and count as the 'same state' if they describe the state correctly.

Simulation and prediction are thus closely related. However, they are not the same. The paper-and-pencil system can simulate the computer, but it will not be very good at predicting its behaviour, because it will be so much slower. Even if the real computer did something years ago, the model still provides a good simulation if it matches the states. This might not be very useful, but it is still a simulation.

There is much more to be said about the features of simulation, but I will address them as they arise in the course of expounding my theory. This introduction should be enough to start with.

Understanding

Suppose, then, that I claim that I understand Macintosh computers, but not Wintel machines. What am I claiming as the difference in my mental states? Clearly, it is more than simply knowledge of the computers. I know that both types of computer exist, and I know quite a lot about Wintel machines. However, I still claim that I do not understand Wintel machines: the knowledge that I have does not constitute understanding. However, my claim that I understand Macintoshes does suggest that I know quite a lot about them: knowledge seems to be necessary but not sufficient for understanding.

So, what is the difference? The most obvious difference is that I know how to use a Macintosh, but not a Wintel machine. This, however, cannot be the full story. To some extent, I know how to use a UNIX box (another kind of computer), but I don't understand them at all. Perhaps understanding grants some ability to use or manipulate the understood thing, but it is perfectly possible to use something that you do not understand.

What about knowledge of internal structure? Again, this cannot be the whole story. My knowledge of the internal workings of a Macintosh is fairly superficial, and I have a similar level of knowledge about Wintel machines. Simple knowledge, then, cannot be the relevant difference. However, I know how the internal components of a Macintosh work together, while I do not know how the various bits of Wintel machines influence one another. If a Macintosh fails to start up properly, I know that the problem is likely to be an extension, because I know that extensions do that sort of thing. If a Wintel machine fails to start up properly, I have no idea what is wrong, although I know that there are types of files called .EXE, .BAT, .DOC and so on. I simply do not know how those files interact, and what sort of effects they have.

This, of course, looks very similar to the ability to simulate. I can, in broad outline, simulate the behaviour of a Macintosh. I can predict what it will do in response to a fairly wide range of actions on my part. If something fails, I can think of possible problems which would lead to that sort of failure, and, sometimes, think of actions which would remove the problem. On a UNIX box, although I know what will happen in response to a limited number of actions, I have no idea what would happen if I did anything else, and if something goes but slightly wrong, I am completely lost. I cannot work out what would make the computer respond as it did, nor what I should do to get it to respond in a certain way.

With ability to simulate, the dividing lines between understanding and its lack seem to fall in the right place. I can simulate the behaviour of the Macintosh, which I understand, but not the behaviour of the Wintel box, or the UNIX box, neither of which I understand. I think that the argument that understanding is sufficient for simulation is fairly solid, in the same way as the argument that understanding is sufficient for knowledge. If I understand something, then I will be able to predict its behaviour under various conditions. However, one example is not convincing evidence that understanding and simulation are, in fact, the same thing. Although, of the candidates considered above, it was the only one that matched up with understanding, there may be other candidates that I failed to consider, or the ability to simulate may be one of the effects of understanding, rather than understanding itself. In order to deal with these possibilities, I shall now argue that there are no circumstances in which we would say that someone could simulate something, without also granting that they understood it.

Before I get into this discussion, I should like to emphasise the point that understanding is not an all-or-nothing affair. It comes in degrees, and even a quite superficial understanding may allow good simulation of a very limited range. Understanding, after all, is measured by the quality of the model, not by the quality of a particular simulation. The quality of the model depends on the quality of its simulations, of course, but on the whole range, not on any particular one.

So, let us first consider those cases in which it might seem that someone can simulate something that they do not understand. One set of possible examples can be dismissed right away. It is possible to simulate the interaction of many things on a computer, and thus simulate a situation which you, personally, do not understand. However, in this case, *you* cannot simulate it any more than you understand it. The computer performs the simulation, not you. Whether the computer understands the situation is an interesting question, but not one that I want to address here: the programmer, however, clearly does not.

Suppose that I know nothing about the internal structure of a black box. However, after careful study of it, I know how it behaves in a wide range of circumstances. Thus, I can simulate its behaviour, to a great extent, but, it seems, in the complete absence of any knowledge of its internal structure, and thus, it seems, in the absence of understanding. Does this constitute a counter-example? I believe that it does not.

Consider the limits on my simulation. If something outside the range of input types I have seen is fed in, I will not be able to simulate it. Granting inductive inference, if I know how it responds to voltages on a certain terminal, I will be able to simulate its response to any voltage. However, if that terminal is heated, I will be at a loss to simulate the result. Similarly, if the box has never been moved, in my experience, my simulations may well be completely upset if the box is turned, or shaken. Thus my ability to simulate the box is quite strictly circumscribed: can I claim a similarly circumscribed understanding?

I think that I can. If the box is part of a piece of scientific equipment, I could probably claim to understand that equipment. Knowing what it does to various inputs, I should be able to say what it could be used for, in addition to its current function. If it goes wrong in certain ways, I may be able to suggest a cause (for example, a dirty terminal on the black box changing the voltage going in to it). This understanding is clearly limited, but if I cannot claim it, then my initial contention that I understood

Macintoshes is false. Further, no-one can claim to understand any other human being, animal, or plant, since we do not, yet, have sufficient knowledge of their internal structures to do more than this superficial kind of simulation.

In summary, I think that a good case can be made that, insofar as we can simulate a thing, thus far we understand it. That is, that understanding is identical to the ability to simulate.

The discussion so far may well leave people with intuitive worries. The ability to simulate and understanding seem to be very different sorts of things, so surely they could come apart in practice? The fact that they seem to go together in many cases is interesting, but it doesn't establish my claim for identity between the two.

The situation is similar to that concerning the kinetic theory of heat. Heat and molecular motion are, intuitively, very different sorts of things. After all, molecules are just like little billiard balls, and a hot billiard ball is importantly different from a moving billiard ball. Certainly, I can imagine a single molecule moving with great speed, and this mental picture is not similar to most of my mental pictures of heat. The problem, of course, is that molecules are not just like little billiard balls, however useful that mental picture may be, and a mental picture of a molecule moving with great speed just is a mental picture of a hot molecule. If our intuitions go against that, then our intuitions are wrong — not an uncommon occurrence.

The identity for heat is supported by the empirical success of the kinetic theory. There is no way to argue directly for an identity claim. To see this, consider the simpler claim that two people, say Clark Kent and Superman, are identical: that is, there is only one person in the case. You might argue that they are never seen together, but then Superman and Spiderman are never seen together either (as one is a DC Comics character, and the other belongs to Marvel), and that doesn't show that Superman and Spiderman are the same. You can't assert that Clark Kent can fly, and that Superman works at the *Daily Planet*, because although both of these assertions are true, you only know them to be true because you know about the identity. Indeed, even if the assertions are accepted, maybe one of Clark's co-workers is Superman, and Clark just happens to have superpowers that he doesn't use much.

Eventually, of course, the accumulation of coincidences will convince people that Clark is Superman, just as the success of kinetic theory convinced them that heat was molecular motion. However, the evidence will never logically entail that Clark and Superman are one and the same, and so no brief, knock-down argument can be given.

In the same way, I would deny the force of the assertion that there is an intuitive difference between understanding and the ability to simulate. There may well be such a difference for many people, but I claim that it is a sign of a mistaken theory of understanding. The only possible response is to exhibit my theory, and argue that it is successful in accounting for the data. That is the purpose of the rest of this book.

Properties of Simulation

In this section, I will develop two further arguments to support my position. First, I will argue that there is a good epistemological reason for relying on simulation. Understanding is something that we can know that we have, and our possession of it is subject to testing. Indeed, the whole purpose of many examinations is to discover whether students understand something, and many scientific experiments are performed to see whether we understand something properly. I will argue that the nature of empirical data means that something like simulation is the only real option, thus blocking the objection that the identification of simulation with understanding is unmotivated. Second, I will consider the objection that simulation does not require true knowledge of internal structure, while understanding does. My reply here is that simulation does, in fact, require such knowledge. The best possible simulation must simulate everything that we can know, and thus it must simulate such internal structure as is knowable.

Observation and Simulation

Understanding is something that I can have reason to believe I have, and reason to believe that others have. Conversely, I can have good reason to suppose that I, or someone else, does not understand something. This means that understanding cannot be something that is inaccessible to the sort of investigation we can undertake. In this section, I will argue that, given the sort of investigations we can, in fact, undertake, this requires understanding to be something like the ability to simulate.

Suppose that I think that I understand something, say heat. Being a responsible epistemic agent, I resolve to test my understanding. There are two things that I can do. The first is to reflect on my understanding. If this reflection reveals great, gaping holes I know that I do not properly understand the subject, no matter how the external world may be. However, even if this reflection reveals a fully detailed, tightly structured understanding, this does not reveal that my understanding is right, but only that it is worth testing. (An alternative route is to take this understanding to define heat, so that I can be sure that I do understand heat. The question then arises of whether there is any heat in the world, that is anything that the model accurately simulates, and I cannot determine this by looking at my understanding. I don't think that the two ways of looking at the problem have any interesting differences.)

The only way to test my understanding is to make observations. In the case of heat, these observations are empirical, and the same is true of many kinds of understanding. There are exceptions: mathematical understanding is tested by the observation, in some sense, of mathematical entities, and these may or may not be empirical. Ethical and modal understanding may also be different, but these issues are sufficiently controversial that I cannot say anything useful without launching into a lengthy digression, and accordingly I shall set them to one side, and concentrate on the empirical case.[2] This does cover a wide range of understanding, and I think that the general lessons will apply in all fields, although the details may be different.

One trivial feature of observations is that they are always, without exception, of the observed. The unobserved is, well, unobserved. The only phenomena against which I can test my understanding are the observed phenomena: the unobserved phenomena are certainly relevant, but, being unobserved, they are unavailable. If my understanding says something about the unobservable, I cannot directly check that part. The phenomena may well exist, but they can never be observed, and thus never have any (direct) influence on my assessment of my understanding. Unobserved phenomena, by virtue of not having been observed, are not available, and thus cannot constrain or test our understanding.

This point is only worth labouring at such length because I am making the utterly trivial claim that, within a class of data, we only know about the data we have observed, as data. I am not making any of the more substantive claims, such as that we can never have any knowledge of unobservables, or that we never really talk about unobservables, or that we never have any reason believe that anything exists while it is not being observed. Any reading on which I am making a controversial claim here is wrong — I am not even putting prior limits on what counts as observation.

The trivial point does have one substantial consequence. Two understandings which make exactly the same predictions, retrodictions and accommodations of the observed data cannot be distinguished (actually and in the present case) by data. They can't be distinguished by *those* data, *ex hypothesi*, and the only other data are unobserved, and thus not available to distinguish the understandings. Of course, further observations may be able to distinguish them, as may observations made with the benefit of more advanced equipment. Right now, that doesn't matter: those data are not available, and thus cannot be used.

There may be other, perfectly reasonable, ways of distinguishing between the two understandings. These other ways must also be observable, and observed, if they are to make a difference. Thus, it is possible to observe the speed with which a simulation works, and then use that evidence to favour it over another candidate. It is not, I suppose, possible to observe the colours of the neurons involved (at least not under normal circumstances and not yet), so while this is certainly a feature of the simulation, it is not one that is of any use for testing it.

In order to simulate a situation, you must predict what will be observed, or show that your simulation gives rise to what was observed. In order to simulate perfectly, you must do this perfectly. The fact that current models

---

2   I do think that this account extends in natural ways to cover mathematical and modal understanding. Ethical understanding is harder, due to the complete lack of consensus as to what is actually involved in ethical beliefs.

of global climate do not predict local cloud cover is regarded as an important shortcoming. On the other hand, you do not need to simulate things that are not observed. Even if you did, those results would be idle. If the simulation does produce the right results, then it is a good simulation, at least as far as this desideratum is concerned. Thus, it is possible to apply evidence to the assessment of the simulation, and understanding is amenable to test.

The worry arises at this point: what if a simulation gets the right results in the wrong way? In that case, it isn't really understanding, is it? I will go into the specific application of this worry to internal structure below, but I will discuss the general issues here. In brief, such a requirement renders it impossible for us to ever know whether we understand something. The claim is that, even if the understanding matches all our empirical data and all our other desiderata, it might still be wrong. Indeed, the match with the empirical data is not taken to be particularly good evidence that we have understood — it only shows that we can simulate. The claim is not that we might be able to simulate some particular data without understanding: this is the possibility of error, and something I am willing to concede. The interesting claim is that, no matter how well we simulate the data, this does not provide any evidence for understanding. And this claim is the same as the claim that data cannot provide evidence for understanding.

This claim is simply false. People reveal their understanding of a computer when they use it, and if they are persistently capable, this shows that they do understand it. If they claim to understand it, and show consistently high ability in using it, this counts as evidence for their understanding. Empirical data can supply positive, as well as negative, evidence for understanding.

The situation is not the same as that for scientific theories. There might be genuine worries over whether we can, really, have evidence for a theory. Understanding, however, is something that we do have evidence for, and it is therefore essential to give an account of it that makes this possible. The simulation account does make it possible, and the idea that we could have perfectly good simulation without understanding makes it impossible. Accordingly, I think that the simulation account is well motivated, and the objection not.

Some readers will now be thinking that I have claimed that we only understand the observable, or that our mental models only deal with observable things. This is not the case. A model may rely on representations of unobservable entities in its simulation of what can be observed. For example, we may simulate the behaviour of a car with tinted windows by supposing that there is a driver. The driver is unobserved, but his representation is no less a part of the model. Indeed, it is likely that many elements of models will represent unobserved things, since we observe so little of the world around us. If we believe that we only observe sense data (I don't, but some people do), then no elements of models represent observed things: in fact, they are all represent unobservables, as none of them are sense data. This is not a problem: the models are assessed on how well they generate representations that match our interpretations of the sense data received, not on whether they are composed of mental representations of sense data. At the other extreme, if we suppose that we can observe electrons there may well be no representations of unobservable elements in our models. If we suppose that we can observe electrons and universals (I am rather sceptical of this end of the scale, as well), then our models probably do not contain any representations of unobservable elements.

Thus, I claim that the worry that simulation is possible in the absence of understanding reduces to the worry that understanding is not amenable to evidential confirmation. Since understanding is confirmable, we must produce a theory that makes it so, and a theory identifying it with simulation succeeds in this. It may not be the only possibility, but it is certainly a possibility, and its status is not affected by this worry. General arguments are not always totally convincing, however, and in the next section I will discuss the specific case of internal structure, to show how simulation handles it.

Internal Structure

Many people have claimed that a really good model of something must mimic its internal structure. Since the internal structure may not be observable (and, in the tight sense in which only sense data are observable, will not be), I do not wish to simply impose such a requirement. In this section, I shall argue that it arises naturally from the constraints imposed by the things that are observed.

There is a very quick way of arguing for this. As I have characterised a good simulation, it must be able to simulate everything that we can know. That is, although we can, if our understanding is poor, know something without understanding it, if our understanding is good we will understand everything we know. Otherwise, it will produce the wrong answers in some cases, or at best fail to simulate, because we will know what is going on, and the model will not tell us. Thus, if we can know the internal structure of things, whether on the basis of observations or some other way, our models must simulate that structure.

The problem with this argument is that it might seem to fall foul of the discussion of the relevance of the observed, immediately above. If models must be tested against the observed only, then maybe we could know about internal structure without having to test our simulations against it. That is, the evidence gives us reason to believe things about the internal structure, but our simulations work perfectly well while postulating completely different internal structures. The history of science suggests that this is wrong: the original motivation for science is to provide better predictions of the observable, and it has ended up with many beliefs about internal structure. However, since it is controversial whether those structures are really needed for the predictions, I will argue for my position from first principles. Thus, even if we consider only the observed data, we are still led to model the (unobserved) internal structure as well as possible.

The ideal model must distinguish between all those inputs and outputs that the thing modelled distinguishes. In other words, the ideal model must have at least as good a resolution as the real thing. If it does not, then there will be simulations that the model gets wrong, because it approximates the input and thus misses the distinction. Of course, this requirement would be satisfied if the model had a higher resolution than the thing modelled, but such models are unnecessarily unwieldy, and thus will usually be abandoned on those grounds.

It might be thought that, if the resolution is higher than that which we can observe, we need merely match the observable resolution. There are two reasons why this is not so. First, we must be able to accurately assign borderline cases to an input category in order to predict the correct output. If the system is sensitively dependent on initial conditions (a chaotic system) a small difference in input can make a very large difference in output, and our models should be able to handle that. It may be that, in practice, we cannot simulate such systems. The ideal, however, should still be to do so. Thus, while we may deliberately simplify the resolution of a model in some cases, this will be a known deviation from the ideal way of simulating that situation.

Second, the broad construal of 'observed' means that differences down to the level of one atomic layer are definitely observable, and will sometimes be observed, for instance when using a scanning tunnelling electron microscope. In order to model the observed results of such a situation correctly, we must have a resolution at the atomic level. It may be that there is no immediate reason to take account of a level of detail which is, at present, technically beyond us. However, if we have reason to believe that such a level exists (for example, the evidence for the atomic hypothesis drawn from Brownian motions), then we should incorporate it into our models, so that we can handle those situations in which it does become observable and observed. Detail which, in principle, can never be observed nor have observed consequences need not be incorporated on these grounds, but it is hard to see how this could be a problem for the theory.

Another consideration concerns the internal structure proper. I claim that if the model is to be functionally equivalent to the thing over a wide range, indeed, in principle, the widest possible range, then the internal structure of the model will have to be functionally equivalent to the internal structure of the thing. Suppose that the thing contains a small group of parts which function together in a certain way, while the mental model contains only one element, representing their joint function. As long as these parts function together, as they normally do, the model will be accurate, and no need to revise it will be seen.

However, suppose that something happens to interfere with those parts, and stop them working together. In order to simulate this situation, the model must have elements for each part, so that their behaviour when separated can be simulated. Thus, in order to simulate accurately, it seems that the structure of the model must mimic the structure of the thing modelled. That is, you really need to know the internal structure in order to have the best possible model.

This is too quick. The model might be able to compensate for the interference without accurately modelling all the internal components. Maybe it models one actual component as two pieces, or, by pure chance, errors in two parts of the model cancel each other out. Models that work correctly by pure chance can be ignored: they might be deceptive, but no theory can avoid being undermined by extreme bad luck or a cosmic conspiracy. In most cases, a model that works correctly by pure chance will fail in other situations, and so the fault will be discovered. Still, there remain a number of possible models which produce the same results as one that mimics the internal structure. How can they be detected and ruled out?

First, the structure must be capable of being developed by refinement of a crude model of the whole. Further, this refinement must follow the lines that are formed when the thing is actually broken. For example, consider a model of a computer, such as the one I am using now. I can connect the monitor to another CPU (and have actually done so), similarly for the keyboard. Thus, my model of the computer must treat the CPU and monitor as separate units: the model must break along those lines. Further, I could remove components from the CPU and install them in other machines. In some cases, this would be easy, in others more difficult, but each bit that I can remove must be a removable part of my model, otherwise simulation will fail. This even applies to such actions as cutting the keyboard in half and throwing one half away. My model of my computer fails at this point: I have no idea what would happen, except that the computer would definitely be broken. If I had a better understanding, however, I would be able to say what effect slicing the keyboard up would have. Thus, the joints in the model must match the joints in the real thing at least down to the limits of the observed: and, as I argued above, this is a long way down.

Second, there must be no idle parts in the theory. These would require resources while not doing anything useful, and thus would be eliminated from the best models. It might seem that this rules out, for no good reason, the possibility that there are idle parts in the world. However, these parts must be *completely* idle, in every context. They must be incapable of detection by any actual or possible method, since if they can be detected, even in the sense in which quarks can be detected, the model must incorporate them in order to accurately simulate those detections — the part is not idle when it is being detected. Parts that are this inaccessible will never be included in any picture of the world, no matter how it is built up, with any justification, because there can never be any evidence that they are there. As soon as the possibility of evidence is allowed, they must be incorporated in the simulation: if there is no possibility of evidence, then the world is simply such that no sentient observer can ever form an accurate picture of it, and the fact that this method has that as a consequence is hardly a criticism of it.

Now, it is obvious that this problem is closely related to the classic problem of underdetermination (see Duhem and Quine). It is not, however, quite the same. In the Duhem-Quine thesis, we have all the information concerning the actual observable states of the world, and we try to construct a theory of it. The claim is that we can construct an arbitrary number of theories, and thus that the empirical data can give us no reason to believe in anything unobservable.

We are not in this situation when we consider the aims of modelling. A model, ideally, should accurately simulate the actual world. Given our limited knowledge, there are many possible futures of the actual world, and although only one of them will be the actual future of the actual world, we have no way of knowing which one. Since we cannot distinguish one of the options, we must try to build a model that will work in all of them. Thus, our aim is a model that would not conflict with any data possible given the laws of nature and our beliefs about the current situation.

This gives us more data than Duhem and Quine allow us. When Quine talks about 'all possible data' he means 'all empirical facts about the actual world'. When I talk about 'all nomically possible data', I mean all empirical facts about all worlds with the same laws of nature as our world. This is a great deal more data, and it is not clear that any sensible form of underdetermination can affect it: the underdetermined theoretical features must be such that, not only did they make no difference to the empirical data in the actual world, but they also made no difference in any other world with the same laws.

It may well be that considerations of underdetermination show that the data accessible within a single world can never uniquely determine such a model. This is fine: I am here concerned with the aims of modelling, not the practicality of carrying them out. My description entails that we should aim to have models that are this powerful, and I have suggested that the only methods available to us as we try to build these models involve simulation. It might be that our methods can never give us what we want: while this would be unfortunate, it would not mean that the description was wrong. Our evidence can tell us whether we have better or worse understanding, even if it can't tell us whether our understanding is perfect.

Thus, I claim that the aim of simulation of the observed under a wide range of possible circumstances requires that we attempt to accurately model the (unobserved) internal structure of the world, all else being equal. Of course, all else is not equal in most circumstances, and in those circumstances I believe that the simulation requirement better matches the facts than the requirement to match internal structure.

Consider a human being. We would normally claim to understand him if we know his likes and dislikes, the sorts of things that annoy him, and so on. That is, we normally claim to understand him if we can simulate him under a psychological description. A strong reductionist, however, might claim that we only really understand him if we can simulate his behaviour on a molecular level. While this seems wrong, he can back up his claim by pointing out that a sudden surge in dopamine levels will have a major effect

A Theory of Understanding

on the person's behaviour, but that our psychological model is completely incapable of simulating it. Dopamine just isn't the right sort of input.

Why is there a perceived tension here? Consider the reductionist, and grant him all the controversial points. That is, suppose that everything in the world is a physical entity, subject to physical laws and only to physical laws. Further, suppose that all the laws are known. Under these circumstances, a full physical model of a person can simulate that person's behaviour under any stimulus. Dopamine would be modelled as molecules of a certain type entering the brain, while an insult would be modelled as sound waves of a certain type entering the ear. There are no surprises.

On the other hand, consider the folk psychologist, working in terms of beliefs and desires. As soon as the subject takes a psychoactive drug, the models will be wrong. If your brain is full of the right neurochemicals, you will be happy, no matter what your current circumstances. (People on Prozac experience this effect.) This is clearly a deficient understanding, so the physicalist model is obviously superior.

However, if we look at this from a different angle, we get a very different picture. The physicalist model is massively complex, far too complex for a human mind to run. Indeed, since it includes a complete model of a human brain, and then some other bits, if it were possible to run the model faster than real time it would be possible to think faster than you can think, simply by modelling your own brain. Further, the model is no good if we are simply told that a person was mortally insulted. We need to know the exact words, the exact pitch of the voice, and the precise previous state of the person's brain, before we can run our physical model. Thus, the physical model is useless for all practical purposes.

The tension between reductionism and anti-reductionism is thus the tension between the ideal and the real. Ideally, a reductionist model is superior (assuming that the materialist's assumptions are correct). It can simulate everything, and is never surprised. Really, a non-reductionist model is superior, because it can actually be used. The reductionist model is great in theory, completely useless in practice. The anti-reductionist model is deeply flawed in theory, but very useful in practice. Indeed, given the ways in which we gather information about the world, only the anti-reductionist model can be used at all, because we simply do not gather data with the precision necessary to run the reductionist model.

The debate between reductionist and anti-reductionist theories of science evaporates on this account. True, in principle we could understand everything in terms of physics, and then we would be able to properly account for any input. In practice, however, this would be absolutely impossible, so we have to understand in terms of chemistry, biology, and psychology. This 'higher level' understanding will not, in practice, reduce to the lower level. There may be translation rules from the concepts of one level to those of another: thus, the benzene molecule is a certain arrangement of carbon and hydrogen atoms. However, performing a simulation at the lower level may well be impossible. As far as I know, the quantum state of the benzene molecule is only approximately known: it is beyond our capacity, even with the aid of computers, to exactly simulate one molecule. Chemistry, however, regularly simulates countless billions.

If there are translation rules, we can bring in a lower-level simulation when it would be helpful. Thus, we can consider the effect of the decay on carbon-14 on benzene molecules because we can treat the benzene as a set of carbon and hydrogen atoms. We will probably have to fudge a bit when translating back to the higher level, but the digression to a lower level was still useful. However, the existence of translation rules is not guaranteed. It is possible that there is no 'bit' in the brain that is 'anger'. That is, you cannot take 'anger' and translate it into a physical brain state. You can take a whole brain state, work out the outputs, and then translate those outputs into social terms (if necessary by creating a simulated video of the acting person), but there is nothing in the simulation of the brain that is the anger. Indeed, it seems likely that some things, at least, will turn out to be like this: money is the standard example. It seems wildly implausible that there is any intrinsic physical property common to coins, bank notes and electronic bank balances that makes them all money. In this type of situation, we might as well ignore the lower level. We certainly can't simulate a whole person or, even worse, a whole society at the atomic level, and in the absence of translation rules we can't even bring in the atomic level in restricted cases. Reduction may be possible and useful in theory, but in practice it is completely irrelevant.

Young[3] makes essentially this point, although he phrases it as a criticism of the use of 'surrogate models' as a means of understanding. A surrogate model is one which matches the structure of the thing to be understood, and he summarises one criticism as follows:

> The surrogate model, although it gives the same answer as the machine to all these sequences, throws very little light on the difficulty. There is no way to examine the model and have it exhibit the cause. One can only 'run' it, just as one can use the machine itself, and watch the problem emerge.[4]

His alternative suggestion is task/action mapping, whereby you create a model that tells you what to do in order to accomplish a certain task. The models that emerge from this process generally involve completely different terms. His example concerns electronic calculators, and while the surrogate model talks about registers and functions within the machine, the task/action mapping is concerned with types of calculation and button-pressings. The task/action mapping allows the user to use the calculator fairly efficiently, but it sometimes throws up problems. Nevertheless, for the purposes of using the calculator it has the advantage of going from a problem to a sequence of actions, which the surrogate model of the calculator does not do. This makes the model superior for many purposes,

---

[3]   Young 1983.

[4]   Young 1983, p 43.

including understanding the calculator *as a tool*. Indeed, Young says that the surrogate model explains the calculator better, but that the task/action mapping is more useful when explaining how people use the calculator, and in the process of design.[5] Thus, the surrogate model of the calculator is of little use in understanding the human/calculator system, because you also need the full model of the human. On the other hand, the task/action mapping allows you to simulate the person using the calculator relatively easily. Thus, the task/action mapping is better for some purposes than the surrogate mapping.

This is, of course, a purely practical limitation, and things will change as computers become more powerful. For example, it is now possible to understand, to a significant extent, fracturing and malleability in metals by simulating the behaviour of each atom individually.[6] No matter how powerful our computers become, however, they will never be able to simulate their own behaviour, at the atomic level, in faster than real time — if they could, they could work faster than they worked, which is impossible. Thus, different levels of understanding will always be useful, even if the physicalist is right, and all the behaviour of a human being could be predicted by considering his atoms. And, as a corollary, we will sometimes understand best by not worrying about the internal structure of a thing. The model will fail under certain conditions, but at least it will be manageable, and we will be able to use it to produce predictions and explanations.

Conclusion

Understanding and simulation, then, go hand in hand, and we cannot have the one without the ability to perform the other, nor the ability to simulate without understanding. Further, the quest for good simulation will push us towards matching the internal structure of things, while recognising that we should not always go all the way to the basic elements.

Distinctions

The positive part of this chapter is now essentially complete. In this section, I will briefly attempt to head off a number of possible misunderstandings of my account.

Understanding and Simulation

Understanding is not simulation. Understanding is the *ability to simulate*. Just as the ability to bake a cake need not be edible, understanding need not

---

5   Young 1983, pp 50–1.
6   Marder 1998.

be a simulation. Thus, it is perfectly possible to have understanding of something that, in fact, you have never simulated. Indeed, it seems likely that we often have such understanding, since our mental models can be combined in a very large number of ways, and we have only explored a small fraction of them. Further, it is entirely possible to understand something that you are not currently simulating. The ability can be unrealised at a given time.

Another consequence is that the quality of understanding cannot be read off from the quality of a single simulation. The ability to bake cakes is not exhausted by the ability to bake lemon meringue pie: similarly, the ability to simulate a person is not exhausted by the ability to simulate them giving a lecture. Someone can be very good at baking lemon meringue pie while only being mediocre at baking cakes in general. Indeed, their carrot cake might regularly give partakers food poisoning. Analogous considerations apply to understanding. As a result, a very poor understanding could produce isolated excellent simulations.

Simulation and Prediction

Simulation and prediction are not the same. A simulation may predict, or it may account for an event. This is not merely a matter of the relative times of the simulation and the real event: there are events which can be simulated, but not predicted.

Consider a truly indeterministic system, containing a single indeterministic event, which has a 90% chance of flashing a green light and a 10% chance of flashing a red one. If asked to predict the outcome in advance, someone who thoroughly understood the system would say something about the inherent problems, but probably opt for a green light. If a red light flashed, however, he can still simulate the system perfectly well. The indeterministic event happened to go one way, and once that fact (unknowable, even in principle, in advance) is incorporated, the simulation can proceed perfectly well.

Epistemic limitations can give rise to similar situations, even when the underlying system is deterministic. For example, the solar system is known to be a chaotic system, if modelled by General Relativity. This means that tiny differences in initial conditions could have substantial differences in results. Suppose that Neptune goes sailing off into the interstellar void one day, completely unexpectedly. The theoreticians go to work, and show that a particular combination of positions, consistent with observations but far more precise than observations could hope to be, have that result, while very similar positions (most of those consistent with observation, in fact) do not have that result. The theoreticians can simulate the disappearance of Neptune, but not predict it.

Similar considerations apply to evolutionary biology and history. To take an historical example, William the Conqueror won at the battle of Hastings. A simulation of the battle will include the fact that Harold's troops were very tired (having fought a large battle in the north and then marched straight to Hastings) as one of the elements leading to his defeat. However, in advance we cannot say that the tiredness of the troops was sufficient to cause their defeat. We cannot predict the outcome of the event, but we can simulate it.

Such simulations are open to accusations of *ad hoc* modifications. This does not, however, mean that such accusations are always justified. In the indeterministic case, they clearly are not. In some deterministic cases, it is similarly clear. The fact that sometimes the modifications are *ad hoc* does not vitiate the point that they are also sometimes necessary. We have to modify the model to match the particular situation, because the particular situation is unique, and sometimes we can only get the necessary information after the situation has played out.

Understanding and Explanation

Understanding is not the same as explanation. An explanation is something that improves understanding (see Chapter 6 for more detailed discussion). The link between explanation and simulation is thus fairly remote: an explanation is something that improves the ability to simulate. To return to the cake example, if the chocolate cake is simulation, an explanation is a recipe. The recipe improves the ability to make the cake, at least in many cases, but it is not a chocolate cake. It isn't even edible.

Thus, my account is very far from claiming that all explanations are simulations: it is likely that very few are. While you might be able to improve someone's ability to bake a chocolate cake by presenting them with such a cake, it is not likely to be a very good method. Similarly, presenting a simulation is unlikely to be a good way of improving the ability to simulate.

These paragraphs are very far from being a full account of explanation — that will have to wait for the development of a theory of the ability to simulate. The following chapters describe such a theory, in terms of mental models, before returning to explanation.

Chapter 3

Mental Models

Introduction

I have now argued that understanding is a matter of the ability to simulate, and claimed that we simulate by means of mental models. In this chapter, I will put some flesh on the bones, and describe my theory of mental models. The next chapter is concerned with the ways in which we use those models: in particular, with how we use them to simulate.

Why do I refer to my account as a theory of mental models? On the face of it, the 'mental' part is easy enough, since I am concerned entirely with things in the mind. This is, however, deceptive, since there is a great deal of debate over the nature of the mental. This account is neutral as between many of the competitors. It is compatible with any version of physicalism. If the mind is identical to the brain, then mental models are collections of neurons. If the mind is functional units supported by the physical structure of the brain, then mental models are such functional units. If eliminative materialism is true, then mental models are things that talk of understanding should be eliminated in favour of.

Dualist views are a little harder to deal with, in large part because few dualist views have much in the way of positive claims. My account is not compatible with any dualist metaphysics which insists that all mental processes must be conscious, as important parts of the operation of mental models are unconscious. The theory is also incompatible with any account on which all operations of the mind are essentially ineffable and impossible to describe, since it describes mental models. It is, however, compatible with dualist views which allow for unconscious mental processes, and that those processes can be described.

One type of dualist view on which mental processes are ineffable is one on which the mind is metaphysically simple. My theory is flatly incompatible with such an account, as it involves analysing the bits of one part of the mind. This conflict has wider ramifications. Although no version of physicalism is consistent with the idea of mental simplicity, there is still a strong tendency to think of the mind as a simple, unitary thing. Dennett[1] refers to this as the 'Cartesian Theatre' idea, in which the simple mind watches all the mental processes on a stage, or carries them out on a workbench. Since my account makes certain parts of the mind inaccessible

---

[1]   Dennett 1991.

to consciousness, it is fairly obviously incompatible with this kind of account.

One basic assumption of my account of understanding is that mental processes, at least the ones that I am interested in, just happen. They are not *done*. There is no agent who does the simulating. This assumption runs directly counter to theories that make the mind metaphysically simple, and to Cartesian Theatre ideas. It would be helpful if I could minimise the chances of confusion. Here, language tells against me. The active voice attributes agency, and it is not practical to write entirely in the passive voice. Thus, I must either attribute agency to the bits of mental models, which is not entirely appropriate, or to something external, which is also inappropriate. The best I can do is point out that the question 'who is doing this?' is almost always the wrong question to ask, because it doesn't have an answer.

My personal inclination is towards physicalism, to the extent that I do not really see dualism or metaphysical simplicity as viable competitors. This does influence the presentation of my theory of understanding. I think of mental models as being supported and instantiated by physical processes in the brain. However, since no version of dualism could be described as well-established, I am not concerned about possible incompatibilities with such metaphysical systems. It is just as likely that the dualist view is mistaken as it is that my account is mistaken, and so each must be assessed on other merits.

What, then, about calling my theoretical entities 'models'? I wish to show that my choice of terminology is sensible, and suggests the right sort of thing about my theory.[2] I will thus consider the main use of the word model, for physical models of cars, ships, and the like, and show that my models have much in common with these central cases.

Models are often made by the designers of large projects. The model is smaller, and thus easier and cheaper to make, than the thing modelled, and it is used for initial testing. The idea is to give the model enough of the important properties of the final product to test how the final product would behave, were it to be constructed. The properties mimicked will vary: in the case of a ship, the precise colouring is unimportant, but the buoyancy and stability must correspond, while a model of a building may be assessed almost entirely upon its colouring. If the model shows that a certain design has serious problems, or is not acceptable to the client, then another design can be created, and the designer is saved a lot of trouble.

Mental models serve the same purpose. The model is intended to simulate the outcome of actions in the real world more quickly, and without any of the consequences. Thus, by mentally modelling a stone boat, I can convince myself that it is likely to sink, and thus not waste time carving one. Like physical models, mental models do not reproduce all the features of the thing modelled. No mental model is complete, and, in any case, mass

---

[2]   See Craik 1943 for an early presentation of similar ideas.

is not modelled with mass. As with physical models, such differences do not necessarily detract from the quality of the model.

It is important to grasp that mental models, in my sense, are like the models in wind-tunnels in that they are concrete, rather than abstract. Their basic elements are like little engines that transform inputs in a certain way, and these elements, which I call mutors, are organised to model things in the world. Their first level of organisation, into what I call effectors, models properties such as mass and colour. The second level, into what I call simulors, models types of things. The final level, consisting of units that I call simulants, is derived from simulors and models specific things.

Mental models, then, are concrete things made up of mutors, which are organised in effectors, which are organised by simulors. In the rest of this chapter, I will set out this account in more detail.

Mutors

Mutors are the basic units of mental models, and the base of my analysis. Thus, while I shall make some suggestions about their internal structure, those suggestions are not centrally important to my theory. As long as the mutors are implemented in some way, the theory could be right. On the other hand, the properties I impute to them are essential to my theory. Thus, it is vital that the properties of mutors be grasped, if the rest of the theory is to make any sense at all. Accordingly, I shall consider this first, before going on to suggest ways in which they could actually exist in the brain.

What Mutors do

Mutors are both the building blocks and the motors of mental models. In this section I shall consider their work as motors: in the next I shall expand on their nature. At the most abstract level, mutors receive input and produce output. The output will depend upon the input, but this dependence will vary between mutors. The important point, at this level of abstraction, is that the mutors are active: they actually *do* the work on the input, and produce the output. They are not rules by which the input can be transformed into the output: rather, they are machines which effect the transformation.

Mutors and logical rules This is the most essential point to be grasped about mutors, and it is impossible to understand the rest of the theory without doing so. Mutors are not logical rules of inference. They cannot be accurately represented in terms of conditionals, universal generalisations, or anything similar. They cannot even be thought of in those terms for heuristic purposes: the analogy is seriously misleading. A much better analogy is a sausage machine: meat goes in one end, and sausages come out the other. Any meat can be turned into sausages, but the sausages will differ, depending on the meat put in (e.g. if you put pork in, you get pork sausages). It is true that a logical system consists of statements and rules, while a system of mutors consists of inputs/outputs and mutors. It is obvious, I hope, that mutors are not analogous to statements, nor inputs to rules, but the analogies between mutors and rules, and inputs and statements, also fail. In the rest of this section, I will spell out some of the disanalogies.

First, I want to introduce a piece of notation. Let us indicate a mutor which takes inputs of the form a and produces outputs of the form b as 'a§b' (pronounced 'a to b'). This representation is not a mutor, anymore than 'elephant' is an elephant, but it does allow for more succinct exposition. (Further, like 'elephant', it is a name rather than a description.) Within mutors, I will use -a to indicate that the input is not of the form a. Thus, -a§b would take any input that was not of the form a, and produce output of the form b. (I will discuss the inputs and outputs of mutors in more detail below.)

A logical rule can do no work in isolation. Consider 'A; If A then B'. Observe that 'B' does not occur outside the scope of the conditional, within the quotes, despite the fact that it is logically implied by those contents. This is an obvious point, and might seem to have no importance. Mutors, however, are different. If you have a mutor (a§b) and its input (a), then you will get the output (b). Logical rules do not force you to apply them; mutors don't need to be applied, and so automatically turn their inputs into their outputs. Of course, this assumes that the input is in an appropriate form, that the mutor is functioning, and so on. However, an inappropriate form would be parallel to 'Q; if A then B', from which nothing follows, and a non-functioning mutor would be analogous to 'A; fat A chartreuse B', from which, again, nothing follows. In short, logical rules require someone to apply them, while mutors do not.

This is related to Lewis Carroll's point in his famous paper 'What the Tortoise Said to Achilles'.[3] Here, the tortoise has Achilles pile up rule after rule, without ever moving, by the rule, from the premiss to the conclusion. This can be taken to show that we cannot treat rules as statements, and that someone so doing has not properly understood the rule. Nevertheless, the disanalogy with mutors is still strong. Severely edited, the corresponding conversation would go something like this:

Tortoise: That beautiful model of equality! You do admire that model, don't you?

Achilles: Yes … [Achilles quickly throws his notebook over his shoulder.] But I seem to have lost my notebook.

Tortoise: No matter. I have the necessary under my shell. Now, [there follows some rummaging] *this* is the mutor 'Things equal to equals are equal to each other', and *this* is the input for 'A

---

3   Carroll 1895 [1995].

and B are equal to equals'. Now, suppose that I have these
and …

Achilles: What's that, that's just appeared in your other hand? It looks
like 'A and B are equal'.

Tortoise: Um, so it is. Never mind. Got any lettuce?

A second disanalogy is also made clear by this dialogue. The tortoise
does not commit a category mistake in believing that he can hold a mutor
and its inputs in his hands. (We will not worry about where he gets his
hands.) Mutors and their inputs are concrete particulars, the sort of thing
that can be held in a location, while logical statements and rules are both
abstract. Unfortunately, a third disanalogy is obscured: the inputs and
outputs of mutors are not inherently representational, unlike the statements
involved in logic. I will return to this point below, when I discuss the inputs
of mutors in more detail.

The differences recounted above are certainly sufficient to establish that
mutors are not identical to logical rules. However, it might be thought that
they are instantiations of those rules. Thus, the mutor a§b would be an
instantiation of 'If A, then B'. We could think about the system in terms of
the rules, but it would really, physically, be made of mutors. This is not the
case. The mutor is not only a completely different sort of thing from the
rule, it also behaves in a different way. The most obvious and important
difference is to do with contraposition. 'If A, then B' can be transformed to
give 'If not B, then not A'. The same cannot be done with the mutor. -b§-a
is a completely different mutor from a§b, and one can easily exist without
the other. Indeed, a§b cannot be transformed into -b§-a even if you also
have lots of other mutors, and only by adding -b§-a itself can you ensure
that the mutor is present in the system. If a§b is presented with the input -b
it will probably do nothing at all: the input is of the wrong sort, and thus the
mutor cannot handle it. Consider the sausage machine: if you put a car in
one end, you do not get a nice little note explaining that there is no meat
out of the other. You get a broken machine.

Finally, a set of mutors need not be closed, in the way in which a logical
system is. Suppose that a logical system contains the rule 'If A, then B'.
This system cannot contain any assertions 'A&~B' without leading to a
contradiction. However, a system of mutors can perfectly well contain a§b
and a value 'a&-b'. If this value is fed into the mutor, then a contradiction
may result, or the output may simply be b. However, there is no reason why
the value should be fed into any mutor, and *a fortiori* no reason why it
should be fed into a§b. Indeed, a mutor of the form -b§-a would happily
take a as an input, as a is not b, and give the output -a. This may be a
problem for the system containing the mutor, but it is not a problem for the
mutor itself, and under certain circumstances it would not be a problem for
the system, either.

A further lack of closure can be seen in the effect of concatenation. A
logical system containing 'If A then B' and 'If B then C' effectively
contains 'If A then C'. However, the mutors a§b and b§c in no way require

the existence of a§c. Indeed, if the b stage was important, there would be good reasons not to include a§c, because that would tend to wipe the b out. Further, a logical system containing 'If A then B' and 'If not C, then not B' effectively contains 'If A then C'. A system of mutors containing a§b and -c§-b not only does not contain a§c, but, given a, it is unable to produce c. Similarly, it is certainly not redundant for a system of mutors to contain both a§b and -b§-a: the two serve different purposes.

Given all this, it should be clear that a system of mutors is not a logical system. However, it might be argued that there is a logical system which is equivalent to the mutors: a system of which the mutors are a model. This is almost certainly true, and certainly irrelevant. My claim is that we do, in fact, understand by using mutors. The fact that we could get the same result by manipulating a certain logical system is not to the point. Further, I think that there are empirical implications that differ between the two cases: I will return to these below, when I have set out my whole theory.

The logic gates that form the basic hardware of conventional computers are a very good analogy for mutors. A not-gate produces a low output if given a high input, and vice versa. It is not the same as the rule for logical negation, although it can often be represented as such. An and-gate produces a high output if both of its inputs are high, and nothing otherwise. Since it has two inputs and a single output, it obviously cannot be run backwards. An and-gate can be useful when trying to perform computations about conjunctions, but it is not, itself, a conjunction. The main disanalogies are that there are only a few types of logic gate, but, I believe, many more kinds of mutors, and that mutors are not structures of doped semiconductor, while most logic gates are.

I have belaboured this point because, in my experience, there is a great temptation, at least among philosophers, to illegitimately assimilate mutors to logical rules. Now that the difference is firmly established, it is possible to discuss other aspects of mutors.

Mutors and their inputs It is impossible to say, at this point, exactly what the inputs of mutors are, as that will depend on the nature of the mutors themselves. They could be activation potentials in neurons, or some sort of disturbance in psychic stuff. It is possible, however, to say something about their structure.

Astute readers will have noted that, above, I used lower case letters to refer to the inputs and outputs of mutors, and upper case for logical variables. This was deliberate: whatever the inputs and outputs of mutors are, they are as concrete as the mutors themselves, rather than being abstract particulars. 'a' is the name of the input or output of a mutor, not the input or output itself.

The first thing that can be said is that the inputs and outputs of mutors are the same sort of thing. The output of one mutor could be the input of another, without needing any intermediate processing. This does not mean that there is some object that gets shuttled through the mutors, being altered by each one in turn (the sausage machine analogy breaks down here). The situation is more like an electromagnetic switch. If a current flows in the input, then a current flows out of the output, but the input current does not flow out with the output: in general, these systems are set up to allow a small current to trigger a much larger one.

Second, the inputs and outputs need not be simple. The use of single letters above was a shorthand. 'a' could represent a state in which channel one is positive, channel two negative, channel three near zero, and channel four a long way from zero, in either direction. 'b' could represent a state in which channel one is near zero, channel two very positive, and either three or four is negative. If a mutor had eight input channels, then it could have input states equivalent to a&b, avb, and so on. Indeed, under these circumstances the mutor bvb§b would, in fact, serve a useful purpose, and might be explicitly present.

From the examples given, it is clear that an input can be -b without being a (if channels three and four are both slightly positive, for example). Thus, the mutor -b§-a could easily have a as its input state and -a as its output state. Given the description here, this doesn't even sound counter-intuitive.

Third, the notation should not be allowed to suggest that mutors are inherently discrete-state devices. That is, there is no reason why, in a§b, b should not be 2a, or, if a is complex, some more elaborate function of the parts of a. Indeed, in many cases such a functional response will be what is wanted.

The final thing to say about the inputs and outputs of mutors is that they are not, inherently, representational. There is nothing about the input or output, considered in isolation, that makes it represent anything. It may well be the case that most inputs to mutors are, in fact, representational, but that is in virtue of things external to the inputs themselves. This situation is very similar to that holding for words. The word 'cat' does not inherently represent feline animals. It does represent them, but it does so in virtue of things external to the word itself. In the case of the input to a mutor, these external factors involve more than just the mutor into which the input is being fed.

This means that mutors do not know what they are doing, even in a vague, metaphorical sense. A mutor might serve the purpose of deciding whether something will fall, but the same mutor (identically the same, not just another token of the same type) might also serve a completely different purpose, without altering its function in the slightest. Further, a mutor doesn't care about the source of its inputs. They could be directly encoded from perception, dredged up from memory, or produced by the imagination: as far as the mutor is concerned, they are all exactly the same.

Mutors, then, can have very complex inputs, and will produce outputs of the same general type, all the while without, necessarily, representing anything.

Mutors and the mind The status of mutors is a little vague, because they are mental entities, and the status of mental entities is disputed. If we assume, for heuristic purposes, an identity theory of mind, the mind is the neurons of the brain, and mutors are groups of neurons. The organisation of the brain is still a great unknown, but a mutor could be a particular group of neurons, perhaps even a particular neuron. Thus, it makes sense to ask questions like 'How many mutors does this person's mind contain?', 'Are any of this person's mutors the same?', or 'Do these two people have any of the same mutors?', in the same way as we can ask those questions about books in their libraries. Two people who have the same mutors possess different tokens of the same type, and their tokens of the mutor type could develop in different ways in the future.

As concrete particulars, mutors are individuated in much the same way as chairs and tables. a§b and c§d are two mutors, while a&c§b&d is only one. At this level, it is not possible to say more than that: mutors are individuals, just as chairs are. In most cases, psychological experiments will be able to tell the difference between different cases: the mutor a&c§b&d cannot act on a alone or c alone, while a§b and c§d, respectively, can. This individuation will be grounded in the implementation of the mutors, but the nature of this grounding will vary between different implementations.

Of course, this theory is not restricted to physicalist theories of mind. The mutors could be bits of mental stuff just as they could be made of neurons. In this case, the same points apply. Even if they are mental, the mutors are not rules which are applied by the 'ghost in the machine': they are mental engines, which carry out their functions quite happily.

One consequence of the theory of mutors sketched here is that the operation of mutors cannot be 'watched'. A mutor only communicates with the rest of the mind via its inputs and outputs, so if the mind needs to know any intermediate states, it must produce two mutors, one leading to the intermediate state, and one going from there to the final state. This is one reason why it might be better to have the pair a§b and b§c, rather than the single mutor a§c. Thus, mutors should match up with a basic level of mental processing, one that is opaque to introspection. This means, directly, that thinking should not feel like using mutors. It should feel like dealing with things and their properties, and seeing what happens next. We should not be aware of the calculations or transformations taking place. I, at least, don't think I am. As I shall argue later, however, mutors are a powerful explanatory tool.

A second consequence is that mutors are, to a great extent, independent of the rest of the mind. If the neurons constituting a mutor were taken from the brain and kept alive in a vat, they would still produce exactly the same response to the appropriate inputs. The converse is not true, however: you cannot have a mind without mutors, and minds with different mutors will be different. This makes mutors sound a lot like mental modules, as described by Fodor and others. They are informationally closed, fast, and automatic. However, they are not all in-born, they vary widely between individuals, and they are a great deal simpler than the systems that modularists normally have in mind, so it would be somewhat misleading to think of them simply as mental modules.

Implementing Mutors

As promised, I will now make some suggestions about the way in which mutors could be implemented in the mind. To emphasise my lack of commitment, I will make two suggestions, one based on connectionist theories (neural networks), and the other on production systems.

Production systems　A production system is a method in Artificial Intelligence programming which has enjoyed considerable popularity (and is thus one of the main targets of connectionist critiques). Both Soar[4] and ACT*[5] are production systems, and I shall have more to say about their general relation to my theory later. Although both production systems are implemented as computer programs, their originators claim that the mind contains similar systems, and so I will talk about productions as mental processes. In this section, I wish to concentrate on the link between the basic elements of production theories and my mental model theory.

A production is a mental thing that fires whenever its conditions are met, producing an output. It is not really possible to say any more in general, as the details depend on the system in which they are embedded. A production is the combination of the rule and the interpreter/processor. However, mutors could be seen as productions. a§b will, when it receives a, fire and produce b. Indeed, it is possible that any possible description of mutors is also a description of a production, and that my theory is a production system. Such a system could include a dedicated processor for each production, but need not.

If it does not, am I then describing interpreted rules? No. Consider one instruction in a computer program, say 'If A=6, then let B=7'. This is *not* the instruction: it is a representation of the instruction. The instruction is a pattern of charge within the processor which, given the structure of the processor, will cause a change should the pattern be of a certain sort.[6] The patterns of charge corresponding to the rules in the program can usefully be considered separately, and it is very easy to talk about them as if they were the rules in the program. Easy, but misleading. Given its environment, the pattern of charge will act in a certain way, and it is no more free in that than a brick is free not to fall. Of course, it is rather easier to change the

[4]　Newell 1990.

[5]　Anderson 1983.

[6]　This distinction was actually enshrined in US law: it was illegal to export strong cryptographic software, but not illegal to export the description of that software. As a result, the source code of the programs was taken legally out of the US, scanned into a computer, and compiled to produce the program. (The example is rather spoiled by the fact that exporting *electronic* descriptions of the software *was* illegal.)

relevant environment for the pattern of charge, but in general the pattern of charge itself cannot do so: computer programs do not rewire silicon chips by running on them.

Consider a sieve, which separates particles with a diameter larger than a certain value from those which are smaller. The sieve is not a rule, but it can be described by a rule. Software charge patterns are like sieves: they are not rules, although they can be described by them. The sieve, the compiled software, and mutors are all dispositions to act, not rules. This distinction is not terribly important if you are a cognitive scientist, and completely irrelevant if you are a computer programmer, but it is absolutely central if you are a philosopher, as I am.[7]

Productions are fairly abstract, program-level entities, and thus this suggestion says little about the physical (or psychic) composition of mutors. Indeed, it is possible that it does nothing but point out an interesting parallel. However, two of the most significant research programs in cognitive science have been happy to take productions as primitive, so, if nothing else, the observation suggests that it is legitimate to take mutors as similarly primitive.

Neural networks Connectionist theory, also known as neural network theory, is currently fashionable in cognitive science.[8] A major reason for this is that the brain seems to be a multiply connected network of simple units, and that, therefore, theories which rely on multiply connected networks of simple units seem to be a good way of talking about it. A neural net is such a network: it consists of a set of input units, a set of output units, and a set of intermediate processing units. Each input unit is set to a value, and this value transmitted along links to other units, mainly in the processing set. These links have varying weights, which multiply the value before it is processed by the receiving unit. The receiving unit will take a value that depends on the total value arriving at it, and then output this value to other units, along more weighted links. The output units receive inputs from a number of other units, and take on a value that depends on the weighted sum of those inputs. The remarkable thing about connectionism is that such networks have proved to be very powerful.

As will become readily apparent, my account is not a connectionist one. My units are far too complex to be the nodes in a neural net, and the links between them are of the wrong sort. However, neural networks are good candidates for the hardware underlying mutors.

Consider a neural network with four input nodes and four output nodes, and an arbitrary number of intermediate nodes. This can be set up with any relationship desired between input and output, and will automatically give the output if presented with the input. Thus, an input of (+1, 0, −1, −1) could give an output of (0, 0, +1, 0).

---

[7]   For examples, see almost any discussion of the later Wittgenstein.
[8]   My characterisation is based on Churchland 1995 and Rumelhart 1983.

The network will not function exactly as I have characterised mutors above: any input will produce an output, and the output will be some sort of function of the input. In many cases, this will be useful, where an output equal to twice the product of the inputs is wanted, for example. In other cases, the spurious outputs would be undesirable. That is, a simple neural net cannot (as far as I know) be made to function purely as a discrete-state device. However, an additional layer of threshold units could ensure that, unless the output was within ±0.1 of the desired value, a null output was obtained. If a more complex 'fail' value was required, a second network could be appended. (It may be possible to do all this within one network: if so, so much the better. The fact that most networks will produce almost the output if given almost the input is emphasised in the literature, however, and I do not know whether this feature can be got around within a single network.)

Neural networks have the additional advantage of flexibility. It is possible to 'program' a neural network with no information beyond the desired response. Thus, if you know that the network must go from (+1, 0, −1, −1) to (0, 0, +1, 0), you can train a network to do so, without having to do anything intelligent: indeed, this task is always done by computer, as it is exceedingly tedious. This is important for my theory, as we must, clearly, be able to learn new mutors and modify old ones over the course of our lives. It need not be particularly easy — indeed, the well-known difficulty of learning fundamentally new ways of thinking suggests that it will not be — but it must be possible. I shall return to this issue when I come to discuss explanation.

On this implementation, all mutors would be groups of neurons. This does not commit me to the claim that all groups of neurons are mutors, much less to the claim that all groups of neurons are mental models. Recall that a mutor can exist in isolation from a mental model, if, for example, kept alive in a vat. In that case, there is a mutor but no mental model. Very simple organisms, such as *C. elegans,* a nematode with around one hundred neurons, do have groups of neurons which respond to inputs by producing outputs. We could, if we wanted, call these mutors. (We may not want to, for various theoretical reasons.) However, unless they were organised into effectors and simulors, they would not be components of mental models. Mutors are the building blocks of mental models, just as bricks are the building blocks of houses. This does not entail that all mutors are in a mental model, any more than all bricks are part of a house.

Finally, there is the question of whether this means that my system could be a neural network. In one sense, yes, it could. It could, physically, consist of nothing but neural network nodes connected in neural network ways. And this would make it a single neural network. However, in another sense it is not. There is not a single network, which is trained to produce all the understanding that the person has. There are a number of small networks, each trained to do part of the work, which produce understanding together. This is another point to which I shall return later, when considering the relationship between my theory and connectionist accounts.

Effectors

Effectors are the level at which meaning enters the system. It is not really possible for a mutor to be wrong: it does its job, and there isn't really any other way of distinguishing it than by the job it does. It isn't even clear that a mutor can malfunction: in order for that to happen, its proper function must be defined. An isolated mutor is not for anything. A mutor within an effector is for something, and thus can fail to do its part. However, it is then impossible to say whether you have the right mutor, but it is malfunctioning, or you simply have the wrong mutor. Effectors can, however, incorrectly model the world: they represent something in the world, and the mutors that make them up could lead to them behaving unlike the thing modelled. If the effector behaves unlike the thing modelled, it doesn't matter whether one of its mutors is malfunctioning, or whether the wrong mutor was incorporated; either way, the effector is malfunctioning.

As with mutors, there are two main respects in which effectors must be considered. First, their internal structure: they are made up of mutors, but how? Here, the things I have to say are an important part of my theory. Second, their role in thought. They differ from mutors in representing, so it is also necessary to discuss what they represent. I will do this first, before discussing their structure and, finally, their role in thought.

Effectors and the World

So, what do effectors represent? Very roughly, those features of the world which we call 'properties'. Individual colours, such as red and blue, scientific properties like mass and charge, dispositions such as fragility and solubility, and aspects of temperament like kindness and touchiness are all examples of properties. Properties are all semantic universals: they can apply to many different things and, on the whole, to many different types of thing. (Note that not all universals are properties: 'man' is a semantic universal, but not a property.) The ontological status of red is, frankly, irrelevant to this question: my contention is that we have constructed something real, and particular, in our minds which is supposed to correspond to red. On a nominalist view of semantic universals, the effector is all that there is to red, while on a realist view the effector sometimes (in fundamental cases) represents a metaphysical universal in the external world. For a trope theorist, particular uses of the effector for red correspond to red tropes, but the general effector doesn't represent anything real. All these views of ontology are consistent with this view of psychology.

Further, I am not claiming that everyone has the same effectors in their mind. Indeed, I would positively claim that different people have different effectors. My mental models contain two sets of effectors called colour: one set represents visible properties, the other represents properties of quarks and gluons, and is not directly detectable by any of my senses. I suppose that most people do not have this latter set, but that does not detract from its status in my model. Similarly, dubious properties, over whose existence there is some debate, will have corresponding effectors in the models of those who believe in them, and won't in the models of those who don't.

It is also important that models of particular things can behave according to their properties. A model of a particular solid object must not let the models of other solid objects pass through it. In order to do this, the mutors making up the effector, as well as its value, must be incorporated into the model. This means that an effector behaves like a universal: it can be wholly present in many different simulants, and yet there is still a sense in which the Temperature of this item is the same thing as the Temperature of that one. Thus, the model account explains why these metaphysical doctrines about properties and things should seem plausible.

This leaves the question of how effectors are supposed to refer to properties. This is far too large a question to cover here, requiring, as it does, a theory of reference for most of language. They can, however, take over most of the existing theories of reference. The component mutors could be taken to define a template, so that they refer to properties that match that template. They could refer to those things that cause them in the appropriate way. They could refer in a way that depends on how they are used. None of these accounts is entirely satisfactory, but they are not particularly unsatisfactory for effectors. In short, the question of reference is no more problematic for effectors than for any of the competing theories. It is also no less problematic but, as I said, that is too large a problem to tackle here.

The Structure of Effectors

An effector is a mental particular which groups together some number of mutors, and has a value. In trivial cases, the number of mutors grouped may be zero, but such an effector would be completely inert. The effector can be thought of as the combination of a variable value, a list of mutors, and the mutors listed. The mutors enable the effector to do things in the model, while the list determines which mutors are in the effector, and the variable value provides the route by which inputs are given to the mutors.

Effectors are, therefore, just as concrete as mutors. Just as a house is a group of bricks held together with mortar and with a door in the front, an effector is a group of mutors held together by the list, and with an associated value. Effectors are a different sort of thing from mutors, but they are not in a different ontological category. In the rest of this section, I will discuss the internal structure of effectors.

The component mutors Given that effectors are made up of a list of mutors and those mutors, the basic question is 'Which mutors are on the list?' It is certainly not the case that any arbitrary collection of mutors constitutes an effector. In this, effectors are analogous to mutors. There are many possible relationships between inputs and outputs which are not encoded in mutors, including, as we saw above, some relationships which are implicit in the system. Similarly, there are many possible groups of mutors which are not encoded in the list of an effector, and some of these groups could be 'implicitly' present. For example, if two effectors were always co-instantiated, any model that contained the mutors in one effector would contain the larger set made up of the mutors in both. Nevertheless, there are two effectors here, not one.

The picture is made more complex by the fact that most mutors will, necessarily, be involved with more than one effector. The effector 'fragility', for example, will have a mutor determining whether something fragile breaks, but the output of that mutor will also depend on the force being put in. Fragile things do not break if touched gently with a feather, after all. Further, the output of this mutor could involve the effector 'broken'.

I suggest that an effector only contains the mutors which take that effector's value as an input. This is to reflect normal usage: a property is normally considered to be characterised by the things it can bring about, not the things that can bring it about. 'Broken' is not generally taken to involve 'having been hit hard or sawed up or pulled apart or partially burned or rusted or decayed or...', although it does involve 'non-functional'. The difference in the model is that the mutors that are part of an effector will react to the presence of a value of that effector. If we consider the effector value a, then a§b will be activated by it, and produce an output. c§a, however, will not.

This makes things fairly simple. An effector contains all and only those mutors which take its value as an input. This has the consequence that most mutors will be part of more than one effector, but that is not a problem. The effector specifies the whole set of the mutors, not just any subset. If we simply consider this in terms of abstract notation, we might now be inclined to limit the variables (a, b, c, etc.) to effector values, so that each letter represents whatever value a particular effector takes, and name the effectors after their values. The effector a might, then, contain the mutors (a§a, a&b§2a&-b, avc§d). The property b would then include a&b§2a&-b, probably among other mutors, but would not include a§a (a simple persistence mutor) or avc§d, and thus would be distinct from a. On this account, -b could well be an active output, indicating that the effector b should be inactivated. If b also included b§b, then there would be a conflict to resolve. This is to be expected: if we turn on a heater and open all the windows, it is not immediately obvious whether the room will warm or cool. I will consider such conflicts and their resolution later.

Mutors and non-interaction   There are some properties that do not interact with one another at all, such as colour and mass, at least for most people. In such a case, I claim that there will simply be no mutor that involves both effectors. The reason for this is very simple. Mutors, as concrete particulars, take up 'space' in the mind. Indeed, if each mutor is a neural net, they literally take up space in the brain. We can only store a finite number of mutors, and so null mutors, which encode a lack of interaction, would be an avoidable waste of space. Further, a null neural net needs to be programmed just as much as an active one, so further effort would be wasted in creating mutors that do nothing.

This means that there is no difference, as far as the mutors are concerned, between knowing that two things do not interact, and not knowing whether they do. In both cases, there is simply no mutor present. This means that there must be some higher level at which there is a difference, because we can wonder whether two things interact and then remember that we know that they don't. The easiest way for this to happen would be for every effector to store a list of effectors with which it was known not to interact: the list could, presumably, be held in less space than would be necessary to hold all the mutors, since the list is a passive thing which does need to be interrogated from outside.

This would probably tie in to type-hierarchies among effectors. For example, anger is a type of emotion, and emotions are a type of mental property. Thus, we might want to say that mental properties do not interact with mass, thus passing this lack of interaction on to all effectors representing mental properties, that emotions do not interact with logical arguments, and that anger does not interact with non-mental properties. (Note that I am not claiming that all these restrictions are accurate, merely that they are possible.) This would also allow for exceptions within a type hierarchy: if most examples of a certain sort of thing do act in a certain way, but one does not, then it is likely to be easier to attach the behaviour to the type, and include an exception for the one example of the type which does not behave thus.

This does not exhaust the discussion of type-hierarchies as they apply to effectors, and I will return to it in the next section

The list of mutors I have been talking about effectors containing a list of mutors, without being explicit about what I mean. Obviously, they don't have little bits of paper with the names of the mutors written on. There are two main ways in which this list could exist, and I will call them *de facto* and *de iure* lists.

A *de facto* list is constituted by the fact that the value of the effector is fed into a mutor. There is nothing more to being on the list than taking the effector's value as an input: the list is not a separate element of the effector. For *de facto* lists to work, the way in which values are transmitted to mutors must be stable and restricted, because otherwise effectors will constantly evoke different mutors, and thus fail to model the regularities that we see in the world.

If we consider effectors in terms of the neural net model of mutors, there is a simple way to implement *de facto* lists. Each effector would have a certain number of input nodes associated with it, on those mutors into which it fed, and the effector itself would be represented by a group of neurons, maybe equal in number to the input nodes, which connected to every mutor involving the effector. In turn, those mutors which involve the effector in their outputs would connect to the effector neurons, altering their state. I should emphasise again that I am not committed to the details of the neural net picture: I am simply interested in building a 'how-possibly' explanation for the implementation of models. The important feature of this neural model is that the value of the effector is provided as an input to all the constituent mutors because it is a value of that effector. The model contains structural features (in this case, bits of nerve cells) linking the mutors of one effector together, and these links carry (literally, in this case) the value of the effector.

A *de iure* list is a distinct element of the effector, and can be used to check up on the mutors to which the effector actually provides inputs. Suppose that each mutor has a unique code, which can be checked against a list of codes contained in the effector, possibly by seeing whether it can physically bind to the code in the list (in the same way as enzymes select their substrates). If a mutor is on the list, it is passed on to another bit of the effector, which gives it the effector's value as an input.

If effectors use *de iure* lists, it is possible for an effector to pass its value to the wrong mutor, or to fail to pass its value to a mutor that should have received it. If the list is *de facto*, this is simply not possible, because a mutor that isn't connected and receiving the input isn't on the list. A *de iure* list allows for better error checking, but has additional processing overheads, since there are two steps: check a mutor against the list, and send it the input. I suspect that effectors actually have *de facto* lists, but this is based almost entirely on my inability to introspect that a mutor is missing from one of my effectors. They could work either way, and still be consistent with my theory.

Whether the list is *de iure* or *de facto*, I do not believe that there is any organisation within the list. A mutor is either on or off: there are no 'important' mutors, or 'pre-processing' mutors. Here, I am motivated entirely by simplicity considerations. It seems that it should be possible to build mental models without needing any more internal structure than is provided by the list, so it is worth pursuing such a theory until it either breaks down, or proves to be successful

Values of effectors Once we have properties, it is clear that some can be possessed in degrees, and that a good mental model must pay attention to those degrees. Thus, one thing can be more massive than another, and one person can be more friendly than another. These are the values of properties. The value of a property will depend, of necessity, on the thing instantiating the property. After all, 'mass' itself is no particular mass. The values of effectors must mimic this, and so I will postpone further discussion of this point until I discuss things and their counterparts in the model, below.

Effectors in Thought

The internal structure of effectors, then, is very simple: they have a value, and a list of mutors to which this value is passed as an input. This organisation sheds some light on the role of effectors: they are principles of organisation. In this section, I shall develop this in more detail.

The uses of effectors Effectors presumably serve a useful purpose: what is it? It cannot simply be that of representing properties, since the existence of real, metaphysical properties is controversial. Besides, even if metaphysical properties really do exist, there are presumably many features of the world that our models do not represent: why do they represent properties?

Effectors serve to simplify our mental models, and bring them down to a size that can be stored in the mind. If there were no effectors, then the model would have to be organised at a higher level. Suppose that it were organised at the level of distinct things: every thing that you can distinguish from other things has its own set of mutors. This would require an enormous number of mutors. For a start, every person you knew well would have to have a set of mutors describing their interactions with every other person that you knew well. A single mutor would not be able to model a person's behaviour, because human behaviour is complex. On the other hand, a single group of mutors could not be used for every person, because people differ.

Further, the model of every distinct thing would need to contain mutors for every other distinct thing with which it could interact. Note that, without effectors, it is not possible to leave some gaps: any two things for which there are no mutors cannot be simulated as interacting. If you had no mutors for how Bill and John would interact, you would be able to say absolutely nothing about what they would do when they met, even if you knew that both were prone to starting fights with other people.

Such an inability may seem implausible, and, indeed, I think it is. However, it is important to see that, as soon as we characterise Bill and John as 'violent', we have introduced effectors into our mental model. Thus, it may be that effectors are not introduced so much because they are useful, as because we cannot avoid doing so. Still, even in that case there must be a reason for the capacity to introduce them, and there their use is a plausible candidate.

It might be thought that we do not, in fact, need so many mutors as this might suggest, even in the absence of effectors. After all, pairs of violent people act in much the same way, so we can link all their simulors to the same mutor. There will be a lot of connections, but it is not so obvious that this is a problem. There is a definite problem with this, however. We cannot know in advance how each pair of violent people will behave: in the absence of belief in properties, there are no grounds for induction here. Thus, we have to build a mutor in each case. To substitute another, functionally equivalent, mutor we would need a mechanism for checking the behaviour of every mutor we possessed, and seeing whether it was suitable. This would require a lot a resources by itself, rendering effectors useful again.

The final observation to be made here concerns novel things. If we see something new, and have no effectors, then we can say nothing about it, beyond reporting what we have seen (assuming that we can manage a language allowing such description). If, however, we can assign properties to it, we can say things about its behaviour. Note, again, that this is not a question of justification: in the absence of effectors we are literally unable to say anything about its unobserved behaviour. Mutors must be assigned to the thing individually on the basis of its behaviour, and the first time we see it it has not (yet) done anything. Thus, it has no mutors, and thus it will not interact in a simulation. This suggests that effectors structure our whole thought, as indeed I think they do.

Hierarchies of effectors   Although mutors may not be organised within effectors, effectors are, almost certainly, organised among themselves. The most important kind of organisation is probably the type-hierarchy. This goes back to the Porphyrian Tree,[9] and even further back to Aristotle's categories. Thus, among properties, anger is a type of emotion, and emotion is a type of mental property. These hierarchies can serve many useful purposes. If all members of a certain type involve certain mutors, then they should all be connected to those mutors. This could be done by connecting each effector to each mutor, but this could get complex. In the abstract notation, there would be many mutors of the form $avbvcvdv...\S z$. The alternative would be to have each effector activate all those higher in the hierarchy whenever it was activated. In that case, the disjunctive mutor could be replaced with the simple $t\S z$ mutor, where t represents that type of property.

In the neural net implementation, the advantages are even more striking. If there is a type of effector, all members of which are governed by six particular mutors, then, if there are eight members of the type, connecting them all directly to the mutors involves 48 connections. If there is a type-effector, however, only fourteen connections are needed: eight from the effectors to their type, and six from the type to the mutors.

This has further organisational advantages, in that a bad mutor can be deleted from every effector in the type very easily, and when adding a new effector to the type, you only need to make one link, rather than modifying the inputs to all the mutors. Possibly equally important, this matches the way in which we think about properties in the world and, since this theory is, among other things, a theory of how we think about properties in the world, it should match up here.

Another kind of organisation is the part-whole hierarchy. It might be thought that properties would not have this type of hierarchy, but consider the property 'striped black and white'. The properties black and white are clearly part of this property, and it cannot be reduced to them, since it

---

9   Porphyry [1994], p 4 (22).

covers many different kinds of striping: narrow, broad, vertical, horizontal, wiggly, and so on. Here, the organisation is required because that is the way the world is (or, at least, seems to be). Some things are stripy.

I do not have a detailed account of how these sorts of effectors will work. Sometimes, at least, as for 'stripy', they indicate that all the part-effectors apply, in some sort of arrangement, in this case in space. 'Flashing' is a property that stipulates a temporal pattern among those properties ('bright' and 'dim', roughly) that make it up. There are likely to be other sorts, and it is probably both safe and (almost) empty to say that such effectors will specify a relationship between the effectors that make them up. Thus, the effector could be a decision procedure: if the effector is considered at a certain place, time or respect, then it acts according to one effector, otherwise according to the other. The alternative would be an effector that was two different effectors at the same place, same time, and in the same respect. This seems, *prima facie, a priori* impossible, which suggests that we do not have such effectors in our models. However, I am not totally clear about the behaviour of this sort of effector, so there may be effectors with other effectors as parts which are not some sort of decision procedure. If so, the overall effector would simply contain all the mutors of the part-effectors as well, and this can easily be incorporated into my theory.

The information about these hierarchies must be encoded somehow, and I suspect that the lists of effectors that represent kinds of the property represented by another effector are likely to be *de iure*, if only because they do seem to be introspectable. However, these lists need not be properties of the effectors themselves, but are more likely to be features of the general machinery that organises simulations.

Effectors and p-prims My theory suggests that we see everything in the world, at least at first, in terms of the effectors that we know. Over time, we may develop new effectors, but at a given time we can only handle the world in the terms that we currently have available. This is because all the mutors, the little motors that let us think about the world, are linked to effectors. Unless you give something an effector, it can do nothing in thought, and once you give it an effector, it automatically gets all the characteristics of that effector. This, in turn, implies that our observations, what we see and hear, are strongly influenced by our beliefs about the world.

Psychologists have done a substantial amount of work on the influence of theory on observation and description, and work by diSessa[10] is particularly relevant. He concludes that people think about the world in terms of what he calls p-prims, short for phenomenological primitives. He characterises them as follows:

---

[10]   diSessa 1983.

[P-prims are] primitive notions which similarly stand without significant explanatory substructure or justification. The system of which these primitives are a part, however, is cognitive, not a scientific theory or axiomatic system. We are after simple knowledge structures which are monolithic in the sense that they are evoked as a whole and their meanings, when evoked, are relatively independent of context.[11]

This is a good description of my effectors. They have no explanatory substructure, since although they do have structure in the mutors, this is not available to introspection. As far as we are concerned, effectors simply behave in certain ways. They are part of a cognitive system, and not, for example, an abstract theory, as I have been at pains to emphasise, and they are certainly evoked as a whole, with context-independent meanings. It should be noted that diSessa was concerned mainly with the way that people do elementary physics, rather than with explanation in general, but that there is no reason to suppose that his results do not generalise. (My theory claims that they should, so this would be a way of testing it.)

The analogy between p-prims and effectors is not perfect, however. diSessa does discuss such p-prims as 'rigidity' and 'springiness',[12] where the analogy seems to be excellent. He recounts an experiment in which the subject would not accept that glass balls bounced because they were springy: springiness requires compression and expansion, while glass is rigid until it breaks, and thus cannot be springy. This maps very well onto effectors in my model. Springiness contains at least two mutors, one which makes the object spring back, and one which makes it compress and expand in the process. Rigidity only needs one mutor in this case, requiring that shape does not change. When an object is believed to be rigid, the conflict between that effector and one of the mutors in springiness is sufficient to entail the rejection of the whole property. That is, the subject rejected the idea that glass balls were springy, rather than simply rejecting the mutor that would have them deform while retaining the one governing bouncing back.

Later in the paper, however, he discusses p-prims that seem much closer to mutors.[13] These include 'dying away', 'force as a mover', and 'force as a spinner'. The first is the Aristotelian idea that motion naturally dissipates over time, without any outside input. The second and third concern the ways in which a force acts on a body. 'Force as a mover' is the idea that something affected by a force will move in the direction of the force, no matter which way it was moving originally, while 'force as a spinner' is the idea that a force which strikes an object off-centre will cause it to spin. The latter two, in particular, both seem to be mutors concerned with the idea of a force. In these cases, diSessa is concerned with persistent false intuitions

---

[11]   diSessa 1983, p 15.
[12]   diSessa 1983, pp 17–23.
[13]   diSessa 1983 pp 30–2.

— ideas about the behaviour of the world which seem to be very difficult to shift, even after education in physics.

From my theoretical perspective, it seems that diSessa is doing different things in the two cases. In the first, he is asking the subject to build a model of a situation, and looking at the elements that get built into the model. In such a case, we would expect to see effectors serving as the basic units — the question is whether the things involved have certain properties, rather than how those properties behave. In the second case, he is concerned with poor models of properties. Even when the right effectors — forces and motion, for example — are incorporated into the model, they do not behave in the right way. This, obviously, points to poor mutors. The difficulty he notes in changing these p-prims is to be expected on my account: mutors are difficult to modify, at least compared to effectors. An effector can be modified simply by changing the mutors that it lists, while a mutor must be carefully reprogrammed.

His conclusions are concerned with the move from novice to expert, and the differences that this will make in p-prims. We can see that such a change will require changes at both levels: experts will become aware of new properties, while rejecting some of the properties believed in by novices, and they will also modify the mutors making up some effectors, while retaining the effector. Since his (sketchy) theoretical framework suggests that the move consists entirely in the modification of p-prims, it is clear why he assimilates the two classes.

Indeed, this is not a particularly severe criticism of diSessa. His paper is largely empirical, concerned with showing that there are these sorts of elements, and that they do differ between novices and experts: the title of the paper is 'Phenomenology and the Evolution of Intuition'. There is little in the way of theory beyond picking out p-prims, and his reasons for believing in them are entirely empirical, as far as I can tell. Since my reasons were entirely theoretical, the two approaches seem to complement one another, and we can take diSessa's paper to provide empirical evidence for my account.

Simulors

According to this theory, things are modelled as groups of properties, by simulors which are groups of effectors. Thus, a book will be modelled as having a certain size, mass, colour, number of pages, certain coloured illustrations, interesting contents, a poor index, etc. The things modelled as simulors are often types, but sometimes individuals will be modelled: people, for example, will often be modelled individually, as may things that a person deals with particularly often. Simulors are linked by a variety of relations — type-token and part-whole for example — but there are no higher level entities in the model, in the way in which simulors are a higher level than effectors, which in turn are a higher level than mutors. In this section, I shall discuss the way in which simulors are made up, and, to some extent, the organisation of the simulors themselves.

The Structure of Simulors

A simulor is a group of effectors, with values. This raises three questions. First, what, if any, organisation is there among the effectors that make up a simulor? Second, how do values work? Third, how, exactly, might simulors be implemented? In this section, I will consider the three questions in turn, and conclude by discussing the relationship between simulors and frames, as discussed by Minsky.

Effectors of simulors A thing has many properties. Even an elementary particle, likely to be simple in a model as in the world, has mass, charge, spin, and energy. These effectors must, somehow, be part of the simulor. Let us first consider a simulor that represents a type of things in the world. The simulor in the model is still a token, a particular. There is a bit of the model that is the simulor, but this simulor can model any token in the world of a type in the world. For example, there might be a simulor in the model that represents dog. This simulor is a particular, but it stands for all dogs, in much the same way as the token of 'dogs' earlier in this sentence. (Again, the details of reference are too complex to pursue here.)

This simulor, then, gathers together all the effectors representing properties possessed by dogs. Within the model, this is true by definition: any property corresponding to an effector not gathered by the simulor is not possessed by dogs *qua* dogs. The aim, presumably — and I will argue for this below — is to have the effectors gathered in the model correspond to the properties gathered in the world. How are they organised within the simulor? The simplest route, again, is to suppose that, as with the mutors of effectors, they are simply listed. Thus, dogs are mammals, four-legged, have a size, are solid, and so on.

There are some cases, however, in which all tokens of a type have properties of a certain kind, but can have different properties of that kind, not just different values for the same property. Suppose, for example, that all dogs have a disposition, so that the simulor contains the effector 'disposition'. This is a type-effector, with such effectors as 'friendly', 'aggressive', 'morose' and so on falling under it. Any particular dog will have one of the particular properties as its disposition. (I neglect such dispositions as 'friendly to people it knows, aloof with everyone else, but aggressive towards postmen', because I don't think that they pose general problems: 'friendly' already comes with an implicit object, since we don't use 'friendly' to describe attitudes to lampposts, and there is no obvious problem with using more specific objects in some cases.) If we do not know a dog's disposition, we still know that it has one, and that it will react to people and other dogs in some way, and that there will be some consistency. If we can substitute a specific disposition, we can say how it will react in more detail.

The same procedure can be carried out in general. If the simulor contains a type-effector, then when we substitute a sub-effector in the model of a specific thing we will increase the specification of the behaviour of that thing. This is because the substitution increases the number of mutors attached to the model of the thing. The mutors attached to the type-effector are still there, as they are also attached to the sub-effector in virtue of its link to the type-effector. The mutors attached solely to the sub-effector are also present, so that the behaviour of the model is defined under a wider range of circumstances.

In most cases, the presence of a type-effector in the simulor will require us to substitute a sub-effector, although sometimes the type-effector itself may suffice. This substitution is no more problematic than the initial attachment of an effector to a simulor, so no new problems arise.

A related problem arises for effectors that represent properties that are usually, or sometimes, possessed by things of a certain type. Most people cannot do handstands, and so the simulor for 'person' will not include an effector that allows the person to balance in an inverted position. This is easy to resolve, as the necessary effector can be added to the relevant simulant when it is created, as described below.

Somewhat more difficult is the question of properties that are normally possessed, but not always. For example, the overwhelming majority of people can feel pain, but there is a medical condition which means that you can't. The simulor for 'person' must contain an effector for the ability to feel pain, but it must also be possible to remove that effector from the simulant representing a particular person. This, in itself, is no problem. Removing effectors from a simulor is no harder than adding them. The complications come when we consider the evidence we would need to remove certain effectors.

Most people speak a language. However, a significant number of people don't, at least if 'speak' is narrowly interpreted to refer to spoken language. Thus, we would be willing to remove that effector from our model of someone on fairly slender evidence — simply being told, for example. We would want more evidence before removing the effector for the ability to feel pain, such as being told, with an explanation, by someone we trust. We would probably not be persuaded to remove the 'mass' effector from someone's model, no matter what. Massless people are just not going to happen. Finally, there may be some effectors we could not remove from the model, because without those properties a thing does not qualify as a token of the type. If those properties are absent, the thing must be modelled by a different simulor.

The problem is that the theory, as so far described, does not have the resources to incorporate these differences. There will have to be more structure than a simple list among the effectors in a simulor. However, although these details are important, they are more important to questions of classification than to questions of understanding. I will return to this briefly, below, but a full discussion of these issues must be left for future work.

Simulors and values While isolated effectors have the capacity to take a value, they do not have any particular value. Otherwise, there would be a certain mass that was typically mass, and any other value of mass would be a deviation from the norm. Simulors, however, will generally attach some sort of value to their effectors. There is a typical mass for a person, and a typical size for a planet.

These values will, in general, be vague defaults. People weigh about seventy kilograms, but can be twice that heavy, or even more. While values will automatically be approximate, depending on the resolution of the model in question, vagueness is a little more complex. It is probably most easily implemented as a property of the whole simulation: if any of the values are relevantly vague, then the outcome of the simulation is uncertain. Thus, in simulating a 'typical person' standing on the bathroom scales, we will not be able to say what the scales will read. However, if they stand on a railway viaduct, we know that it will not collapse. The mass of the person is vague, but it is clearly less than that of a train, and the viaduct is strong enough to carry a train.

Default values will usually be easy to over-ride when a simulant is produced from the simulor, as described below. We often know the properties of a particular instance of a type of thing, and thus do not need to rely on defaults. However, some defaults will be very hard to over-ride, just as for the presence or absence of certain effectors, described above. Further, there are values for some properties that are impossible for some types of things: people do not weigh several tonnes, or less than a kilogram. This suggests that a default value will also come with an expected range of variation, and that it will be easy to over-ride it with values within that range, but hard if we step outside it. Such a range also allows descriptions in relative terms. Without a range, a description of a person as 'very heavy' and an elephant as 'very light' should lead to modelling the person as heavier than the elephant, which is almost certainly wrong. Instead, the 'very heavy' person is modelled at the top of the human range, while the 'very light' elephant is modelled at the bottom of the elephant range. Since the ranges do not overlap, the elephant is still heavier.

The larger the class of things that a simulor represents, the larger the range of its values is likely to be. The extreme case is a simulor that represents a particular individual. This may well be worth doing for things with which we have to deal often, as it provides a convenient way of remembering the precise values of all its properties in a form that is immediately useful for modelling. In this case, many values will have zero range, so that changing that value requires updating the model held in memory.

I believe that we remember types of things by building corresponding simulors. Do we remember tokens by building specific simulors? Here, I am much more agnostic. I suspect that, at least in some cases, we do, but I am not sure that this is the only way we do it. It is not, after all, too hard to remember a list of specific values to substitute when creating a simulant from a general simulor. This question can only be answered by psychological studies, so I will leave it here.

Implementing simulors At least in the abstract, a simulor can be implemented quite simply: it is a list of ordered triples of effectors, values and ranges. As with effectors and their mutors, these lists could be *de facto* or *de iure*. I suspect that, in this case, they are more likely to be *de iure*. For one thing, we can usually list the properties of a thing, which suggests that we have access to the list of effectors attached to the simulor. For another, I cannot see an obvious way to implement a range in a *de facto* list. There must be some way to check the value used against the range for that effector in this simulor. It might be possible to 'hard-wire' the range into the simulor, producing a structure that cannot go outside the range, but that would make it absolutely impossible to simulate a person with a mass of one ton. It seems that this can be done, if we decide to over-rule the range, although we know that we are thinking about an impossible situation. Further, the need to rank the effectors in terms of their centrality in the simulor also seems to require a *de iure* list.

In a production system implementation, simulors would be literal lists of ordered triples. In a neural net implementation, it is much harder to describe the implementation, and doing so probably wouldn't be very helpful. Neural net circuits that remember things can be designed, but they are fairly complex, and a circuit storing a list of ordered triples would be more complex still.

Simulors and frames Simulors, in my theory, bear a striking resemblance to frames, as described by Minsky.[14] He describes them as follows:

> A frame is a sort of skeleton, somewhat like an application form with many blanks or slots to be filled. ... Default assumptions fill our frames to represent what's typical.[15]

Do they differ from his account? At this level of abstraction, no. However, as Minsky himself says,[16] at this level the account is more of a suggestion than a theory. Minsky 1985 is an attempt to set out a real theory containing frames, and while there are further suggestive similarities (he has simple, active agents: I have mutors), the two theories are extremely different. Most importantly, Minsky is trying to cover different areas: primarily perception, memory and action.

Thus, it is only sensible to consider the situation at the level of the general suggestion. At this level, simulors in my model are frames in Minsky's sense. The list of effectors forms a skeleton, which is filled out

---

[14] Minsky 1985, Ch. 24.
[15] Minsky 1985, p 245, original italics suppressed.
[16] Minsky 1985, p 259.

by the assignment of particular values when a simulant is created. The simulor is not, however, completely devoid of content: the effectors connected to it are still connected to their mutors, after all. Thus, even a simulor, in my account, carries a lot of information about the world. Indeed, in many sciences the concern is entirely with simulors: with the general properties of a type of thing in the world, rather than with any particular instances.

Frames have been seen as very important in many theories of cognition, organising thought and capturing important information in their own organisation. This is also true of my simulors, as I will discuss in the following section.

Simulors in Mind

Simulors serve an important purpose in our models, and are organised in such a way as to fulfil this purpose most effectively. The purpose is that of codification, and thus similar to that served by effectors. Unless we organise our thoughts in some way, we cannot handle the mass of information coming from the world, and, according to this theory, we organise in terms of things. Thus, when we think about a thing in the world, we think using the simulor, and can conveniently review everything we have learned about it. On the other hand, this means that, should there be any features that all simulors must have in order to be part of the model, we will, on careful consideration, attribute these features to all things in the world.

The point of simulors   The main purpose of simulors is to encode knowledge about the world. They do provide some gains in simplicity, especially in memory, since they obviate the need to store all the effectors every time you want to refer to a thing. This, however, is probably not a major consideration. Storing the names of all effectors is not as big a job as multiply storing all the mutors making up an effector, and so in this respect it may be that we could have managed without things.

Simulors are absolutely essential for simple (and complex) sorts of observational discrimination, however. Suppose that your retina is stimulated in a particular way. In the absence of things in the mental model, the best you will be able to do is recognise properties. Thus, you might be able to say that there is a redness, maybe a separation of some sort, a loudness, maybe even a transparency. You certainly couldn't see that a cricket ball was heading towards you through a window, and that someone was shouting a warning. All of these things contain unobserved but observable properties, properties which are highly relevant to your actions, but not necessarily connected with the observable properties. Thus, a red cricket ball is red, hard and solid, while strawberry cordial is red, liquid, and wet. There is no particular correlation between redness and hardness, by themselves, so the simple observation of redness does not allow us to infer that something is hard.

Simulors allow us to gather together a group of effectors, and assert that the corresponding properties come as a package. Thus, redness, roundness, and a certain size tend to go with cricket balls, so something displaying those observable properties is probably a cricket ball, and thus probably has the other properties. Without simulors, then, most moment-to-moment inferences would be completely impossible, and we would be not long for this world.

At this point, I should head off a possible misapprehension. I am not suggesting that we first notice the observable properties and then infer that a thing is present. We do have simulors as parts of our mental models, and the processes of recognition probably go on in parallel. Thus, if redness and size are present, that makes it somewhat likely that the thing is a cricket ball, which makes it more likely that the (somewhat indistinct due to speed) shape is round. Thus, we see a round ball, but we inferred that it was round from the observation that it was a ball just as much as vice versa. (Note that we do not see tennis balls squash as they hit the ground, despite the fact that we see them hit it, and thus can clearly resolve events of that duration. On this account, this could be because the shape is indistinct, due to rapid changes, and that, therefore, our recognition circuits decide that it is round, because, after all, it is a tennis ball. Accordingly, we see it as round just as immediately as we see it as moving.) I do not think that this recognition process takes place *in* our mental models, but I do think that it must draw on their resources, as they are the only ones available.

Hierarchies of simulors   Simulors, like effectors, are organised into type-hierarchies and part-hierarchies. Unlike effectors, where type-hierarchies seem to be far more important, both hierarchies are of equal weight. Type-hierarchies serve many of the same functions as they do for effectors. If all things of a certain type have a certain set of properties, it is more economical to link all the effectors to the type-simulor than to link each simulor individually to the full set of effectors.

Part-hierarchies serve a more important function, in one sense. As the model is described, it is not possible for a thing to have contradictory properties. Thus, if a bird is to be white with a black head, the body and the head must be represented by different simulors. However, since they are part of the same, larger thing, they must be linked as parts of a whole. The whole may still have properties of its own, however. Thus, a man may have black skin, white teeth, and brown eyes, but *he* is intelligent: no part of him has that property.

Both hierarchies could be implemented as lists of other simulors carried by the simulor. One list would be those simulors that it was an example of. Thus, for example, the simulor representing me would indicate that it was a kind of man. The simulor for man would indicate that it was a kind of human, that of human a kind of mammal, and so on up. The other list would list the parts. A human being has a head, arms, legs, body, liver, kidneys, and so on. A full model of a particular human being would involve filling out all those parts for one case, while a full model of human beings would involve full models of each part.

Part hierarchies introduce similar issues to those mentioned under effectors, above. While most people have all the parts represented by the parts of the 'person' simulor, not all do. People do lose hands or legs in accidents, and developmental defects can lead to some parts never growing at all. Once again, however, some parts are more firmly attached than others. We might be quite willing to believe that a person had no left hand, but a claim that someone had no skeleton, or no brain, would be much harder to accept. Indeed, in the absence of a brain we might be inclined to say that the thing in question wasn't a person.

Both of these hierarchies also help when we encounter things for the first time. If we can class something as an instance of a certain type, then we can give its simulant all the default properties of that type. This includes those properties that tokens of that type possess which we have not yet observed in this case, and so is the fundamental kind of recognition discussed above. On the other hand, if we are unable to say what type of thing it is, but can say what it is made up of, then we are still able to build a better simulation, because we can treat it as an assembly of its parts. If we can use information from neither hierarchy, we can only attribute the properties that we have already observed the thing to have, a poor situation to be in.

Simulors and classification As I mentioned above, the question of classification is somewhat tangential to my main discussion, so I will keep my remarks brief. Consider the simulor for a type of thing, and the problem of deciding whether an observed thing is of that type. There will be some necessary conditions, corresponding to effectors, parts and values that cannot be revised, but these conditions are likely to be held in common with other types. For example, the simulors 'bird' and 'mammal' will have very similar limits on their mass-values. There will also be sufficient conditions: if the model of a specific thing exactly matches all the default values of the simulor, then it is a token of that type.

In between, there is a large grey area. It will be a matter of judgement whether the degrees and respects in which the thing differs from the default state of the simulor are small enough and inessential enough for it still to count as an example of the type. This entails an exemplar theory of classification.[17] A thing very close to all the default values will be a particularly good example of the type, and easier to classify, while a thing further away will be a poor example, a harder to classify. There is a significant body of experimental data supporting exemplar theories of classification, which can accordingly be taken to provide some support for my theory.

---

[17]   See Medin and Ross 1997, pp 380–2.

Simulants

Models need to represent particular things, as well as types of thing. Types, on the whole, are represented by simulors, as described above. Tokens are usually represented by simulants. A simulant is an 'active version' of a simulor, ready to work in a model. All its effectors have definite values, which may or may not be equal to the default values held by the simulor. Even if all the values of effectors in a simulant are equal to the default values in the relevant simulor, the two are still different: they play different roles in the model. The way in which simulants play their roles will be discussed in the next chapter: for the moment, they should just be distinguished from simulors.

The distinction between simulor and simulant is not, then, the distinction between type and particular. All simulants will represent particulars, but so will some simulors, as discussed above. The distinction between simulors and simulants is theoretically motivated, and concerned with the way in which models work. Our intuitive distinction between types and particulars is, I think, based on whether a simulant derived immediately from a simulor is complete or not. A vague default value may cover the whole of the range available in that simulor. If the simulor represents an individual, it will specify values, and so the simulant will be 'ready to run'. Otherwise, the simulant will need to have values fed into it in order to turn it into a particular, demonstrating that it was not a particular before this was done.

Simulants are all created from existing simulors. The simulor specifies a lot about the simulant, and also fixes the gaps that need to be filled. In some cases, the gap will be a need for a definite value for some effector. In others, it will be the need to select an effector that falls under a certain type. It may also be necessary to add or subtract effectors and parts, to ensure that the simulant matches the thing in question. Setting up simulants is the main process involved in starting a simulation going — this is the level at which outside information, about what items are present, for example, is fed into the model.

Implementation

How can simulants be implemented in the mental model? When a particular thing in the world is under consideration, the simulor is recalled, and a simulant created; sub-effectors are substituted for type-effectors, while some default values are replaced by more specific ones. This, it is clear, tells us very little. However, I don't think that it is possible to say much more at this point.

Let us turn to the neural net implementation, in order to be a bit more specific. The simplest way to implement a simulor would be to have a cluster of neurons connected to the effectors of which the simulor was made up. These connections would set the values of the various outputs of the properties, and thus start the simulation going.

Unfortunately, there are obvious problems with this. First, it is not possible to have more than one simulant based on a given simulor at a time, because the neurons can only take on one value at once. Second, the only way to substitute sub-effectors for type-effectors is rewire the neurons to connect to a different effector. If, as seems entirely possible, sub-effectors may have different numbers of connections from the type-effector, this will also require adding new neurons to the thing.

At this point, I will simply give up. It is not possible to design an entire computer architecture in the space, and time, available to a single person. The precise details of my neural net implementation must be wrong, but it still serves the purpose of showing how something along these lines could actually exist. The key point here is that simulants could perfectly well feed values to effectors. If I put the simulors in a black box, this box could be connected to all effectors and decide what values to send where based on the things within it. Of course, this isn't a description of a possible implementation, but since it only requires the ability to think about more than one thing at once, it certainly doesn't invoke implausible capacities.

Knowledge without Understanding

I began Chapter 2 by clearly distinguishing understanding from mere knowledge. In this chapter, I have claimed that we cannot even know that something is present without having a simulor corresponding to it. Since such a simulor is part of a mental model, we seem to have a conflict.

The conflict is only apparent. It is possible to have a simulor containing no effectors, or effectors containing no mutors. Such structures will allow us to think about a thing, and to know that it exists, but in the absence of mutors, they will not allow simulation. Since understanding is the ability to simulate, this gives us knowledge without understanding.

The conflict is not real for a second reason. There are very few things that we know about without having any understanding at all. We might only understand them on the level of 'physical object', but that is a sort of understanding. However, we might have no understanding of a computer as a computer. In that case, we still have a model of the object, but it is a model of a beige box weighing a few kilograms. We might even know that it is called a computer, but since our model contains no effectors relevant to its operations *qua* computer, we have no understanding of the computer.

An extreme example of such a case can be found by considering gamma ray bursters. These are pulses of energetic gamma rays that appear from apparently random parts of the sky at apparently random times. Until recently, it was not known whether they originated in our solar system, or at the other end of the universe, and there was a corresponding uncertainty about their power — if they came from the other end of the universe, they would have to be very bright to be as strong as they appeared from earth. Scientists knew about gamma ray bursters, and could predict how they would interact with instruments, because they knew that they were gamma rays. However, they could say nothing else about them: where they came from, when they might appear again, how they were generated, or whether they might be dangerous. Recent discoveries have improved this situation: it is now known that they come from the other end of the universe. There are a number of theories about the mechanism, and astronomers are still trying to work out which is correct. We now have a very poor understanding of the phenomena, because they have their own model, which contains a few mutors.

Summary

Mental models are hierarchical structures, with three main levels. The lowest level consists of mutors, which are concrete particulars: little engines which transform their inputs in a particular way, and send them on to other parts of the mind. Effectors organise the mutors into groups that tend to come together in the outside world, with a property, and represent that property. Thus, the 'mass' effector would include mutors covering gravitational and inertial effects. Simulors are groups of effectors, gathering all the properties that a particular type of thing in the world has, and representing that type of thing.

There are further hierarchies within this: some things are parts of another, and some properties are kinds of other properties, as red is a kind of colour. These hierarchies serve to make the models manageable, and as useful as they can be given the limited information we get about the world.

Chapter 4

Mental Models in Action

Simulations

Simulation is the *raison d'être* of mental models. The models are used to simulate the world, to assist their possessor in his interactions therewith. To define the process of simulation is to define an architecture for understanding, in the sense used in cognitive science.[1] Doing so properly would require more space than I have available, and would not be directly germane to the purpose of the book. The properties of interest arise from the levels of the theory already described: the precise way in which they interact to perform simulations is not central.

That is not to say the subject is uninteresting or unimportant. It is possible that certain features of the architecture would require alterations in the basic theory given above, but such a discovery would require many hours of computer time, spent working with a fully implemented version of one potential architecture. At present, I have neither the skills nor the resources to carry this out, so I will leave it for the future.

It is possible, however, to consider some of the architectures that have been proposed in cognitive science, and see how they mesh with my theory. I will do this for two different proposals: Newell's Soar architecture, as described in Newell 1990, and a connectionist architecture, as characterised in Rumelhart 1989. In neither case do I have space to fully set out the base forms of the theories: these can be found in the references cited. I do hope to include enough detail for my discussion to be comprehensible. First, however, I will make some general remarks.

Self-Sufficiency and Control

Mental models perform simulations from their very nature. This can be seen by considering the character of mutors. Mutors are active things, which transform inputs into outputs. Thus, once the inputs of a mental model are fed to the mutors, the simulation will proceed without any 'outside' intervention. The act of feeding in the inputs is presumably what we do when we decide to work out what would happen in a certain situation. Indeed, since we seem to predict some things without conscious effort, it may be that thinking about some ideas starts the process of simulation without further conscious intervention.

---

[1]   See Anderson 1983, Newell et al. 1989, Newell 1990, and Rumelhart 1989.

This raises an important point. Simulation is only automatic once it has been started, once the decision about what to simulate has been taken. Mutors are, I suppose, capable of being stored in an inactive form, or, at any rate, of being passive when not provided with input. The activation of mutors is probably not under conscious control: once we have decided which situation to simulate, they will be activated automatically if required, but the process must be set in motion before the mutors will do anything.

This is related to the problem of the control of cognition, one that the theories of cognitive architecture are intended to address. That is, how do we decide what to think about, and avoid getting stuck in useless loops? In discussing the process of simulation I will be concerned with some aspects of this question, namely those concerned with the control of the process of simulation.

The decision to start simulating, however, is not one that I shall be concerned with. It is a decision taken by the person involved, and analysing it would involve analysing the will, a different problem, and one harder than that which I am considering. The important point is that, given mental models as I have described them, there are no deep problems concerning how they are used to simulate. They are designed to do simulations if simply left to themselves. This is deliberate, and an attempt to avoid invoking any mysterious ghosts in the machine.

A Connectionist Architecture

One problem with discussing connectionist architectures of cognition is that they have almost no general features. That is, the units are specified, as are the sorts of ways in which they can connect, but nothing general is said about the sorts of networks that can result. Thus, I am almost completely free to speculate. Nevertheless, there are some important constraints on a connectionist model, and I will take them into account.[2]

First, the individual nodes are simple. They take a value that is a function of their inputs and pass this value to other nodes. And that is all that they do. Second, everything is made of these nodes. There are no other functional bits. Finally, it is permissible to take certain functions of the mind in isolation. This last point may seem controversial, as some authors, such as Churchland,[3] talk as if the mind is just one huge network, with everything delocalised. This is unlikely, however, as neurological studies have provided convincing evidence that functions are localised in the brain, often, but not always, in corresponding locations in different people. Further, the time required to train a neural network goes up faster than a linear function of the units involved. That is, it is faster to train two networks with n nodes than to train one network with 2n nodes. It seems likely that the human life span would not be long enough to train a single

---

[2]   This section is based on Rumelhart 1989.
[3]   Churchland 1995.

network the size of the brain, so that we must suppose that it is broken down into units.

The first part of this architecture has already been described. Mutors are small neural networks, with inputs from some effectors, and outputs to others, depending on the specific mutor. The automatic processes undertaken by mutors are characteristic of neural nets, and so the identification seems reasonable.

This means that mutors have a fixed location in the brain. Copying a mutor means making a new set of neurons that match it, moving it means physically moving the neurons involved, and so on. Since such movement and copying is not physiologically plausible, the ways in which I can talk about mutors are limited.

Effectors could also be little nodes of neurons, as described earlier. They need not be, but this is the simplest way of incorporating them, and so I shall pursue it for the moment. The limits applying to mutors, therefore, apply also to effectors.

I do not think that simulors can be represented in the same way, however. Simulors need to give rise to simulants, the particular things with particular values involved in particular simulations, and it is not clear how this can happen if they are neural nets. Further, it is frequently the case that two different simulants based on the same simulor are involved in the same simulation. If things were neural nets, this would require multiplication of physical neurons, which is, as noted, implausible (and thus simulants are very unlikely to be groups of neurons).

Let us now consider the whole 'understanding organ' in the brain. There are three sections: the mutors, the effectors, and the simulors. The mutors and the effectors are fairly well defined, as are their connections to one another. The simulors are less so, and thus I will try to develop this area a bit. Suppose that there is a single network, providing inputs to all the effector units. This network accepts its inputs from whatever has overall control of whether, and what, to simulate. These inputs could be described as names of simulors (although they are certainly not verbal). When the name of a simulor is sent into the network, it generates a simulant and the outputs send appropriate values to the effectors in that simulor. If more than one simulor is named, the effectors of more than one simulor will be activated, by multiple simulants. If any mutor receives all its inputs, it will process them, the result will be sent back to the effectors, then back to the simulor network. This will then decide whether the simulants are still present, and whether new ones have appeared. The process will then repeat.

This is obviously a very crude description, and it cannot handle such common cases as multiple things with the same type of property. Thus, two massive objects could not be simulated. Similarly, it has problems with multiple instances of the same type of thing, since it can only send one set of values to the effectors. Finally, it does not seem to have any way of representing spatio-temporal information, other than by making it a property of specific things. I cannot fully resolve these problems without actually producing an architecture, but I will make some suggestions.

The problems with multiple things of the same type is the easiest to handle. The simulor network could be hard-wired to deal with a certain number of simulants, with a number of sets of connections to all the mutors. Thus, a network hard-wired to deal with six simulants would have six connections to every mutor, each set of connections forming its own network. Each simulor-name given to the network results in a certain state of one of these networks, and thus a certain set of inputs to each mutor. This means that it is impossible to simulate an indefinite number of things, but this limitation is psychologically plausible: just try simulating a crowd of one hundred people by considering the actions of each individual, without considering it one sub-unit at a time.

This leaves the problems arising from the need to activate the same effector multiple times. A similar solution may work here. Some effectors do not affect themselves, such as colours. A red thing has no influence on the colour of another red thing. For these effectors, there simply needs to be an inhibitory mechanism so that only one set of inputs is handled at a time. Thus, if three different simulants are trying to activate 'red' with three different values, the effector will take on each value in succession. This sort of behaviour is possible if there are feedback loops.

Properties that do affect themselves, such as mass and charge, require a different approach. There must be as many physical instances of the effector as there are inputs of that type on any mutor. Thus, if a mutor can handle seven different masses at once, there must be seven mass effectors. The connection patterns will have to be calculated to allow all the necessary combinations, but this is the sort of thing that neural networks are good at.

Finally, the mutors bound to effectors will also need feedback loops so that only one set of inputs is processed at once. These can work in the same way as the loops governing effector connections.

Space and time remain problematic. They could, in principle, be represented by space and time in the neural net, but this seems unlikely. The best option may be to have each cycle of the system cover one time unit, with the size of the unit depending on the situation under consideration, while areas of space are considered in turn, in a similar way to the organisation of competing needs for the same effector.

These suggestions are very vague, and I am not in any way committed to them as accurate descriptions of what goes on in the brain. They do allow me to make a number of observations about the process of simulation, however. First, the only point at which another mental process can intervene is the pause between cycles. Once the simulants have been created, everything else simply happens. Second, the process is very parallel. Only when the same resource is needed by two parts of the process will there be a serial bottleneck. Third, one cycle of simulation will take approximately a constant amount of time, neglecting the bottlenecks. Thus, there will be a point at which the only way to get through more simulated time in a given period of real time is to move to longer units of simulated time. This could be very important, especially if the simulation must, in order to be of use, run faster than real time — as is true of any simulation being used for prediction.

Models in Soar

Soar is a symbolic architecture developed by Newell and others, and set out as a unified theory of cognition in Newell 1990. 'Symbolic architecture' means that it is couched entirely in terms of symbols, and that Newell has very little to say about possible neural implementation. I will follow him there to some extent, but I want to keep the distinction between the representation of a production and a production clear, and will conclude this section with some very tentative remarks on possible implementation.

Soar has a simple structure. There are two memories, working memory and production memory. Values are placed, somehow, in working memory, and then those productions whose conditions are present in working memory are activated. Every production writes new values to working memory. If the process comes to a halt, the architecture devotes itself to finding a way out of the problem, but I cannot detail the methods used here: suffice to say that they seem to work in most cases. There is also a learning process, in which the conditions found at the beginning of a problem are made the conditions for a production that produces the solution to the problem, but this is not relevant to my discussion here, as I am not concerned with learning.

Soar is obviously different from my account, as it does not contain effectors or simulors. The productions could be described as mutors, however, and this seems the best place to start my suggestions for how my theory could be implemented in a Soar-like architecture: every mutor corresponds to a production.

Simulors and effectors can be introduced as ways of structuring mutors. Let us say that simulants are the items placed into working memory. A special set of productions is then tested: these productions call the effectors relevant to each thing, and put them and their values into working memory. Each property brings with it another group of productions, the mutors, and in the next stage these productions are tested against the contents of working memory, and the values of effectors altered appropriately. The cycle then continues, with any new effectors required being called before all the mutors are checked.

This model departs in fundamental ways from Soar. In particular, the simplicity and homogeneity of the production memory has been sacrificed. In 1990, at least, Newell would probably not have accepted this as a version of his theory: it is a different theory inspired by his. It also seems to have one key advantage. A major problem with Soar is that it needs to match all productions in memory against the contents of the working memory: it has no way to choose which productions to check. It seems likely that this pattern matching would require immense computational resources,[4] and might well be beyond the real-time capacities of the brain. (Newell himself assumes that it can be done in one cycle, completely in parallel, but others disagree.) On the model I suggest, a subset of productions is selected in advance, thus greatly reducing the workload. Further, there is nothing mysterious about the way that the selection takes place, as all and only those productions associated with active effectors are considered, so that there seems to be no prior reason to suppose that things do not happen this way.

The productions of this account could be charge patterns, or activation patterns over neurons, or other patterns of energy, which are rather easier to copy than patterns of matter. Thus, the problems with effectors and simulors noted for the connectionist architecture do not arise. Space and time could be handled in the way suggested there: there are defined cycles in Soar, and a second working memory could be added to store the objects in those areas of space not currently under consideration.

This does, however, lead to the comments I wanted to make about implementation. It seems to me that the symbolic architecture described here could be implemented in the connectionist architecture described above. The act of placing the simulants in working memory is the act of generating simulants from the neural simulor-clusters. The effectors are then invoked when the simulants send their values to effectors. The mutor-productions are activated if they receive appropriate inputs from the effectors, which is to say, if their conditions are matched. And then everything feeds back to working memory. If this is right, it suggests that the oft-stated opposition between connectionist and symbolic architectures is completely misguided, although there may be pragmatic advantages to working with one rather than the other.

I have thus considered two ways, which may turn out to be the same, in which simulations could take place within my system. There are many missing details, and it would be valuable, in the future, to attempt a full-blown software implementation of one or the other. The sketches should, however, serve their purpose in this book: that of giving the reader an idea of how I suppose my models to work.

Simulation on Stage

There is one theoretical issue that should be addressed explicitly at this point. In *Consciousness Explained*,[5] Daniel Dennett has argued against the 'Cartesian Theatre' picture of consciousness. This is the idea that the mind carries out various activities, and that the conscious ones are those which parade across a stage for the delight of the inner observer. As he notes, this theory is, when explicitly described, ridiculous — if nothing else, it leaves the question of the consciousness of the inner observer completely

---

4   See Anderson 1983, Ch. 1.
5   Dennett 1991.

untouched. He also notes that many discussions of conscious and unconscious processing seem to be carried out under its spell.

It might seem that my account of simulation falls foul of his strictures. The models for a situation are selected from the stores, and put on stage, where they do their stuff for the benefit of the conscious audience. The audience can see what the models do, but cannot see inside them to see how they do it. This is, I confess, one way of looking at my mental models. If, for example, they were implemented on a computer, and produced a display mirroring the behaviour of the program, then they would indeed work this way.

However, this is not necessary to the account. Just as no ghost is needed to apply the rules, no ghost is needed to interpret the results. The simulors of the model are not symbols needing interpretation any more than the mutors are rules in need of application. The simulors are, instead, referential, intensional objects. They are the thoughts that refer to things and, in many cases, they are the conscious thoughts that so refer.

This assertion rests on a huge promissory note. I have not given any argument for the claim that things in the model are referential and intensional. On some accounts of these notions, it is trivial that they are not: if (abstract) propositions are the only referential entities, then things in models cannot be, because they are concrete tokens. I believe that such accounts are wrong (in part because my thoughts are concrete episodes in my head, and they refer) and that a good theory of reference can be given that has the result that simulors are referential. There is, however, no way that I can even sketch that account here — it is enough to aver that I believe it to exist, and that, if it does, there is no need for a Cartesian Theatre in which models perform.

Quality

It is clear that simulations and models can be good or bad. A model of the world which supposed that fire was cool and quenched thirst would be very bad, while one that had it cool but deadly poisonous to the touch would be better, but still poor. What is not clear is how, exactly, we can decide on quality. Clearly, we are primarily interested in good simulations, and in order to achieve this, we need good models. However, the quality of particular simulations is, in part, what determines the quality of the models. In what follows, I hope to disentangle these two and set out a clear notion of quality for mental models.

Quality of Simulation

It is clear that the basic notion in assessing the quality of mental models must be the quality of the simulations that they allow. Very roughly, a good mental model is one that produces lots of good simulations. I will want to greatly refine that characterisation, but first I want to explicate the idea of a good simulation, as I do not think that it is sufficiently obvious to be made into a primitive notion.

To start with a very rough notion, a simulation is good if it is right. That is, if the actual events are accurately reflected by the simulated events, the simulation is a good one. However, we do not want an all-or-nothing measure: there should be degrees of goodness. Is there a way of characterising a simulation as 'a little bit wrong, but basically good'?

Let us refine our rough notion. Simulations are supposed to be used to help with decisions in the real world. Thus, there is a second criterion of simulation quality: the speed with which it supplies its answers. Thus, a simulation which was highly accurate but slow might be as good as a quick and dirty one that got some of the details wrong. Alternatively, perhaps the two desiderata cannot be conflated: if you have unlimited time, then the speed of a simulation becomes unimportant, and you would regard the most accurate as the best. On the other hand, if time was highly limited, then any simulation that produced an answer in the time available would be quite good, and any simulation that took longer would be no use at all, no matter how accurate it was.

I shall keep the two measures separate in my discussion here, since I cannot see any easy way of combining them into a single measure. The speed of simulation is the easier of the two to characterise, and so I shall look at it first. It might be thought that this could simply be measured by the length of time that the simulation takes to perform. This, however, is a little too simple. Bear in mind that the mind is likely to be doing more than one thing at once. A complex simulation given your full attention could proceed faster than a much simpler one that was competing for attention. Since we do not want the two simulations to come out as equally fast, nor, indeed, for one simulation to have different speeds on different occasions, we need a more constant measure. Fortunately, there is a candidate which is still fairly simple, at least conceptually. Every simulation will require a certain allowance of mental resources: mutors activated, values of effectors stored, etc. Thus, the amount of mental power that a simulation uses could be measured, and compared between simulations.

One issue concerns variability of the simulation between people. There are two ways in which such variation could arise. First, people could have different models. This is not a problem: although they may be simulating the same things, they are running different simulations, and differences in quality are most important in this sort of case. Alternatively, people could implement the same model with different degrees of efficiency. This might be a way of characterising one aspect of intelligence, but it does make it harder to compare models. The best way out is to compare the efficiency of two models, when both are run by the same person, one after the other. That way, variation in the simulator is controlled for, and variation in the simulation will come to the fore.

A complication does arise here, unfortunately. It may be that there is more than one type of mental resource used by the simulations. In this case, there may not be any way of comparing the use of a certain amount of one type of resource to the use of a certain amount of another type. In this case, the speed of a simulation will also become a multi-dimensional thing. However, this problem may not arise, as it will depend on just how the mind works, a question which I am not qualified to address.

While measurement of simulation speed may be technically difficult, it does not seem to pose any conceptual problems. The measurement of accuracy, however, does. Consider the sort of thing that is produced by a simulation. It certainly need not assign numerical values to various properties, and there is no obvious way of saying how accurate, or otherwise, a simulation which claims that the temperature is 'high' is, compared to one that says it is 'quite high', in a scale that goes from 'really very cold indeed' to 'incredibly painfully hot'. It would be an easy way out to assume that somewhere, buried in the models, there are numerical values, but I do not believe that this is the case.

A first step towards resolving the problem is to say that we encode our perceptions in the same sort of way. That is, an experienced temperature would be classed as 'hot' or 'quite hot', not with a numerical label. Now, it seems reasonable to assume that the categories used in the simulation will be the same as those used in the encoding of perceptions. Thus, a simulation is accurate if the categories in which it predicts that perceptions will fall are those in which the perceptions do, in fact, fall.

The first thing to note here is that the model makes its predictions by activating certain models, with certain values. Perception is interpreted by the activation of the same models. If the prediction matches perception exactly, then *identically* the same model is activated. If it's close, then it will be identically the same model, just with a different value. In other words, the need for similarity comparisons is greatly reduced. In most cases, the question of accuracy is the question of whether the simulation and the perception activated the same models. This is no more philosophically problematic than determining whether two people are holding the same metre rule. That isn't to say that it is completely unproblematic, but it is nothing like as problematic as trying to assess the degree of similarity between, say, the first and final drafts of a book.

Some categorisations are finer than others, and, all else being equal, a simulation employing finer categories will, presumably, be superior to one that uses coarser. That is, the more tightly the range of experiences is constrained by the simulation, the more it tells you. That is not to say that finer categories are always better, of course. Suppose that there are two models, one of which has categories four times finer than the other. However, although the coarse model always gets the predictions right, the finer model doesn't. Its solution is always within the correct category of the coarse model, but it gets the right fine category no more often than pure chance would allow. Clearly, the finer model is trying for a precision that cannot be supported. Maybe the distinctions don't exists in the world, or maybe the data acting as input isn't good enough to distinguish them. Either way, resources are being wasted, so the coarser model is better.

We must now return to considering the possibility that the perceptions will not fall in the same category as the simulation predictions. That is, we must consider the possibility that the simulation is wrong. It still seems plausible that a simulation with a categorisation five times finer than another will be superior, even if it is often wrong, but never by more than one category, while the other is always right. Indeed, it seems that we could add an error theory to our simulation, if we wished, producing a set of overlapping categories. The first simulation would always get these categories right, and they are smaller than the categories of the second simulation.

If the outputs of two simulations can be grouped into categories, about which the simulation is right, then the simulation with smaller categories is better. If we consider simulations with categories the same size, then it is clear that they can only be distinguished by their error rate. Note that this is not subsumed in the above. Both may have the same size of spread for possible errors, but one may have the right answer fall in the correct small category significantly more often than the other. Indeed, this could even confuse the issue of category size, since a simulation with a large possible error, but which most often produces a very precise and correct prediction, could be better than one with a moderate possible error, but which is never that precise.

Thus, perhaps a detailed error theory could be developed for these categories, allowing the detailed comparison of the accuracy of two simulations. It does, at least, seem possible. However, I think that it is also likely to be highly technical and complex, and so I do not wish to pursue the details at this point. Indeed, given that we most likely assess the quality of our own models, there may not be a precise theory used: simply a set of criteria, much as outlined here, that we balance as best we can. It is enough, for my purposes here, that I have argued that both the accuracy and the speed of a simulation could be measured, and compared between simulations. High accuracy and high speed make for a good simulation: low accuracy and speed make a bad one.

Quality of Models

The quality of a mental model depends on the quality of the simulations it can produce. We now have a (relatively) clear account of what makes a particular simulation good, so we can take this for granted and look at the features that the model should have in addition.

The fundamental consideration is that a model which can produce more good simulations is better, *ceteris paribus*, than one which produces fewer. This has two main consequences: good models are wide-ranging, and they are robust.

A model is wide-ranging if it can provide good simulations for many initial conditions. That is, a model that can simulate one situation very well, but which is hopeless if anything is changed in the slightest, is not a good model. Thus, if a model could only handle the impact of the cue ball on the red ball in a particular set up on a snooker table, it wouldn't be very good. The more things that can be changed, the better. Thus, if the model is equally good for any colour of target ball, it is better. If it can handle different arrangements of the other balls on the table, it is better still, while being able to cope with different initial velocities of the cue ball, different angles, and different positions relative to the sides of the table makes for a pretty good model. Of course, that model couldn't cope if the red ball was nailed down, or if the cue ball was hit with a laser disintegrator gun just before it struck the red, but a wider model might be able to.

Robustness is related, but different. A model is robust if it produces good simulations, even if the initial conditions are inaccurate. Thus, it can handle perceptual error, mistakes of estimation, and so on, without rendering the simulation useless. There will be definite limits to robustness: if you are sufficiently wrong about the inputs, you ought to get the wrong result, because otherwise you would get the wrong result if the inputs really were as you thought, and you were right about them. Despite this, some degree of robustness is essential. If the model of the snooker table relied on getting the velocity of the cue ball exactly right, then it wouldn't be much use unless you had appropriate measuring equipment.

To a certain extent, robustness relies on the world's co-operation. If the situation is such that a tiny variation in initial conditions causes a massive later change, then your model will have to reflect that if the simulations are to be any good. However, some systems, especially those with cybernetic feedback, will be more robust if considered in certain ways than in others. Thus, if I treat a thermostat as simply fixing the temperature, I will have a fairly robust simulation, while if I insist on simulating its every detailed action, I will probably not get an accurate picture of the ongoing changes in temperature.

A good model, then, is one that produces good simulations, robustly, over a wide range of initial conditions. This concludes the presentation of my theory, but before I go on to consider empirical and theoretical issues there are a couple of issues concerned with terminology to consider: is it sensible for me to call my mental constructs 'mental models', and can my theory account for other uses of 'understand', in particular in the context 'understanding English'?

Giere: Explaining Science

In his book *Explaining Science*[6] Ronald Giere intends to provide a theory of science. That is, he wants to give an account of what scientists are doing, and how they go about deciding what they believe. He explicitly sets his theory up in the tradition including the logical empiricists, Kuhn, and the

---

6   Giere 1988.

Strong Program in Sociology of Scientific Knowledge.[7] He describes his new approach as naturalistic and cognitive, and mental models are an important part of the structure. In *Science Without Laws*[8] Giere discusses other aspects of his account of science, particularly its relationship to the 'science wars'. He does not, however, discuss explanation and understanding in any more detail, and his account of theoretical models is almost identical to that given in *Explaining Science*. Accordingly, my account is drawn primarily from the earlier book. In this section I will consider what Giere has to say about mental models, and consider any implications that this has for my theory, or that my theory has for him.

Giere's Theoretical Models

Giere does not refer, strictly speaking, to mental models. His term is 'theoretical models'. However, these entities are not physical things, and are mainly dealt with in the mind. Commenting on the characteristics of these theoretical models, he says:

> Indeed, the texts often explicitly note respects in which the model fails to be isomorphic to the real system.[9]

These mental entities are supposed to form the basis of scientific knowledge and understanding:

> Theoretical models are the means by which scientists represent the world — both to themselves and for others.[10]

What, then, are Giere's theoretical models like? He characterises them as follows:

> I propose that we regard [theoretical models] as *abstract entities* having all and only the properties ascribed to them in the standard texts. The distinguishing feature of the simple harmonic oscillator, for example, is that it satisfies the force law $F = -kx$.[11]

Having specified theoretical models as closely as he ever will, Giere then turns to the relationship between them and the world. He rejects isomorphism, as noted above, and proposes the term 'hypotheses' to cover the statements of this relationship. He then says:

---

[7]   Giere 1988, Ch. 2.
[8]   Giere 1999.
[9]   Giere 1988, p 80.
[10]   Giere 1988, p 80.
[11]   Giere 1988, p 78, emphasis in original.

The appropriate relationship, I suggest, is *similarity*. Hypotheses, then, claim a *similarity* between models and real systems. But since anything is similar to anything else in some respects and to some degree, claims of similarity are vacuous without at least an implicit specification of relevant *respects* and *degrees*. The general form of a theoretical hypothesis is thus: Such-and-such identifiable real system is similar to a designated model in indicated respects and degrees.[12]

He then goes on to use theoretical models in his theory. He proposes for them a role in scientific explanation:

What science provides for 'scientific explanations' is a resource consisting of sets of well-authenticated models.[13]

He makes most use of his notion of theoretical models, however, in his account of scientific judgement. Theoretical models are taken to be the units of currency in scientific work: scientists choose to accept, reject, or pursue them. He argues that scientists do this in a satisficing manner, choosing the best of the satisfactory options from among those available to them.[14] The only place at which he goes into any detail about the reasons that there might be for regarding a model as satisfactory is when he is considering experimental tests. There, he says:

The connection between the models under investigation and the output of the experiment is provided by the fact that the physical system being modelled must be a causally relevant part of the experimental set-up. Moreover, for any model under investigation the experimenters must be able to determine what range of outputs would most likely result if that model in fact fits the system being modelled.[15]

This emphasis is not unreasonable: other factors that he mentions in passing include professional commitment, personal attachment, availability of research equipment, and the like. It would, quite obviously, be extremely difficult to say anything both general and useful about such factors.

The main vagueness in Giere's account is due in part, I think, to his methodology. He considers three case studies of scientific practice and theory change in considerable detail, discussing the way in which models were changed in those cases. As a result, he has a tendency to rely on what the scientists say about their models, and the similarity between them and the real world, without a great deal of analysis.

---

12   Giere 1988, p 81, emphasis in original.
13   Giere 1988, p 105.
14   Giere 1988, pp 157ff.
15   Giere 1988, p 165.

Models Mental and Theoretical

How, then, does Giere's picture fit with mine? The central distinction is that my models are concrete, while Giere's are abstract. In this section, I will consider how this affects the usefulness of his theory, compared to mine.

A point of similarity can be seen in the application of Giere's theoretical models to explanation. My mental models also provide a resource which can be used to understand a situation, and thus to provide an explanation. The process of providing an explanation will be considered in more detail in a later chapter.

The main area of interest, however, must be Giere's account of scientific decision making. I propose to adopt a simple methodology here: I will argue that my account of mental models can be seen as a properly articulated version of Giere's theoretical models, and can serve the function that he wanted his to serve, while being sufficiently detailed to make proper predictions possible. That is, I claim that my account allows us to model science in a way that Giere's account does not.

Such an approach involves, essentially, rejecting Giere's account of theoretical models. They are not defined by the equations written down in textbooks, but rather by the mutors held in the mind. The equations may be an accurate description of the models, in some cases, especially in the case of mental models of sophisticated theories, but that need not be the case, and the disanalogies between mutors and logical rules strongly suggest that the equations will only rarely be a wholly accurate description. With this rejection, the big problem with Giere's account simply fades away. I no longer need to claim that mental models are similar to the thing modelled, and to treat that similarity as primitive. Instead, I can claim that mental models provide good simulations of the things modelled, and use the criteria of quality given above to characterise a good simulation, and, more broadly, a good model. I could claim that a good model is similar to the thing modelled, but I can flesh that out: it is similar because, in a certain, defined sense, it mimics the behaviour of the real thing. The terms in which I characterise a good model are clearer and easier to apply than a primitive notion of similarity, are based on comparisons that are less philosophically problematic, and also, I think, give more insight into what exactly is going on.

A further advantage of this change is that it allows us to extend the theory of decision making from science to general, every-day life. People do not usually have theoretical models, in Giere's sense, of their car, or their postman, but they do, often, have mental models, which they change over time as more information comes in.

This advantage comes with a balancing disadvantage, however. Scientists often consider models that cannot be run by any human mind. The models of the earth's climate which are currently being developed are a good example of this. These involve so many calculations that no human being could possibly do anything with them. However, while this is a problem if they are to be seen as providing understanding, it is not a problem in the scientific context. Here, I can allow models implemented on computers, or which can only be worked out with the aid of paper and pencil. They still aim to simulate the system under consideration, and can be tested in the same way. Indeed, given the current popularity of object-oriented programming, the computer models may well be extremely similar to the models described above. Individual instructions serve the role of mutors, and the objects (functional units in the program) serve the role of simulors and effectors.

I shall, however, follow Giere's lead in neglecting to say anything about factors other than experimental tests which influence the choice of model, for the reason that this is a complex field, only tangentially relevant to my thesis. Let us consider experimental tests, then. In brief, the experimenters simulate the experiment using their mental models, and then see if the results agree with the simulation. If they don't, they usually look for ways to correct the simulation.

This clearly shows that a model cannot be tested alone. At the very least, our models of our own perceptions will be involved, and there will generally also be models of experimental apparatus cluttering up the works. If the model fails to provide an accurate simulation, it is not immediately obvious what part of the complex has gone wrong.

This gives scientists a strong motivation to test two models against each other, in a context in which they predict very different results. It is necessary that the scientists have models that only differ in the area being tested, but this is, I think, the normal situation. In this case, if the results are consistent with one model, and inconsistent with the other, it is very likely that the problem with the failed simulation is that the model of interest was incorrect, while in the other case, everything seems to be fine. If there is no competitor for the model being tested, there is no indication, from the results, of where the error may be.

Similarly, they have a good reason to adopt a satisficing strategy. If a model can adequately simulate all the situations in which it is put, there is no reason to go looking for another one. Further, the relevance of previous commitments is clear. If you are used to using a certain mental model, there will be a great deal of effort involved in changing to a new one. Thus you will need to be convinced that there are major benefits to be had by changing models, otherwise it will not be worth your while.

To return to the experimental results, Giere notes one feature of the factors cited in support of a theory of nuclear structure in particular. It is not simply the fact that it predicts the values of a certain set of measurements well, but that, if the values in the model are set from one set of measurements, the model then predicts a second set very well, without any alteration. The time element does not seem to be important, here. The important point is that the model only needs to be calibrated against one set in order to accurately simulate both.

On my account of mental models, the reasons for this are easy to see. If the model produced on the basis of one set of simulations proves to be good at simulating other aspects of behaviour, there seems to be good reason to suppose that this model is capturing something of the structure of the modelled thing. Indeed, I argued earlier that this is the only way in which we can decide whether a model does provide an accurate picture of the internal structure of a thing. We would not expect the relative timing of the simulations to be important, but the independence of the design of the model from one set of data is important.

In summary, I do not think that Giere's account of models is sufficiently detailed to be considered as competing with mine. Indeed, it says so little about models that it is, at times, difficult to see how they can play the central role to which he assigns them. If, however, my theory of mental models is used in his theory of scientific judgement, then we get a theory that seems to hang together sensibly, with many factors appearing as eminently reasonable which, before, may have seemed unscientific. For example, the tendency to retain one's current model in the face of contrary evidence is seen as a reasonable position, given the work involved in changing a mental model. Further, the move from abstract to concrete models, and thus from considering the similarity between the model and the situation to considering the productions of the model, solves the most serious problem for Giere's account. Thus, I am inclined to agree with Giere about the importance of mental models in explaining science, but to disagree with him about the nature of these models.

Other Meanings of Understanding

I have, so far, been concerned with one sense of 'understanding': the sense in which we understand things or people. The word is used in other senses, in particular that of understanding language. In this section I will discuss how these senses relate to mine.

Understanding Words

A common use of the verb 'to understand' is in the context of understanding a language. Now, while it is possible to understand a language in the sense described above, such understanding is the province of linguists, not of normal speakers of the language. However, these speakers are commonly said to understand the language, so there must be a slightly different sense of the word operating here. In this section I shall argue that this sense, although different, fits well with my theory. I shall argue that this sense of understanding can be regarded as parasitic upon the sense discussed above: while different, it is close enough that the use of the same word for both things is understandable, and not unreasonable.

Roughly speaking, someone understands a language when they understand most of the words and grammatical constructions used in that language. Perfection is obviously not required: simply being vague on the distinction between epicene and epicure does not mean that one does not understand English. However, when individual words and grammatical constructions are under consideration, the situation is much more all-or-nothing: a failure to cope with all the nuances of a word is grounds for attributing a lack of understanding of that word. Thus, I shall concentrate on understanding words and constructions.

As a first approximation, a person understands a sentence when, as a result of hearing or reading that sentence, they can construct an appropriate mental model. Thus, someone understands 'The dog is red' when, as a result of reading or hearing that sentence, they can construct a model of a red dog. A word is understood if the model so constructed responds appropriately to it: a grammatical construction is understood if the model is constructed according to that construction.

This formulation is vague, and subject to a number of problems. I do not want to get drawn into an attempt to answer them fully, as that would require developing a theory of semantics, something which deserves at least a book to itself. However, as it stands, the approximation is surely too vague, and thus I shall expand on it somewhat, to support my contention that this form of understanding is also dependent on mental models.

First, the understanding of a sentence is primarily a capacity: the ability to understand that sentence whenever it is uttered. Thus, if, through the use of orbital mind control lasers, I induce the correct mental model in someone when they hear a given sentence, they do not thereby understand the sentence. Even if I do it every time, since they do not have the capacity to form the model from the sentence, they do not understand the sentence. It is, however, possible to understand a sentence without understanding the component words or grammatical relations. For example, I know that the Japanese sentence 'Onakagapai' means 'I am full, I have had enough to eat'. Whenever I hear that sentence, I can generate an appropriate mental model. However, as the way I wrote it indicates, I don't even know where the word divisions are, let alone what the individual words mean, and I certainly have no idea about the grammatical structure.[16]

If, on the other hand, I only knew how to respond when someone said that, by not giving them any more food, and clearing their plate away, for instance, then I would not understand the sentence. I cannot form a mental model, because I have no idea whether it means 'I am full', or 'This is revolting', or 'I cannot eat this for religious reasons', etc.

As an aside, on this model Searle is correct to say that neither the person in the Chinese Room, nor the room itself, understand Chinese. Bits of paper are passed in and out, and the room can carry on a conversation, but at no point is a mental (or, perhaps, roomal) model of the situation represented by the sentences created. The conversation may be good, but it is purely mechanical, carried on without any understanding. His critics, however, are right to say that this has no bearing on the possibility of artificial

---

[16]   Since first writing these sentences, I have learned rather more Japanese, and discovered that it should have been 'onaka ga ipai'. The point still holds, however.

intelligence, since a computer could, in theory, be programmed to build a mental model based on what it hears, and then to respond based on that model.

This brings us to the other half of understanding language: being able to form sentences. In this case, someone is able to use a sentence, with understanding, if they are able to express a mental model in that sentence. So, on this account, I understand 'Onakagapai' in this way as well. When my mental model is of me being full, I can say it, and convey my mental model to the world (the Japanese-speaking part thereof, anyway).

It is worth noting that, on this model, the ability to understand a language and the ability to speak it are separate, and could have radically different levels in the same person. To understand a language, one must be able to go from the words to the model: to speak it, one must be able to go in the other direction. If the links between words and models are governed by something like mutors, there will have to be separate mutors for the two functions, and thus it would be possible to understand a language very well, but not be able to speak it at all. It seems that the reverse state should also be possible, but perhaps the ways in which we can learn languages rule it out.

So, understanding a language consists in the ability to go back and forth from mental models to sentences in the language. Thus, since we understand sentences when we can build the appropriate mental model, and understand a thing when we can build the appropriate mental model, the close relationship between the two meanings is evident.

Other Understandings

'Understanding the world' and 'understanding a language' are, I think, the two main uses of 'understanding'. However, they do not exhaust the field, and in this section I shall briefly consider two other uses. The first is when we speak of understanding a theory such as relativity or quantum mechanics. The second is when we speak of understanding a fact; 'I understand that the bank is closed', for example.

In the first case, this is clearly distinct from understanding the world. If someone claims to understand quantum mechanics, they are not claiming that they understand all the systems with which quantum mechanics deals. Indeed, some of those systems are so complex that no human being alive today understands them, and some may remain forever beyond our powers. What, then, is being claimed in such statements?

It should not come as a surprise that I think that the speaker is claiming a capacity to construct mental models. Specifically, she is claiming that, given a quantum-mechanical description of a situation, she can build a model of that situation. This does not imply the ability to simulate, because the constructed model may be too unwieldy (and thus not terribly good). It may not even be possible to complete the task of construction, due to time constraints. However, if she does understand quantum mechanics, then she will be able to model and simulate any reasonable sized quantum mechanical system that is described to her.

Understanding a theory, then, is, in a way, a meta-modelling ability. It is the ability to construct models of a certain type of situation. As such, it is likely to imply understanding of a number of things that are in the world. In the case of quantum mechanics, I doubt that one could understand the theory without understanding photons and electrons to a significant extent. The emphasis, however, is on the ability to build more models, not on the models already possessed. Someone who understood quantum mechanics could build a mental model of a new fundamental particle, given some information about it, and I think that this is the capacity that is being referred to.

The second case, that of understanding facts, is rather more difficult. This is because I am not sure what is actually being claimed. One sense of 'I understand that the bank is closed' seems to be 'I have been told, by a source generally reliable, that the bank is closed'. This is the use made of the phrase in contexts such as going into a shop and saying 'I understand that you do repairs', or something similar. Here, the usage seems to be by leakage from understanding language: you have understood someone else telling you this, or the model that you built as a result of their words has this as a consequence. This, however, is very definitely a peripheral use of the word.

There does, however, seem to be a sense in which the fact can be understood in a more central sense. Here, my intuitions fail me, in that I am not even sure that there is such a sense, much less how it fits into my general theories. If there is such a sense, however, it is likely, I think, to refer to the possession of a model of a particular aspect of a thing. Thus, understanding that grass is green would involve the possession of a model of its colour. This would be more involved than simply knowing that grass is green, which only requires the fact, without a model. If this does capture this putative sense, then it clearly fits into my general model.

Models and Inference

Simulation, according to this account, can be a kind of inference and prediction. Accordingly, understanding and prediction have a very close link. A similar link was proposed by Hempel, in his Structural Identity Thesis.[17] I have already, in the sections on mutors and implementation, emphasised the difference between my theory and one based on propositional inference, and it is a subject to which I will return again. Hempel saw both explanation and prediction in terms of propositional inference: I see neither in those terms. In this section, I will draw out the consequences of this difference.

---

[17]   Hempel 1965b pp 364–76.

This discussion will fall into three parts. In the first, I will discuss the reasons for the difference — the ways in which prediction by propositional inference is different from prediction by models. In the second, I will consider, briefly, those kinds of inference that do not fall under simulation. This section will be mainly concerned with acknowledging their existence, rather than attempting analysis. Finally, I will consider the extent to which I could be taken to have, in fact, given an account of propositional inference.

Propositions and Mutors

Propositional inference can cover a wide range of activities, only some of which correspond to simulation in my sense. Those which do concern inferences from known general principles to specific cases. For example, if I know that all fire burns items placed in it, and that it is painful to have part of my body burned, I can infer that it will be painful if I put my hand in a fire.

Many of the differences between simulation and propositional inference arise from the difference between mutors and logical rules. If I believe that all fires are hot, then I can infer that anything that is not hot is not a fire. If I have the mutor fire§hot, I cannot necessarily say anything about non-hot things. These differences were covered at length in the section on mutors, so I will not go over them again here.

There is another important class of differences, however. Consider classic cases of common cause: the electrical discharge in the atmosphere causes lightning and thunder. All electrical discharges are accompanied by lightning; all electrical discharges are accompanied by thunder; all flashes of lightning are accompanied by crashes of thunder. As far as a system of propositional inference is concerned, these generalisations all have exactly the same status, even if we are fully aware of the causal pattern. Even though I know that the discharge causes the lightning and the thunder, I can still infer from the sight of lightning that thunder will shortly follow.

In a system of mutors, this is not the case. If I know about the causal structure, there will be no mutor linking lightning and thunder. A simple simulation of the lightning flash will not include thunder, unless I actually start the simulation with the discharge. This is as it should be: a lightning flash is simply a bright flash of light in the sky, and such things are not necessarily associated with thunder. Once it is identified as a *lightning* flash, we have identified the presence of the discharge, and can start our simulation from there. In the propositional case, we still need to identify the light as lightning before we can perform the inference, but the electrical discharge is idle in that inference. Indeed, we could make it even if we didn't know about the discharge.

This is a specific example of a general class. In a propositional system, any correlation is good for inference. As long as all members of Newnham College are female, I may infer from someone's membership there that she is female. In a model, the only inferences permitted are those that would, roughly, become true if the antecedent were brought about. Since it is not the case that, were I to join Newnham (by lying about my sex, say), I would become female, this link cannot be included as a mutor. The reasons for this will be discussed later, in the section on causes and mere correlations.

It is important to note, however, that the reasons are not directly concerned with inference. It is inferentially useful to be able to rely on indicator properties. If I see a name in the *Cambridge University Reporter*, in the standard form of surname and initials, followed by an italic *N*, indicating Newnham, I know that the person in question is female. I could not make this inference by running a mental model. Similarly, if I meet a male member of the university, I know that he is not at Newnham, since all members of Newnham are female. This is a (slightly) useful inference, and I could not make it by simulation even if Newnhamite§female were a mutor in my mental model — the mutor can only run forwards, and so cannot go from a male input to the belief that he is not from Newnham.

Thus, the fact that some fact can be deductively inferred from the beliefs involved has no direct bearing on whether that fact will be produced by running the model of those beliefs. Simulation is, at best, a subset of possible inferences of this sort. It is, however, a very important subset and, as I argued above, there are reasons why we want to distinguish this subset from others. The standard problems for the Deductive-Nomological model of explanation show the problems that you get by assimilating explanation to inference: my model does not face the same problems, as I will show in Chapter 6.

It is clear, however, that we do perform the other types of inference. I do (occasionally) make judgements about my colleagues' Collegiate membership based on their sexes, even though I cannot make such inferences in my models. In the next section I will briefly discuss ways in which these other types of inference might fit with my theory.

Types of Inference

There are, I think, two main types of inference, apart from simulation. The first is the process by which we improve our own mental models, while the second is the process by which we build models of situations. Both of these are inferential, as the result of neither process is given in its inputs.

The first type covers the classic cases of inference: inferring that, since all emeralds so far observed are green, all emeralds are green, or inferring from the observations of planetary positions that they are governed by an inverse square force.

This is a type of inference which proceeds by improving your mental models. As such, it is very closely related to explanation, and can be regarded as the process of explaining something to yourself. Indeed, the slogan 'Inference to the Best Explanation' has clear applicability here: the process of induction is the process of building the best mental model of the situation that you can: of gaining the best understanding possible. Of course, this means that some inferences of this sort could proceed by deduction. If I deduce something from my background knowledge, and then include that in my mental model I have engaged in this sort of inference.

I shall discuss explanation, and the ways in which it can proceed, below. Most of this discussion will, I think, transfer to these inferences. There is one major problem that will not be covered, however. When I explain something to someone else I may, and in most cases will, simply take my current model of the situation to be the correct one, and try to bring the other person into a state in which they have the same model. Clearly, when I am performing an inference I cannot get the final model in this way: if I already possessed it, I would not be performing an inference. Thus, the question arises of from where we get the models to which we infer. I will not address this question in this book, as it deserves more space than I can give it.

On the other hand, the discussion of the quality of models does suggest how we might check our inferences. Since they produce models, we can simply check those models for their quality, and only accept those which are pretty good. If we have a choice between two, then we will choose the better. Thus, this book can be taken as providing an account of induction, as restricted to the context of justification.

The second type of inference concerns the process by which we go from observations to mental models: it is obvious that my head does not contain, say, the Andromeda galaxy. Irrespective of the size of one's ego, human heads are simply not that large. Thus, there must be some process by which the mind goes from its sensory input to the presence of an enormous universe. I believe that this central process is actually applied more widely than in the analysis of sense data, and I will return to this below.

I will not say a great deal about the mechanisms of this second kind of inference, for the simple reason that I have very little idea as to what they could be. They are the processes by which we construct our mental models of our currently observed surroundings. Thus, they are distinct from simulation, which involves the running of these models, and from the first kind of inference, which involves improving our modelling resources, or the unobserved aspects of a current model. These processes are, I think, even more automatic than the processes of simulation, in that we cannot even decide whether to use them (beyond the decision of whether to open our eyes, and where to look). Nevertheless, they can clearly be altered, given enough time: when I look up at night, I see stars scattered over a universe, not lights on a crystal sphere.

This is, I think, indicative of various degrees of such processes. There are very basic ones, which are probably impossible to alter. These are the ones which allow perspective to work, and which underwrite optical illusions. Further up, it is probably possible to change the processes which determine that I see trees, possibly by the simple process of changing my models of trees. I think that the process of understanding testimony probably comes in around this level: accepting testimony involves building a mental model based on words, rather than on sense input. This is clearly less basic than the sense based process, since I can learn new languages, but it is still fairly automatic, since I do not spend time thinking about how to understand a language which I speak fluently. I suspect that there are very loose processes of this type, ones which, perhaps, we need to consciously use.

This final type covers such inferential processes as going from the fallen barometer to the coming storm, and similar inferences using indicator laws. These inferences do not proceed by simulation, nor do they involve the improvement of mental models. They consist in going from perceptual data to a model of the current environment, and this is exactly the process covered by this type of inference. As I have no model of the processes of observation, I cannot say much more than that. However, these inferences are of the same type as other inferences that we must make, and are of a different type from the other kinds of inference described above (simulation and induction). Thus, it seems reasonable to suppose that they use the mechanisms developed to enable us to go from observations to models, in some way.

These are, of necessity, extremely sketchy remarks: a book could be written on either of the above subjects without any trouble. They serve simply to indicate that I do not think that simulation covers everything that we describe as inference, and to gesture at the places where I think accounts of the other types could be found.

Propositions Redux

I have spent a great deal of effort on distinguishing mental models from beliefs and inferences. It might seem that this is unreasonable, that what, in fact, I have done is give an account of beliefs and of one type of inference. That is, our beliefs consist of our models, and one way in which we make inferences is to run simulations in those models.

At this point in the book, I have no problem with accepting this. I think that most, if not all, of our beliefs take the form of models, and that we perform many inferences by simulation. However, this identification can tell us nothing about mental models, although it may tell us a great deal about beliefs.

The following chain of reasoning and parallel ones are not valid, even given the identification between models and beliefs: 'Beliefs are propositional attitudes; mental models are beliefs; therefore mental models are propositional attitudes.' Rather, we can reason as follows: 'Mental models contain mutors; beliefs are mental models; therefore beliefs contain mutors.' Mental models are defined by the theory given above: if the consequences of the theory differ from the standard theory of belief, then either the standard theory of belief is wrong, or mental models cannot be equated with beliefs.

If it turns out that mental models cannot be equated with beliefs, this only proves that the two theories are in competition. It has, in itself, nothing to say on the question of which is true. Newton's mechanics and Special Relativity disagree on many predictions, but this disagreement is not evidence against Newtonian mechanics: only the disagreement with the empirical data is such evidence. Similarly, if my theory disagrees with the theory of beliefs, we must then ask which one better describes the data, and we cannot know, in advance, which will win — the history of science demonstrates that neither antiquity nor novelty is a good predictor of success.

If my theory is right, and it turns out that beliefs simply cannot be mental models, then we have fewer beliefs than is generally thought. We most likely have no unconscious beliefs at all, simply forming conscious beliefs by inspecting our models, as and when we need a belief for some purpose. This would be an odd way of talking, true, but we would get used to it. My own feeling is that it will be reasonable to assimilate beliefs to mental models, and that this assimilation will tell us a great deal about belief. Ultimately, however, the theory will be tested by how well it accounts for the relevant data, not by how well it agrees with previous theories.

Two Examples

At this point, I will present a couple of examples of understanding something by means of mental models. The first is taken from everyday life, and the second is a real scientific process. Obviously, this discussion will be somewhat simplified, as I do not want to have to explain a whole field of science. However, the discussion will only go down as far as effectors: I will not discuss the mutors at all. There are several reasons for this.

The first is purely presentational. I cannot actually include mutors in the text, and the confusions between mutors and their representations is so common that I do not want to encourage it, if at all possible. (Simply naming the mutors, as I did earlier, would add nothing to the presentation.)

The second is more substantial. Mutors are not, I suppose, available to introspection. Thus, their nature can only be discovered by empirical psychological experiments. Further, such experiments could only be performed after the simulors and effectors involved in a particular model had been identified, which would mean assuming that the theory was correct. Such experiments are probably not the first priority. Moreover, the details of mutors are likely to vary from one individual to another. Thus, any precise description I could give would be both entirely made up, and unlikely to be true of more than one individual in any case.

The only purpose of a description of mutors would be to prove that the model is possible. In this case, that is not necessary. Object-oriented computer programs work in a very similar way to mental models as here described, and they can successfully simulate complex environments (computer games are perhaps the most accessible example). Thus, it is well established that a mutor can be described for almost any conceivable behaviour, and there is no reason to suppose that any I did describe would correspond to ones really held. Under these circumstances, the presentational considerations win out.

There is one further interesting feature of the presentation here. I have to explain the scientific example I am using, since I cannot assume that the reader will understand it. At the same time, I have to describe the structure that corresponds to such understanding. The purpose of the explanation is to allow the reader to build a mental model of the described situation. The purpose of the description is to allow the reader to build a mental model of the mental model of the described situation. Clearly, the mental model and the mental model of the mental model will have many similarities, and thus the explanation and the description will be very similar. Indeed, it would tell against my theory if they were not.

A Rubber Ball

Consider a red rubber ball. A good mental model must be able to tell us a number of things: what it will look like, whether it will fit into a pocket, and what will happen if it is dropped. The ball itself will be represented by a single simulor, so the question concerns the effectors that are attached to this structure.

It is a solid object, so it needs the effectors for solidity and size. The solidity effector has a value for hardness, while the size effector is a type effector, which has sub-effectors covering various shapes, each of which has at least one value for extent. The rubber ball is pretty solid, and spherical, so it has a single size value.

Visually, we only need to specify the colour now, so the effector for red is added to the model. At this point, we can simulate its appearance, as we know its shape and colour, and work out whether it will go in a pocket. It is slightly squashy, so a model in which we try to put it into a space slightly smaller than it is will give the result that it will go in, with a bit of a push.

However, we still have little information about what will happen when we drop it. The effector for 'bounciness' needs to be added, with quite a high value. When a moving object with this effector encounters a solid barrier, its direction of motion is reversed, and its speed is reduced. The extent of reduction depends on the value of the effector: a high value gives a low reduction. Thus, the bounciness effector is given a high value.

Since we already know how big the ball is (from the size effector) we can now start it moving around in an environment, and the bounciness effector will change its motion as it bangs into things. Thus, we now have an elementary understanding of the ball.

Apoptosis

Apoptosis[18] is programmed cell death, the process by which individual cells commit suicide. This usually occurs in response to damage of some sort, although it is also an ordinary feature of development. As is normal for biochemical processes, it is very complex, so I will concentrate on one part of it, in the nematode *Caenorhabditis elegans*.

The first stage in understanding cell death is a simple model of a functioning cell. The functioning cell is a simulant derived from a simulor representing cells in general. We can take this model to involve three further elements, as parts of the cell: the genetic material, the enzyme, and the cytoskeleton. Each of these elements corresponds to a simulor — the numerous proteins are modelled by a single element for simplicity's sake, and similarly for the other elements. The genetic material simulor includes the effector 'encodes for proteins', while the enzyme simulor includes the effector 'decodes genetic material'. When these two effectors interact, they result in the persistence of all the elements in the cell model. If they do not interact, all four elements will disappear, as each contains a 'decay' effector, probably inherited from the type-simulor 'biological molecule': such molecules are not completely stable. The cytoskeleton simulor contains an effector which enables the persistence of the simulor corresponding to the whole cell: cells are actively maintained structures. Both the enzyme and cytoskeleton simulors are kinds of protein, which is why the production of protein as a result of the genetic material's effector will maintain them. This model will simply maintain itself in a steady state, although it is clear that if any of the parts disappear, the whole will soon follow: if the cytoskeleton goes, the cell disappears right away, and if the enzymes go the genetic material will not be decoded to replenish the cytoskeleton, so the cell will, again, disappear.

Now we can consider apoptosis. The main player is CED-3, a kind of enzyme called a caspase. This enzyme is a protein, but it has the property 'destroys proteins': it is a fairly indiscriminate protease. So, one effector in its simulor is 'destroys proteins'. Now, it is clear that adding this to the model of the cell will rapidly result in simulated cell death. The cytoskeleton will be destroyed, and so the cell will cease to be maintained. This is not quite what happens, however: CED-3 is normally present in cells, but they do not die.

Enter CED-4. It turns out that CED-3 is not normally active, but that CED-4 can activate it. CED-4, then, is another simulor, including the effector 'activates CED-3', and CED-3 must be modified so that the effector is 'destroys proteins when active'. However, this is still not quite right, since CED-4 is usually present. In order to activate CED-3, it must be phosphorylated. There are lots of enzymes that can do this, so the effector 'phosphorylates CED-4' can be added to the simulor for enzymes, while

---

18   The details of the example are taken from Medema 1999.

'activates CED-3' has to be replaced with 'activates CED-3 when phosphorylated' in the simulor for CED-4.

However, a model with CED-3 and CED-4 still results in dead cells, as the enzymes automatically phosphorylate CED-4, and death soon follows. Enter the final player, CED-9. This has the effector 'dephosphorylates CED-4'. Changing the effector in CED-4 to 'activates CED-3 when phosphorylated for two consecutive cycles' sets up the final conditions.

Start the model running in the normal state. On the first cycle the enzymes produce more protein, and the cytoskeleton keeps the cell in existence. The enzymes also phosphorylate CED-4, but that's all that happens this time. On the second cycle, CED-9 dephosphorylates CED-4, and the enzymes and cytoskeleton maintain the cell. The third cycle is the same as the first, so the situation is stable.

Now signal the cell to die, by removing CED-9. (The details of how this is done are still being worked out at the time of writing: anyway, they would complicate the example.) The first cycle goes on as before. On the second cycle, CED-9 is not present, so CED-4 remains phosphorylated. On the third cycle, CED-4 activates CED-3, and on the fourth cycle CED-3 destroys CED-4, the enzymes, and the cytoskeleton, and, probably, itself. On the fifth cycle, the cell disappears, because the cytoskeleton no longer exists. Cell death has occurred.

This model enables us to say quite a bit about apoptosis. (All the details above are correct, with the possible exception of what happens to CED-9: it may be inactivated rather than removed. As far as I know, this is not currently known.) First, it is kept at bay by an active process. In one sense, the default state of a cell is to be dead. Second, we can see that mutations that prevent CED-9 from working will be lethal, as all cells will apoptose. Third, we can see that mutations that prevent CED-3 from working will prevent apoptosis. (Analogous mutations in the human apoptosis system are important in the origin of many cancers, so this is of more than purely scientific interest.) Finally, we can see that there are two possible mutations in CED-4. One would make it permanently phosphorylated (or, at least, functionally equivalent), and that would be lethal. The alternative would make it permanently inactivated, thus leading to no apoptosis.

This does have practical consequences. If there is no CED-4, it may be possible to activate CED-3 some other way, so alternative activators can be sought. However, adding more CED-3 will have no effect, because the additional protein will also not be activated. If the problem is that CED-9 cannot be removed, then adding something that removes it will start apoptosis. We have thus, on the basis of the model, ruled out one therapeutic strategy, and discovered two others that may work.

I would like to emphasise two things. First, this is an example. It is not an argument. The above process could be done by rule-based inference, but it also could be done by models with mutors and effectors. It is my contention that, as a matter of fact, we do it the second way, and not the first. Second, the labels I gave to the effectors are descriptive labels, not the effectors themselves. They are certainly not the mutors.

Conclusion

I have now described the structure of mental models, suggested how they might be implemented, discussed which features are important to their quality, how they relate to other uses of the word 'understanding', and their relationship with theoretical models and propositional representations more generally.

It should be clear that, in this chapter and the one preceding, I have set out a theory with implications for psychology as well as philosophy. The claim that we do, in fact, possess mental models as described here is an empirical one, and so in the next chapter I will consider some of the evidence bearing on the question.

Chapter 5

Empirical Issues

Introduction

The theory of understanding that I developed in the last two chapters is a theory of human cognition, as well as a philosophical account of understanding. Accordingly, it is apt for empirical study. As I am primarily interested in the philosophical aspects, I will keep this discussion brief, but it is worthwhile considering some of the empirical matters that bear on my theory.

The first concerns the possibility of implementing my theory in the brain: its compatibility with what we know about neurons. Second, I consider the ways in which such a capacity might have arisen. The third section of this chapter discusses three different sets of empirical evidence, all of which seem to support the broad outlines of my theory. Finally, I consider some of the predictions that I can make on the basis of my account.

Neurological Constraints

If my account is to be plausible as a theory of the way that people understand it must, given present theories of the mind, be such that the brain could implement it. I discussed some elements of this while setting out the theory, above. In this section, I will discuss the most pressing empirical constraint. We do not know a great deal about the mind. It is not even certain that the brain functions as a neural network, in the sense used in theoretical work, as there is no evidence for some features that are essential to most current networks. We do, however, know a great deal about the speed at which neurons function, and the speed at which humans work.

Newell[1] sets out the relevant facts: an individual neural action takes ~~1ms. The '~~' prefix indicates that the value may be a factor of three larger or smaller: there is a lot of variability between neurons. Thus, there can be around 1000 individual neural actions over the course of one second. For a small neural circuit, the time taken becomes ~~10ms. According to the account given above, this is the level at which mutors would work. Thus, I seem to be committed to an account in which mutors

---

[1]   Newell 1990, pp 123–5.

can operate no faster than ~~10ms. One neuron almost certainly has insufficient structure, and while larger circuits would be possible, it isn't clear that they are necessary at this level. The part of the model that handles simulors and simulants is rather more complex than the mutors, however, and it seems reasonable that it will operate at a speed of ~~100ms.

This puts us under tight constraints. Cognitive behaviour, in which we deal with models of the world, takes place at a time scale of ~~1s. For example, if faced with a new door, it takes me around a second to work out how to open it: which side to manipulate, whether to pull, push or slide, and so on. On my account, this requires me to build and run a mental model of the door. Of course, if I am familiar with the door, things are a lot faster, at a speed of ~~100ms. The faster case may involve skills that bypass mental modelling, so I will leave it to one side. The fact remains that it must be possible to build and run a simple mental model in ~~1s.

We can assume that my perceptual processes are capable of recognising doors and handles, and feeding them into the set-up network. This then has to generate the situation, with the appropriate simulants. This takes, we suppose, ~~100ms. The simulants must then activate their effectors. This is a single neural circuit activity, and so takes ~~10ms. The same time is required for the effectors to activate the mutors, and the same again for the mutors to run. This brings out one of the great advantages of the theory: it is naturally highly parallel. In each ~~10ms period, dozens of effectors and mutors can be activated. The mutors must then send their outputs back to the effectors, and the effectors back to the simulants. One cycle of the model thus takes ~~50ms. If this cycle results in the creation of a new simulant, the set-up network must be activated again, but otherwise the model can be run through another time tick immediately. In simple situations, new simulants are unlikely to arise as a result of the simulation. Thus, it is possible to set up a model and run two cycles in ~~200ms. This would allow us to run at least three models when faced with a new door: if these correspond to push, pull and slide, that would allow us to make the decision.

It seems, then, that my mental models can run fast enough to handle real situations in real time. This, of course, doesn't show that I am right, but it does show that it is not obvious that I am wrong. We can see that this is important by briefly considering an alternative theory.

Suppose that mutors are to be represented by conditionals, and inputs and outputs by statements. Each conditional is processed by the brain, and the output states concatenated. Suppose that there are ten conditionals, and five inputs — a very simple situation. Checking one input with one conditional takes ~~10ms (this is possibly generous, but no matter). One cycle of one model thus takes ~~500ms. If we suppose that a typical effector governs three mutors (this seems a bit low), and that a typical simulor has three effectors (again, a bit low), and that a typical model contains three simulants (low, once more), then the equivalent conditional system contains about 15 conditionals, one per mutor and allowing for shared properties (e.g. two things with mass). There are nine inputs for these conditionals (the value of each effector for each simulant), and so a total of 135 pieces of processing. That would take ~~1s, which is too slow: there is no time for perceptual processing, or fixing motor responses, or running more than one cycle, or running a second model if this one fails. Of course, this does assume that there is only one 'location' in the mind capable of processing conditionals, but this seems reasonable. The processing unit, after all, must be capable of parsing strings, comprehending language, and applying arbitrary logical rules. (A massive look-up table is no use, as it would take ~~10ms to check each entry, of which there would have to be thousands, if not millions.) Thus, there is no way that we could possibly think by applying conditionals in anything remotely resembling the way that they are used in logic. We are simply too quick.

Of course, there are ways of implementing conditionals to get around this problem, although the combinatoric explosion of logical consequences probably guarantees that no such implementation could actually be of conditionals, strictly speaking. Nevertheless, one superficially appealing model can be shown to be definitely wrong: we do not think by consciously applying theories to propositions. And, since one theory fails the test, the fact that my theory passes does count as a point in its favour: it remains a candidate.

Origin and Development

I am claiming a complex capacity for the human mind. While it is obvious that the mind has some complex capacities, claims for particular ones need rather more support. In this section I shall give a possible origin account for this capacity, arguing that its existence is not really surprising. In giving this argument, I shall assume that modern biology is roughly correct about the origin of human beings: that we arose by neo-Darwinian evolution. If the mind is something separate from the brain, and non-physical, then, I am assuming that it did, nevertheless, evolve. If this assumption proves to be false, then the argument in this section will likely be worthless: however, given the strength of support for Darwinian theory, I am not too worried about the possibility.

Consider, then, a creature in a world larger than itself. It has to act in this world, if it is to find food and reproduce. Those which do not will die, and natural selection will exclude their genes from future generations. Of those which do, those who do best will, on the whole, leave more descendants, and their genes will become common. There are many adaptations which can help with this: sharper teeth, better muscles, and better senses, for example. The possible adaptations that I am interested in are mental ones.

When a creature enters a situation, it must settle on a course of action. The simplest way of doing this is to simply act in the same way in all situations. Plants, on the whole, seem to use this level of sophistication:

they just sit there. This, of course, is not a terribly good strategy for the individual, as the ease with which individual plants can be destroyed shows. More sophisticated strategies, and the capacities to use them, will thus be favoured by natural selection. (Albeit not exclusively: plants also employ reproductive strategies which make the survival of the individual of minimal importance to the survival of its offspring.)

The next simplest kind of strategy is to have a limited repertoire of behaviour, and to react to certain stimuli with one behaviour. This is exemplified by many insects. Certain wasps, for example, drag their prey to near their burrows, and, when the prey is a certain distance from the burrow, they leave it, go and check the burrow, and then return for the prey. If the prey has been moved back a bit in the meantime the wasp will drag it to the same distance, and then go and check the burrow again. It responds to the stimulus of being a certain distance from its burrow with this behaviour, and so it can be made to repeat this almost indefinitely.

The next step up is to have two possible kinds of behaviour, used for the same stimulus, but depending on the state of the organism. Thus, if you find water and you are thirsty, drink, but if you are dirty, wash. There are very definite limits to how far you can go in this direction, for two reasons. The first is the limited time-resolution of natural selection.[2] Only correlations that are constant over several generations can be built into such simple conditional behaviour. The second is combinatoric explosion. Before long, you would need a vast number of learned responses, and even then you would have to have an 'otherwise ...' behaviour to cover the situations that you missed.

The best way to deal with this is to allow the organism to combine units, and act on the balance of their consequences. Thus, if you are both thirsty and dirty, and you encounter water, you can set up the situation, and learn that you should drink and wash. It is not possible to do both of these at once, and it is best to drink before you wash if you are planning to use the same water for both. At this point, natural selection cannot, in general, select the best solution. Creatures will get themselves into completely new situations, and need to know how to act. It is possible to select for the ability to predict the future, and this will be the route taken. An animal that can work out that washing will produce dirty water, which it cannot drink, while drinking will not make it impossible to wash, can then choose to drink first.

At this stage, the animal need not have anything resembling an idea of water. There can simply be stuff that you drink, and stuff that you wash with, and it may not even notice that these two keep turning up in the same place. What it has, effectively, is a set of mutors, but no effectors or simulors. This allows it to consider a course of action, albeit in a very limited fashion, before taking it. Any element of the environment that is not primed by natural selection will simply be ignored.

---

[2]   See Plotkin 1994.

This is clearly not the best strategy, as some new situations may be quite importantly different from old ones. The response to this is to allow learning: learn which mutors go together in which effectors, which effectors in simulors, and, finally, which simulors need to be in a model of the current situation.

Initially, then, mental models are used to predict things of everyday utility. Drinking water slakes thirst, and eating food staves off hunger. Eating particular kinds of food, however, causes serious illness. Dropping a rock will lead to it falling, and possibly hitting the sabre tooth tiger below. While these mental models are simple in content, it may well be that, in form, they are no simpler than models of nuclear processes in the heart of stars. Thus, a capacity could evolve for purely practical reasons which has much wider potential application.

We are clearly not born with many mental models and, indeed, there are good reasons for this. Inborn mental models would only be useful in the environment in which they arose, and, since the environment of people changes much more quickly than the evolutionary time scale, they would tend to be a disadvantage.

This is not to assert that intelligence is a *tabula rasa*.[3] While we do not start with many (or, perhaps, any) particular models, we do start with the whole framework of mutors, effectors, and simulors. Thus, we cannot avoid seeing the world as composed of things, which have persistent properties, and will respond to similar stimuli in similar ways. This is quite a lot of structure, and we do not discover this by observation: we are born with it. I discussed the reasons for many parts of the structure in Chapter 3, but the consistency of mutors can now also be explained. Unless something's behaviour can be predicted in the future on the basis of the past, we cannot use our experiences of it to help us in the future. Thus, those creatures that assume that things can be predicted, and keep looking for ways to do so, will tend to survive better. If there is complete unpredictability, there is no advantage in realising that fact: you still have no idea how things will be. Thus, in order for knowledge to be useful, the world must be predictable. Therefore, as far as evolution is concerned, we might as well assume that it is, because there is absolutely no point in learning about total unpredictability.

Despite this initial structure, we still need to build mental models. Since people who build more and better models will be better able to survive, there are good reasons for a drive to understand. Indeed, this model puts curiosity at the same sort of level as hunger, thirst, and sexual drive: it is a basic urge, a legacy of our past. The existence of this drive means that, when we have leisure time, we will tend to start modelling things that are not immediately relevant to our survival, or, in the case of trying to understand the past, will never be so relevant.

---

[3]   See Plotkin 1994 for a spirited denial of *tabula rasa* theories.

One important feature of this story is that every intermediate stage has some use. Indeed, most possible intermediate stages are useful. If we have mutors alone, we can make some predictions, and thus do better than creatures with none. If we have mutors and effectors we can deal with a wider range of circumstances, again an advantage over maxims alone. Having access to mutors, effectors, and simulors provides further advantages, as described in Chapter 3. It must be possible to tell such a story for any complex feature, if it is to be supposed that it arose by evolution.

A parallel story can be told about the eye. Light sensitive cells are useful by themselves: they will not let you see, but you will at least be able to tell whether it is day time. Some form of protective coating is useful, because then minor abrasions will not destroy the sense. Given such a coating, it should be as transparent as possible. Now look at a parallel line of development. It is better to have many cells than one cell, because one cell would be prone to error. With many cells, you can detect lines of shadow that fall on the patch, and a rapidly moving shadow might be dangerous, so that is worth knowing. If you sink the cells in a depression, with a small opening, you can see which direction light is coming from, which makes it easier to find, or hide from, light. Once you have such a depression, and a transparent coating, the covering can thicken in such a way as to partially focus the light falling on it, thus giving you better resolution. And now you have an eye.

The essential feature is that the complex organ must be built up of components that can be independently useful. While all natural organs have this feature, not all possible ones do. Take, for example, the use of logical inference rules. In order to use such a rule, you need, at least, the capacity to interpret signs, and to analyse and transform syntax. Neither is any use by itself: with the first, I can think about sabre-tooth tigers, pain, death, and running away, but I can't link them; while with the second I can know that if A leads to B, B is to be avoided, and A can be avoided by C, without being able to apply this structure to the case of the sabre-tooth tiger now in front of me. Further, each capacity seems extremely complex, and only of use as part of a system. If I can recognise sabre-tooth tigers, and know that they are carnivorous, dangerous, and so on, this is little use unless I can also work out that this means that I should be somewhere else. The system only does useful work when it is all there, and so could not have evolved.

This does not mean that we cannot perform logical inferences. However, it does mean that we must perform them by using a more basic system, which did evolve, and which evolved for another purpose — evolution is blind, and could not know that the system would allow logical inference. I will consider, below, how logical inference could be based on mental models as described in this book. Accordingly, propositional inference *per se* cannot compete with my theory as a description of the mind: it must be based on something like my theory (in that it could have evolved), and that something must be produced if the challenge is to be assessed.

Thus, we can see that the capacity to build mental models would be useful to an organism. Further, parts of the capacity would also be useful, so that the whole complex could have evolved gradually, facing positive selection at every stage. Since it must be responsive to a changing environment, we cannot be born with all our models already there. This means that we must build new models, and thus be endowed with a drive to do so, and a sufficiently flexible basic structure to make it possible. Since we cannot know what might be useful in the future, this curiosity should extend even to things with little immediate practical import, as should the flexibility. In sum, it is plausible that human beings could have evolved both the desire and the ability to understand black holes, even though such understanding has never been relevant to our survival.

Empirical Evidence

Bailer-Jones: Radio Sources

In her Ph.D. dissertation,[4] Daniela Bailer-Jones sets out a detailed case study of scientific modelling, specifically concerned with the modelling of extended extragalactic radio sources. The scientific details are quite involved, and I cannot reproduce them here — I will, instead, concentrate on the conclusions that Bailer-Jones draws about the model itself.

The situation is somewhat complicated by her distinction between the scientific model, the philosophical model, and the mental model. Roughly, the scientific model is her object of study, and the philosophical model is what she produces. The mental model is something that must exist, underpinning the scientific model, but about which she has little to say. Accordingly, I will be concerned with what she has to say about the philosophical model, and whether my account could provide the mental model that underlies the whole structure.

She highlights four features of the model: a lack of account anywhere in the model is perceived as a problem, the search for accounts to fill the lack starts from familiar accounts, complex problems are split into smaller models, and visualisation plays an important role. I will not have much to say about the last point, because I have not said anything about the link between mental models and visualisation. The other three points, however, do seem to fit quite well with my theory.

A lack of account anywhere in the model would correspond to an absence of simulors, effectors, or mutors at that point. Since the simulation process would simply stop when it ran out of components, a lack of account would obviously be a problem. Bailer-Jones says that the modelling process aims at completeness, even if it is thought that this will never really be achieved. Further, gaps can be filled by placeholders: hand-

---

4   Bailer-Jones 1998. This case study is also described in Bailer-Jones 2000.

waving arguments that do not really show how the gap can be filled in detail, but allow it to be handled. This is easy to motivate on my account: a mental model that is simply missing parts will not be able to simulate at all. A vague filler will let the model continue, but since it will, most likely, be error-prone, there are strong motivations for replacing it with a more detailed model. Nevertheless, the placeholder will be a real component of the mental model, and will allow the simulation to continue.

It is also easy to see why we should start from the familiar. The easiest example, as Bailer-Jones notes, is one in which a model from another field is simply imported wholesale. This corresponds to simply incorporating an already-existing simulor or effector into the model. Analogical inference is harder to deal with, but could involve the use of some effectors from a simulor that already exists, or some mutors of an existent effector. The details of this process would need a book to themselves, but it is, at least, highly plausible that an account of this type would arise from my theory.

The last point that I want to discuss, about sub-models, is also the one that flows most naturally from my account. The sub-models could be models of properties, in which case they would be effectors in the model, or of things, in which case they would be simulors that served as parts of the overall model. In the case of properties, the architecture of the model mandates considering them as independently as possible. It is necessary to know with which other properties a given property will interact, but it must operate independently of co-instantiated properties if it is to be represented by an effector. That is, an effector is an independent group of mutors that can appear, if not by itself, at least in combination with a fairly arbitrary group of other effectors.

For models of parts, things are a little more complex. It might be thought that there was no real need to break a thing down into parts, although it is easy to do so. However, since simulations are run on simulants, and those simulants need to be tolerably complete before any simulation can be run, there is an obvious advantage to developing models bit by bit. If you can get the model of a part running, you can test that model even if the rest of the model is still in the very early stages of development. If you tried to develop the whole model at once, nothing would happen until you had finished, and if the model then failed to simulate accurately you would not have many clues as to which part had gone wrong.

Overall, then, it seems that my theory can account for the features of scientific modelling observed in Bailer-Jones's case study.

Johnson-Laird: Mental Models

In his books *Mental Models*[5] and *Human and Machine Thinking,*[6] Philip Johnson-Laird has put forward a theory of cognition based on the use of

---

[5]   Johnson-Laird 1983.

mental models. Johnson-Laird sees mental models as a sort of internal tableau.[7] The model is a picture of the things modelled, and their relationships, but it is, to a great extent, abstract. Only those features of the tableau that are immediately relevant are portrayed. For Johnson-Laird, the following diagram is an adequate representation of a mental model of the two statements 'All the athletes are bankers' and 'All the chemists are bankers':

$$a \quad = \quad b \quad = \quad c$$
$$a \quad = \quad b \quad = \quad c$$
$$a \quad = \quad b \quad = \quad c$$
$$(b)$$
$$(b)$$

(see Johnson-Laird 1983 p. 131: note that this model is not the only one necessary to represent these premises). From what I have already said about mental models, it is clear that, on my theory, such a diagram would, at the very least, be missing large amounts of information. Of course, Johnson-Laird does not claim that the diagram captures all the detail of the neurological implementation of the model: he does, however, claim that is captures all the important structural features. Even on purely structural features, such a diagram cannot capture my mental models, as it does not refer to the mutors, nor to the ways in which they are linked.

This difference is probably explained by the difference in the main cases that we are considering. While I have concentrated on explanation and understanding, Johnson-Laird concentrated on the solving of syllogisms. Syllogisms are static entities, concerning relationships that hold either at a specific time, or at all times. Explanation and understanding are dynamic, dealing with things that change, and with those very changes. It is thus unsurprising that my mental models are much more complex than his.

In his books Johnson-Laird develops a full theory of syllogistic inference, backed up with a substantial amount of experimental data. He also develops accounts of the parsing of language, induction, and creativity, but I shall not discuss these. Most of the discussion of language parsing is technical, and not very relevant to my arguments. Similarly, I am not, at present, concerned with creativity. His discussion of induction is, potentially, very relevant. However, I have not developed my account of induction (as opposed to simulation) to a sufficient extent to be able to make meaningful comparisons.

While I have nothing original to say about syllogistic inference, Johnson-Laird's theory of this process is self-contained, and well developed. Thus, if I can argue that my mental models can serve the purposes of his models, I can argue that my theory can account for another

---

6   Johnson-Laird 1993.

7   Johnson-Laird 1983, p 97.

area of thought, and claim his experimental evidence as support for my theory.

Mental models and deduction Johnson-Laird develops his theory of syllogistic reasoning in Chapter 5 of *Mental Models*. Very briefly, it runs as follows. First, construct a mental model of the first premise. This requires only a single mental model. Next, add the information in the second premise to this model. This may require the construction of several models, since there may be several ways of adding the information. Finally, the conclusion is anything interesting that is true in all the models.

This theory correctly accounts for the difficulty of various types of syllogism: those syllogisms which require more models are harder. It also accounts, in a natural way, for a number of observed systematic errors in syllogistic reasoning: it can explain why people draw the conclusions they do, even when those conclusions are wrong.

The question, then, is whether my mental models can serve in this theory. Clearly, if they do so they will not be functioning at full power. There is no need to simulate the behaviour of an artist when considering the premise 'All artists are beekeepers', after all. In general, the mental models that my theory says that we have of objects will be largely idle in these situations. The dispositions and manifold properties of the object, all of which are encoded in the model, are irrelevant to most deductions. All that is necessary, in order to build one of Johnson-Laird's models, is the model of the situation described, with the things in the situation represented purely by their names. Thus, Johnson-Laird's models are like the models that I propose for situations, with all the details of the models of the constituent objects suppressed.

Given this constraint, it seems obvious that my mental models can serve the function of Johnson-Laird's. He requires that tokens representing the items involved in the premises be arranged in a sort of internal tableau that structurally mimics the situation described in the premises. If you ignore the internal structure of the models of objects, then the process of building a model of a situation is the process of constructing an internal tableau that structurally mimics the situation described.

It will be noted that I have not said a great deal about how these tableaux are constructed. It must be said that Johnson-Laird doesn't either, but that is hardly a defence. The real accusation here is that my theory adds nothing to Johnson-Laird's, at least as far as syllogistic reasoning is concerned, and so my attempt to take over some of it as further evidence for my account is unfair.

This is not an unanswerable accusation. First, I claim that mental models are there so that we can understand the world, not so that we can do syllogisms. I also argued that we understand language by building models of the things described. Given that models evolved as our way of representing the world, and that language is a way of transferring a representation of the world from one person to another, this is a very unsurprising claim. The combination of these two claims, however, makes

Johnson-Laird's theory of the syllogism seem obvious. The syllogism is not, as formally stated, a natural form of reasoning. It required Aristotle's genius to formalise it, after all. Thus, when untrained people deal with syllogisms, we should expect them to deal with the problem in the same way that they deal with all problems. That is, we should expect them to build a mental model of the situation described, and then inspect that model for the results. In short, Johnson-Laird provides substantial evidence that people reason in this way. If the mental models are situational models, as described in my theory, then we can explain why people reason in that way.

The second point is that my model makes predictions that are not made by Johnson-Laird. If you build the situational model with simulants, as they exist according to my theory, then all their effectors are present. Since the simulation process is, to an extent, automatic, people should simulate the situation, and thus draw conclusions based on the simulation.

Thus, if you are told that all the artists are bankers, and that some of the artists are chemists, then you may conclude that some of the artists have degrees. Now, from All A are B, and Some A are C, there is no way to get, syllogistically, to Some A are D. However, since most bankers have degrees, and the same is true of most chemists, and since some of the artists are both bankers and chemists, it is an entirely reasonable conclusion that some of the artists have degrees. That is, if someone knows about the things involved in the syllogism, they are likely to draw conclusions based on simulation, rather than on what is actually entailed.

Is this prediction borne out? As I am not able to do any experiments, I cannot provide any definite evidence. However, as far as I am aware, most experiments on syllogistic deduction have to take pains to stress what is going on, or use purely abstract terms. That is, the subjects either have to be told not to simulate the situation, or they have to be given empty tokens which, since they have no model, cannot be simulated. Certainly, if you present someone with syllogistic information and ask them what they can tell you about that situation, they will not simply provide the deductive conclusions.

In fact, in *Human and Machine Thinking*,[8] Johnson-Laird provides some evidence that this is the case. He presents the following premises:

Three children are standing in a line.

At least one of them is a girl, and at least one of them is a boy.

And the question is 'Is a girl standing next to a boy?'. This problem is unanswerable on the normal constraints placed on answering deductive problems, because we do not know the sex of the third child, nor do we know that boy and girl are exhaustive characterisations. Indeed, since true hermaphrodites are not unknown, they are not, and the question is genuinely unanswerable. However, most people quickly answer 'yes': if the third child must be a boy or a girl, then obviously a boy is standing next to a girl somewhere. Thus, when they build the model, they clearly include

---

[8]   Johnson-Laird 1993, pp 45–6.

at least some properties of the things in the model which have not been explicitly invoked: specifically, the sex of the third child. It would be interesting, if practically impossible, to see if people with a lot of experience with hermaphrodites tended to regard the question as impossible.

In fact, I can make a stronger prediction based on my theory. The syllogistic conclusions are not the natural ones to draw. The natural procedure is to simulate the situation, and say what transpires. Only in situations that cannot be simulated will the deductive conclusions occur first. This prediction would be hard to test, since the protocol for the experiment should avoid suggesting that a deductive conclusion is required, but should also avoid suggesting that such a conclusion should not be drawn.

If this account of how my theory and Johnson-Laird's fit together is correct, and both of the individual theories are also correct, then the status of deductive reasoning becomes clear. Far from being a fundamental part of our reason, it is an artificial way of using mental techniques developed for entirely different techniques. This would explain why people find it difficult to learn deductive reasoning, while inductive reasoning, which is not taught, poses very little problem.

Conditionals In *Deduction*[9] Johnson-Laird and Byrne present a mental model account of conditional reasoning. This account is of a piece with their accounts of other kinds of reasoning, involving internal tableaux. However, my theory explains much conditional reasoning by the operation of mutors: to see what would happen if X, you set up the mental model of X and see what happens. Part of their discussion concerns the Wason selection task, to which I shall return below. Here, I will discuss their account of some other conditionals, and argue that mine is superior.

Their first observation is that the conditional 'If there is a circle, then there is a triangle' is held to be true if there is a circle and a triangle, false if there is a circle and no triangle, and irrelevant otherwise. On the other hand, the conditional 'If there is no circle, then there is a triangle' is held to be true if there is either a circle or a triangle, and false otherwise.

Johnson-Laird and Byrne's explanation is that, when presented with the first conditional, the mental model we build only explicitly represents the existence of the circle. It thus has nothing to say about the case in which there is no circle. On the other hand, the model for the second conditional includes the case in which there is a circle, because negations tend to bring their positive counterparts to mind. This seems rather *ad hoc:* it might be true, but it certainly doesn't follow from their account.

I would suggest that we possess a mutor designed specifically for generalised conditional reasoning. We set this mutor up by providing a standard and an output. If the input to the mutor matches the standard, then

---

[9] Johnson-Laird & Byrne 1991.

the output is produced, and added to the model. The conditional is then assessed by comparing the situation to this model.

When presented with 'If there is a circle, then there is a triangle', the standard is 'there is a circle' and the output is 'there is a triangle'. If 'there is a circle' is presented as input, then 'there is a triangle' is presented as output, and the model assembled includes both a circle and a triangle. Thus, if there is a circle and a triangle, the conditional is assessed as true, while if there is a circle but no triangle, it is assessed as false. If the input provided is 'there isn't a circle', nothing is produced, and we have no model to compare the situation to (recall that absences are not usually modelled explicitly). Thus, we cannot say whether it is true or false: the situation cannot agree or disagree with the absence of a model.

In the second case, the input is 'there is no circle', and the output is 'there is a triangle'. If the input is 'there is no circle', the model produced is 'there is a triangle', so the conditional will be judged true if there is a triangle, and false if not. If the input is 'there is a circle', then the mutor will produce nothing, and the model will be 'there is a circle'. Accordingly, the conditional will be judged true if there is a circle — which there is, as that was the input. This seems, to me at least, much less arbitrary. There are good reasons, in general, to compare whole models to the world, rather than just fragments, and the difference flows entirely from that requirement.

The only concern might be over the reason why we should have a generalised conditional model, as described. Since Johnson-Laird gives no reason why we should have mental models, other than that they are useful for deduction, there is no rhetorical need for me to answer the question. However, a return to the Darwinian account sketched above does allow me answer. It is likely to be hard to create new mutors, no matter what the specific implementation may be. Thus, it is only worth doing so if a situation becomes common, and is likely to remain so. However, there are many temporary situations about which we want to reason. If they include novel relations, it is useful to have a way to reason about those relations without having to create a new mutor. Indeed, the generalised conditional model could even represent the first stages of creating a new mutor. This is a long way from a rigorous demonstration that we would have such a thing, but it does, at least, show that it is not surprising if we do.

Johnson-Laird and Byrne go on to discuss causal conditionals. In this case, I would say that we reason by using the relevant effectors and their mutors: the general conditional model is not used. I will discuss the relationship between mutors and causation in Chapter 7, so here I will restrict myself to criticising Johnson-Laird and Byrne's account.

They present three types of causal relation, specified by models of actual and counterfactual situations. The first is strong (necessary and sufficient) causation, the second weak (sufficient) causation, and the third the 'Allowing relation' (necessary causation). I will restrict my discussion to the strong case. According to them, we build two models to represent this, an actual model and a counterfactual one. In the actual model, both the cause and the effect occur. In the counterfactual model, neither do. The occurrence of one without the other is not a possibility.

The problem is that this account cannot distinguish between strong causation, and strong common cause. Thus, if there is a cause that is both necessary and sufficient for each of two effects, then, if we consider the two effects, they both occur in the actual world, and the only possible counterfactual world is one in which neither occurs. Similar examples can easily be constructed for the other two cases, and have been, at great length, in the literature on causation. Johnson-Laird and Byrne's account is thus hopeless as a description of our causal reasoning.

Theoretical Comparisons   The programmatic statements made by Johnson-Laird are really remarkably close to the claims that I make. For example, in the first chapter of *Mental Models* (entitled 'The Nature of Explanation') he says:

> [H]uman beings understand the world by constructing working models of it in their minds.[10]

Indeed, he claims that this is the foundational idea underlying all his work: everything is understood in this way. It is thus somewhat curious that he has almost nothing to say about understanding in either book. In fact, I can quote almost his entire discussion of the subject. This is found in *Human and Machine Thinking*.

> You can describe a phenomenon without understanding it, but you cannot explain a phenomenon unless you have some putative understanding of it. A descriptive mental model of the phenomenon merely simulates it, although such a model may be useful in predicting certain events. An explanatory model of the phenomenon, however, embodies underlying principles, so even if it is incomplete or partially erroneous, it is more powerful than a simulation. If you have an explanatory model, you may know what causes the phenomenon; what results from it; how to influence, control, initiate or prevent it; how it relates to other phenomena or how it resembles them; how to predict its onset and course; what its internal or underlying structure is; how to diagnose unusual events; and, in science, how to relate the domain as a whole to others. Scientific explanations characteristically make use of theoretical notions that are unobservable or that are at a lower physical level than descriptions of the phenomena. An explanation accounts for what you do not understand in terms of what you do understand: you cannot construct a model if the key explanatory concepts are not available to you.[11]

---

[10]   Johnson-Laird 1983, p 10.
[11]   Johnson-Laird 1993, p 66.

It is clear from this passage that our motivating ideas of understanding are very similar indeed. Since I read both of these books some time before I developed my theory, it is likely that these passages were among the seeds for my account. Thus, my account is not quite so isolated from previous considerations as may have appeared at first.

On the other hand, Johnson-Laird does not provide a theory of understanding: the above single paragraph is, at most, a sketch of the form that a theory might take. Further, the theory sketched is not the one that I have produced. Johnson-Laird makes a distinction between simulation and understanding, while I do not. He requires that a model embody underlying principles to grant understanding: I argue that, if a model grants understanding (i.e. the ability to accurately simulate over a wide range of conditions), then it probably models underlying principles.

His gestures towards explanation, such as they are, are even less satisfactory. He refers to the possession of an explanatory model, without any indication of the relationship between such a model and an explanation. Since his models are not verbal, or even propositional, entities, the model and the explanation clearly cannot be identical. According to my account, it is misleading to characterise a model as explanatory: models grant understanding, and explanations improve models, but are not models themselves. Further, the features that he claims are characteristic of scientific explanation, appeal to unobservables or lower physical levels, are, on my account, only contingently so characteristic, and may be missing in a perfectly acceptable scientific explanation. Finally, he seems to be unaware of the problem of the why-regress, claiming that you can only explain something if you understand the explanation.

It might seem a little unfair to apply this level of criticism to a sketch in passing of a theory. If my aim was to show that Johnson-Laird was wrong about explanation, it would be unfair. My aim is slightly different, however: it is to show that, despite the programmatic similarities between our accounts, my account of understanding is both original and superior. While it is motivated by the same ideas, it is not, in any sense, a development of Johnson-Laird's theories.

Our theories of mental models are, in fact, very different. In summary, then, Johnson-Laird's conception of understanding is very close to mine in broad outline, although it differs in even the few details which he does develop. If his account of syllogistic reasoning is assimilated to my theory, we gain an explanation of why we solve syllogisms in that way, and also predictions for other types of 'errors' that may be made in those circumstances.

Wason: The Selection Task

Wason's selection task is one of the best known results in cognitive psychology.[12] The subject is given four cards, each with a letter on one side and a number on the other. The visible faces read 'A K 4 7'. The subject is then asked which cards she needs to turn over in order to test the hypothesis 'if a card has a vowel on one side, it has an even number on the other'.

Most people correctly turn over the 'A' card. Almost no-one bothers with the 'K'. Thus far, things are as would be expected from elementary logic. However, a lot of people turn over the '4' card, and very few check the '7'. This is wrong: no matter what is on the other side of the '4', the rule is unaffected: it does not say that a card with a consonant on one side cannot have a vowel on the other. If it did, it would be necessary to turn over the 'K' card. On the other hand, the '7' should be checked, since if it has a vowel on the other side, the rule is false.

This result fits in very well with my theory. The conditional will be plugged into the conditional model, as described above, so that 'has a vowel on one side' is the standard and 'has an even number on the other' is the output.

Given such a mutor, numbers simply produce no result when used as input, and odd numbers never come out. The mutor itself says nothing about the circumstances surrounding odd numbers, and so we would expect people to overlook the importance of the '7'.

The selection task can be varied in such a way as to make it easier. If the rule is 'if you are drinking beer, you must be over twenty one' and the cards are 'drinking beer', 'not drinking beer', 'over twenty one', and 'under twenty one', people generally pick the right cards. That is, they know to check that the people drinking beer are old enough, and that the youngsters are not drinking beer. This effect is observed whenever the situation involves permission.

Things can be made more complex, however. If the rule is 'if you have spent more than £100, you may take a free gift', then the cards are 'more than £100', 'less than £100', 'free gift', 'no free gift'. People still check two cards, but which two depends on how the situation is described. If the description suggests that the shop is cheating, they check 'more than £100' and 'no free gift'. If it suggests that the customers are cheating, they check the other two.[13] Of course, these selections make perfect sense, even though, strictly speaking, you cannot tell whether anyone is cheating: the customers are not *forced* to take a free gift, so someone who spent more than £100 and has no free gift may simply not have wanted one, while there is no indication that spending £100 is the only way to qualify for a free gift,

---

12   This account is based on the summary in Medin & Ross 1997, but the task is also mentioned in Plotkin 1994 and Johnson-Laird 1983, as well as many other places.

13   Manktelow and Over, referenced in Medin & Ross 1997.

so a customer who spent less than £100 and has a gift may have qualified another way.

Thus, the situation is not that people become better at logical reasoning when a concrete situation is presented. Indeed, in the last example it seems that the overwhelming majority of people were wrong, in logical terms, since they thought that it was possible to test the rule with the data given. It does, however, strongly suggest that a general conditional mutor is not being used. Instead, people seem to be using a general 'permission/prohibition' model, as Cosmides suggested.[14] This model takes a social rule as input, and tells you how to check that the rule is being followed. Given the ubiquity of such rules in daily life, the possession of such a model is completely unsurprising, on my account. Thus, the results of these experiments are entirely consistent with my theory.

Williams, Hollan, & Stevens: Heat Exchangers

Williams, Hollan, & Stevens[15] provide a descriptive account of the mental models used by an experimental subject while he reasoned about a simple heat exchanger. While my account and theirs were developed independently, they show striking similarities. They define a mental model as follows:

> A mental model is a collection of 'connected' autonomous objects. Running a mental model corresponds to modifying the parameters of the model by propagating information using the internal rules and specified topology.[16]

If it is assumed that the internal rules have their own impetus, so that the model runs itself, this could be taken unchanged as a quick description of my models. Williams *et al.* seem to assume that the rules do have to be run by some outside force (although this is not entirely clear: see below), so their account may differ from mine in this respect. They also say:

> We think mental models assist human reasoning in a variety of ways. They can be used as inference engines to predict the behavior of physical systems. They can also be used to produce explanations or justifications.[17]

These are the two uses that I have proposed for mental models in this book, so I am inclined to agree with them here. Their account of an 'autonomous object' is also worth quoting:

---

[14]   Referenced in Medin & Ross 1997.
[15]   Williams *et al.* 1983.
[16]   Williams *et al.* 1983, p 133.
[17]   Williams *et al.* 1983, p 136.

Autonomous objects are mental objects that have definite boundaries. The behavior of autonomous objects (defined as changes in parameter values) is governed strictly by internal rules reacting to internal parameter changes and to highly constrained external provocation. The internal operations (rules) by which objects achieve their input/output characteristics across object boundaries are not directly introspectable (nor meaningful). This results in the object having a certain opacity.[18]

On my account, this definition would seem to confuse simulors and effectors, just as diSessa's account confused mutors and effectors. Nevertheless, this is very close to my account, and, again as in diSessa's case, the model seems to have been developed from experimental evidence, rather than for theoretical reasons. The evidence that they discuss in the article consists of a protocol obtained from a subject reasoning about a simple heat exchanger. This consisted of a device which took hot oil and cold water in at one side, and sent cooler oil and hotter water out of the other. The subject was asked various questions about the exchanger, and developed models to answer them.

The first model consisted of a single container with three rules: changing the heat going in led to a corresponding change in the total heat in the container, and a change in that total heat led to corresponding changes in both of the output heats (oil and water). This would seem to be modelled by a simple 'substance divider', rather than something specific to heat and temperature. Further questions provoked the use of more complex models, first one in which a constant amount of heat was transferred within the exchanger, and finally one in which the rate of transfer depended on the temperature difference.

These results can be interpreted on my account, but the interpretation differs slightly from that given by Williams *et al*. In the first and second models, the subject is not using the effectors for 'heat' or 'temperature'. Instead, he is treating heat as a generic 'stuff' and using very simple models for the transfer of stuff between inputs and outputs. This can be seen easily in the first model: the rules would, *mutatis nominibus*, apply equally to a system in which water flowed in at one pipe and out at two. The constant transfer model has stuff flow in, some swapped between channels, and then stuff leaving. Only the third model actually relies on the properties of heat. Why should this procedure be followed?

The simplicity of the earlier models provides the reason. As long as the situation can be simulated without dealing with the many properties of heat and temperature, which the subject may not be entirely clear about, it is a good idea to do so. This uses fewer mental resources, and thus allows for faster answers. Only when the model proves to be inadequate is it worth using the more complex one that is available. This does seem to be a common procedure. In normal use, I treat my computer as a grey box. I hit

---

[18]   Williams *et al*. 1983, p 134.

keys, and words appear on the screen. I do have a more sophisticated model available, in which the signals pass from the keys to the processor, and thence to the screen, but I only use that one if my first one stops working: if I hit a key, and the screen remains unchanged. The more elaborate model leads me to consider various possibilities, such as loose wires or a system crash, that the simpler model does not involve. On the other hand, if I thought about that possibility before striking every key, I would never get anything done.

This analysis also helps to handle the points that Williams *et al.* raise about reasoning outside the scope of mental models.[19] The first concerns constraints and limiting cases. In particular, their models cannot handle limits: what would happen in an extreme case. This is something that my models can handle very easily, however. The model can easily be run with extreme values for the various parameters and, crucially, they can be run repeatedly and rapidly to simulate maintaining something for a long time.

The use of multiple models, as discussed above, is also easy to explain. It is a simple matter of wanting to use as little mental energy as possible. While the mechanisms for doing this are not part of the models themselves, they obviously exist. I do not, however, have the space to say much about them here.

Finally, they talk about the use of experiential knowledge. On my account, this is not an external factor. Mental models *are* experiential knowledge. To a great extent, this is how we remember what we have learned about the world. That is, my knowledge about heat is not gathered from memory and applied to my mental model of heat: my mental model of heat is my knowledge about heat. Whenever we build a mental model of a new situation, we use our experience of similar situations indirectly, by relying on the models we built to handle them. (Williams *et al.* do canvass this possibility, briefly, later in the paper.)

In their concluding section, Williams *et al.* discuss several problems for their account. Most are problems of implementation, and thus are equally problematic for my account. The most important one, however, is not:

> First, it is quite difficult to distinguish in any evidential sense the theoretical ideas that we put forth (objects, runability, etc.) from the particular models we use to account for the subject's protocol. We are much more committed to these underlying ideas than we are to the particular models we have presented. Yet we don't know of any technique to explore or test the basic concepts independent of particular models.[20]

Essentially, this entire book is devoted to exploring and testing the basic concepts, independent of particular models. It is my belief that the fundamental ideas underlying their work come out of this process quite

---

[19]   Williams *et al.* 1983, pp 147–9.

[20]   Williams *et al.* 1983, p 150.

well, although the same cannot be said for the particular models they attribute in this case. On my side, the problem is more the provision of empirical evidence for my theory, and Williams *et al.* do this admirably.

Predictions

In this section I will take my philosophical life in my hands and venture a few predictions. First, however, I would like to pay the insurance premiums so that I am covered if it does blow up in my face. It should be obvious from all the recent work on theory confirmation that the failure of any one of these predictions would not refute the theory as a whole. If they all proved to be completely wrong, that would suggest that I had missed the mark, but if one were slightly in error, that would point rather to the need to refine the theory — something which, given its current state, it will obviously need even if every suggestion I have made is completely accurate.

Also, it is not possible to make terribly specific predictions at the moment, in the absence of a fully detailed account of the implementation of models in the mind. This is an inherent problem of high-level theories: even Newtonian mechanics makes few predictions without information about initial conditions. More to the point, none of the competing theories make specific predictions. Hempel explicitly denies any intention to say anything about actual explanations, Lewis requires that explanations be causal except when they're not, and Kitcher's characterisation of unification has so many place-holders that any explanation could be fitted into it. These shortcomings do not militate against the theories in question, however, because empirical predictions are not their primary aim. The same is true of my account, but I find that I get a few empirical predictions 'for free', as it were.

Chapter 6, on explanation, can be seen as devoted to testing the theory against the evidence of our explanatory practices. In this section, I will concentrate on applications to simulation in general.

The simplest prediction is that we will, in fact, simulate the world. That is, we will work out what is likely to happen next, both under the current conditions, and if something changes. Obviously, we do. This result is only interesting because it is predicted by a theory of explanation. If a theory of inference had the consequence that we were constantly making predictions, that would not count in its favour, since it must explain this in order to be a candidate. However, there is no obvious reason why a theory of explanation should have this consequence, and only Hempel's comes close to doing so in the literature, due to his structural identity thesis (to which I will return in Chapter 6). The fact that mine does, then, is a mark in its favour.

The division of the world into properties and things was much more a datum for the theory than a prediction of it, so I cannot really claim that as evidence. Some of the details of the division do count, however. First, my theory suggests that a simulation will be harder if there are more things involved. There may even be a limit, which could vary from person to person, on the number of things that can be handled simultaneously. This is plausible: I can simulate two billiard balls on a table, but not a hundred. It is also open to empirical investigation.

A second consequence is that, on the assumption that the basic mental capacity of human beings is constant to within an order of magnitude, any differences in simulatory ability beyond that must be due to differences in the model, and that those differences will be in the things and properties considered. That is, if someone can simulate a hundred billiard balls as easily as I can simulate one, this will not be because he has clever tricks for simulating a billiard ball extremely quickly, but because he can treat a hundred balls as a small number of objects. This should show up in experimental protocols: the poor simulator should talk about the behaviour of each ball, while the good simulator talks about the behaviour of the mass — which will, of course, have very different properties from a billiard ball.

A third consequence concerns 'trick questions'. If someone is known to have an aggregate simulor, as well as simulors that represent its parts, then simulation of the aggregate should be faster and easier than simulation of the parts. Thus, if a question could be phrased to disguise the involvement of the aggregate, people should be much slower in answering it. This could even make the difference between possibility (simulate one thing) and impossibility (simulate ten million things).

Specific implementation proposals have more specific consequences. One consequence of the neural network account given above is that it should take longer to simulate a group of items all of which have the same property than to simulate highly distinct things. This is because the same effector has to be used for each item in turn in the first case, while the simulations in the second case can take place in parallel. Similarly, the same model suggests that the time taken for a simulation should be independent of the number of effectors involved, as they are all activated in parallel. The energy used, on the other hand, should increase, because more bits of brain are being activated. Thus, you should get tired faster simulating things with lots of properties.

The Soar implementation has different consequences. Because it allows many copies of a mutor to be made, simulations should be no slower when lots of similar properties are involved than when they are all different. This emphasises the point about high level theories not making specific predictions: there is no possible discovery about the relative speeds of the two types of simulation which, taken by itself, could count as evidence for or against my theory. Nevertheless, the evidence is highly relevant to the theory, since it can constrain the possible implementations. Many pieces of evidence of this type could have the consequence that there is no possible implementation, and that would certainly count as evidence against the high-level theory.

My theory is, to a certain extent, a theory of the way the mind actually works and, in that capacity, it can make some predictions. However, it is more properly considered as a philosophical account of understanding, which means that the predictions it can make are not highly specific.

Conclusions

In this chapter, I have quickly surveyed some of the empirical issues and evidence relevant to my thesis. This is generally favourable, although the nature of the theory prevents it being conclusive at this stage. Nevertheless, fortified by the belief that I am, at least, not flying in the face of the evidence, I will continue in the next chapter by developing a theory of explanation based on my account of understanding.

Chapter 6

Explanation Rebuilt

I began this book searching for a theory of explanation: now, with the additional equipment of a theory of understanding, I hope that I shall be able to provide one. In this chapter, I shall first set out the general form of my account of explanation, before considering the pragmatic factors that influence particular occasions of explaining. I shall then consider how my account handles some of the classic problem cases for theories of explanation.

Providing Understanding

In my account, I take my theory of understanding to be basic. An explanation, roughly speaking, is anything which increases understanding. This is, however, very rough, and in this section I shall develop the notion and make it rather more precise. It should be noted at the outset that the final restrictions may not be well motivated by theoretical considerations, other than the desire to conform to our normal use of the word 'explanation'. This is to be expected: only the most naive would suppose that our use of words will necessarily conform in detail to theories of that area.

The first point to note is that, on this account, there is no way of assessing whether something is explanatory *simpliciter*, in isolation from everything else. Since an explanation must improve understanding, its explanatoriness depends on a certain starting level of understanding. Similarly, an explanation which is completely incomprehensible to someone, simply because it is given in a language which he does not understand, will not improve his understanding, and thus is not an explanation, for him. Even if we cast explanations in terms of propositions rather than particular words, someone may still, perhaps, lack the concepts necessary to grasp a particular explanation.

However, this problem is not as serious as it might appear. Within a culture, such as modern Western society, there will be enough in common between people for broad assessments of explanatoriness to be made: there will be potential explanations which would improve the understanding of a wide range of people. It is cases such as these that I will have in mind for most of the discussion in this section.

Following normal philosophical procedure, I shall refine my definition against putative counter-examples. The first restriction I need to make is not unique to my account, however. This is the idea of an explanation of something. An explanation of something must improve understanding of that thing. It may improve the understanding of other things as well, but it must improve the understanding of the thing that it purports to explain. Thus, although being told about relativity theory may well improve my understanding, it does not serve as an explanation as to why that student was late for a supervision, as it does not improve my understanding of that situation. Some such restriction is, of course, necessary in any theory of explanation.

The next problem is, however, specific to my formulation. Suppose there is a 'clever pill'. When you take this pill, your mental acuity is increased by a factor of six. Clearly, since speed is a desirable feature of mental models, taking this pill is going to improve your understanding of everything. However, we certainly do not want to claim that the pill constitutes an explanation of any particular situation, much less one of every particular situation.

Can we get around this problem by requiring that the explanation increase understanding of the thing explained more than it increases the understanding of other things? I suspect not. It seems plausible that you could explain something, and incidentally provide a large boost to the understanding of a different area. For example, in explaining the actions of a security guard you might provide a modest improvement in understanding of the guard, but a great improvement in the understanding of the operation of shop alarms. On the other hand, thought experiments with the 'clever pill' suggest that it might affect one kind of simulation more than another, thus improving some understanding more than others. Thus, this restriction seems to fail both ways.

Perhaps this is the wrong approach. Another example suggests that it may be. Suppose that you are struck on the head, and this blow knocks your neurons into a pattern which gives you an excellent understanding of Mahler's personality. We would, I think, be reluctant to describe such a blow as an explanation of Mahler, despite its specificity.

Peter Achinstein's[1] characterisation of explanation as an illocutionary act might help here. On this account, an explanation is a form of words uttered with the intention of explaining: the intention is important. If we include this requirement, then someone must intend to improve your understanding of a particular situation by their explanation in order for it to count as such. Alas, this requirement clearly falls prey to slight modifications of the previous examples: if the clever pill were given with the intention of improving someone's understanding of their car, it still would not count as an explanation of the car.

One possibility, then, is to require that explanations be linguistic, either spoken or written. After all, it is indisputable that most things which we call explanations are such entities. This is, however, too strong in my

---

[1]   Achinstein 1983.

opinion. Consider the following example. Your car has stopped working, and the mechanic is looking at it. He beckons you over, and points to a certain part of the engine. You look, and see that the fan-belt is broken. I think that few people would balk at saying that the mechanic had explained to you what was wrong with your car, but he has not used any language at all.

There is a way around this example. It can plausibly be claimed that the mechanic's ostension, while not linguistic, does have content — specifically, the content that the fan-belt is broken. Thus, we can focus on the content of the explanation in an attempt to draw these examples together. Now, it is not sufficient that the explanation simply have content. Implausible philosophical examples make that clear: suppose that the statement 'Ganymede has a magnetic field' has the same effect on me as the blow with a hammer, giving me a superb understanding of Mahler. Even if these words were uttered with the intention of giving me such an understanding, we would not say that 'Ganymede has a magnetic field' explains Mahler. The required refinement is easy to find, however. We must intend that the content of our explanation be incorporated into the model, and that that incorporation should improve the model. I cannot think of anything that fits this requirement which we would not class as an explanation.

There still remains a problem, however. Consider the assertion that the broken fan-belt explains the malfunctioning of the car. The broken fan-belt itself does not really seem to have content, and it certainly has no intention of improving your model. Further, no-one, in normal circumstances, will give you the fan-belt with the intention of improving your model. Is this a problem? I think not: rather, it raises the need for another distinction.

There are clearly two senses of 'explain' in English. One is the sense in which the mechanic explains the problem with your car, the other is the sense in which the fan-belt does. These senses are clearly different. On my account, someone explains in the first sense if they offer an explanation, as described above. For X to explain Y in the second sense, however, requires that (the model of) X could be incorporated into the model surrounding Y, in such a way as to improve it. That is, if X explains Y, then a statement which had X as its content could be offered as an explanation of Y.

Another possible English phrasing rears its head now: we could, under these circumstances, refer to X as the explanation of Y. Since X probably doesn't have a content (because it is, for example, a fan-belt), and may well not have been offered by anyone with any intention, it doesn't fit my account. This is not a problem: we have simply discovered that 'explanation' is used in two different, but closely related, senses. Since, on my theory, explanation is not a fundamental notion, this is not a problem: both senses of 'explain' and 'explanation' have clear relations to understanding, and thus there are good reasons why the words are used as they are.

An explanation, in its primary sense, then, is something provided with the intention that its content be incorporated into the recipient's model of a particular situation, thus improving his understanding of that situation.

Improving Mental Models

The above characterisation relies heavily on the notion of improving understanding, that is, improving a mental model. While I have provided an account of what makes a mental model good, that is only part of the work necessary to elucidate means of improvement. A building is good if it stands up in storms and earthquakes, and keeps the occupants sheltered from the elements, but that does not tell us anything about the practicalities of home improvements. In this section, then, I will give a more detailed account of the ways in which mental models can be improved. I shall start with the least far-reaching, when understanding of a particular situation is improved, and then consider improvement of the model of a thing, before considering broader still improvements, when the models of properties are altered. It should be noted that this is intended as a taxonomy of explanations: the names that I give to them are terms of art, and the descriptions should be taken as defining the scope of the terms. The aim is to provide a way of breaking explanations down into categories that flows naturally from the theory, and provides insight into some of the differences that occur.

Situations

The simplest improvement in understanding occurs when the understanding of a situation is improved, without any impact on wider understanding. That is, no new models are added to the person's repertoire: rather, the details of those activated to simulate the situation at hand are altered. Simple as this kind of improvement is, it still comes in several varieties.

First, the explanation could point out that another thing should be added to the simulation. Thus, if you see two notoriously lazy students working very hard in the library, rather than goofing off as normal, you might be puzzled. If someone pointed out that their supervisor was present, you could understand the situation by adding the supervisor to your model. In general, this type of explanation can be offered when the person has failed to take account of something that he does understand. He must already have a model of the thing to be added to his model, and the models involved must already be capable of simulating the relevant interactions. If these conditions are met, however, this is a very easy type of explanation to give, as the recipient of the explanation already has all the relevant parts of the model, and merely needs to be told which to use.

Explanations of events which the questioner did not see often fall into this category. If I ask why a window is broken, and I am told that it was hit by a cricket ball, then I understand the situation. I already have a model of a window, and of cricket balls, and I can easily put them together to simulate the situation. I think that most causal explanations will fall into this category, since if I do not know how to simulate the proffered cause I am likely to ask for more information. In effect, a simple causal explanation, one which merely cites the causally active thing, is simply telling you to add that thing to your model of the situation.

A slightly more complex case involved the re-identification of something involved in the situation. Thus, the deferential behaviour of all the College authorities to an elderly woman whom you have never seen before may puzzle you: if you are told that the woman in question is the Queen, then everything will make sense. When you are told this, you do not add anything to your mental model, as you are still modelling the same number of things. Instead, you substitute your model of the Queen for your model of a typical elderly woman.

This kind of explanation applies in many cases in which a misconception is corrected. For example, if someone has got drunk and you think that they have been drinking water all night, you will be considerably enlightened if someone tells you that they have been drinking 'little water', the translation of 'vodka'. In some sense, many of these explanations will also be causal, but I think that they are worth distinguishing from the previous type, as they involve correcting a mistake, not just rectifying ignorance.

The most complex type of explanation which affects only your understanding of a given situation is one which modifies the characteristics of one of your models, but only for this case. This differs from the previous case in that you have correctly classified all the things in your model, and you have picked out all the relevant things. However, you have given one of the things the wrong value for one of its properties.

For example, suppose that you see someone break a steel bar with their bare hands, and you want an explanation of how on earth they did it. An example of the first type of explanation would be to point out the hydraulic press connected to the ends of the bar, cunningly hidden behind the man. An example of the second type would be to tell you that the man in question was Superman. An example of this type, however, would be to say that the bar was made of very brittle steel. That is, everything is what you thought, but the properties of the steel bar were not quite as you had supposed.

This type of explanation is less common, I think, than the other two, mainly because we are quite good at assigning properties well enough for the purposes of our simulations. However, such explanations as pointing out that something is, in fact, switched off come into this category.

All of these three types of explanation function in the same way. They elaborate or alter our model of the situation so that running that model produces a result which corresponds more closely to what actually happened. Variants are possible in which, for example, we are told that a present, potential cause was not the actual cause, and thus we modify the way in which the simulation produces results, without actually modifying the results. These explanations fall into this category, although the improvement in understanding of the situation must come about because the model is now better in counterfactual situations: we can now say what would have happened, had things been a bit different.

Thus, if the increase in understanding is limited to one situation, there are three basic types of explanation. A thing can be added to the simulation, one of the things involved in the simulation can be substituted with something else, and the value assigned to a property of one of the things in the simulation can be changed. Of course, there is no rule which says that only one thing can be changed in an explanation: more than one thing could be added, or a thing could be added and another substituted.

Simulors

Explanations can have wider impact, however, if they result in an alteration in the model of a thing, a simulor. Since the simulor will be used in simulating any situation in which that thing, or type of thing, is involved, these explanations can effect a larger increase in understanding. As with explanations which affect only the situation in question, there are several ways in which these explanations can work. The simplest is the addition of an effector to a simulor, then the substitution of one effector for another, and finally the creation of a completely new simulor.

The simple addition of an effector to a simulor will occur most often, I think, in explanations of behaviour. If someone's actions seem strange, it might well explain them well if you are told that this person has a bad temper, or is very vain, or is extremely generous. In this case, you add another property to your description of the person, and they will be modelled with the corresponding effector every time that you wish to simulate them in the future. Similar cases could arise with inanimate objects: you could be told that petrol is flammable, for example, in order to explain a certain event.

These explanations will make permanent changes to the mental models that a person has, but these changes are not particularly major. The model for one thing is linked to an additional effector, together, perhaps, with a default value for that effector. Such a change will not, I think, be very hard to make.

Substitution of one effector for another is slightly more complex, but not much more. Again, examples are easiest to come by when dealing with people. If someone whom you thought was bad tempered behaved extremely politely, this might be puzzling. If you were told that he was racist, rather than bad tempered, this could well serve as an explanation of his behaviour, and would result in an alteration in your model of him. Here, one effector is unlinked from the model of the thing, and another linked in its place. Again, this is unlikely to be very complicated.

The last type of simulor-related explanation is much more complex, and likely to take rather more than a sentence to convey. This is an explanation which introduces a completely new type of thing to the recipient. In this case, all the relevant effectors, with their default values, must be specified. None of the effectors themselves will be new, but only because if any are, I classify the explanation differently: see below.

A common type of such explanations would be the introduction of a new person: the person would be named, and several properties specified. This person would then be added to your mental models, ready for simulation in the future. Of course, you need not be told everything about them at once: the possibility of refining your model of this person in the future still exists. The same applies to models of new inanimate objects, such as computers. The first time you deal with a computer, the explanation of its behaviour is likely to be quite involved.

Indeed, this feature explains why it is harder to explain your latest work to someone completely unfamiliar with it than to someone who has seen what you have produced earlier. If a person is already familiar with your work, you need only add or subtract an effector or two for their model of your work to be quite accurate. If they are a complete novice, you have to build the whole edifice from the ground up, something that you may not be readily able to do.

Similarly, it explains why '*virtus dormitiva*' explanations seem empty. A new thing is introduced, and the only information you are given about its model is that it causes the behaviour that you have already seen. As this information says nothing about the conditions necessary for such behaviour to be displayed, you do not end up with a good model of the thing in question. As your understanding is lacking, so is the explanation.

These sorts of explanations are likely to be complex, but mainly because of the quantity of information that has to be conveyed in order to make them satisfactory. There is no reason why a particularly involved explanation of a thing already modelled, one which adds lots of effectors and substitutes for others, could not be equally complex. Thus, the difference in complexity between explanations of this type is one of degree, rather than of kind.

The difference between these explanations and one which only affect individual situations is one of kind, however. These explanations require that things be added to your mental models as they are held in memory: explanations of particular situations only require that you use another bit of your stored model to simulate the current situation. That is, situation-explanations only require manipulation of short-term memory, and recall from long-term: simulor-explanations require creation of long-term memories.

Effectors

The most complex explanations are those that involve the modification of effectors. Indeed, these explanations are much closer to teaching: there is no way that they could be conveyed in a single sentence, and it is sometimes difficult to convey them at all. Nevertheless, they come in types corresponding to those outlined for the other types of explanation above:

addition of a mutor to a given effector, substitution of one mutor for another, and creation of an entirely new effector.

This type of explanation is further complicated by the fact that most mutors are attached to more than one effector. If one effector has to be modified, then, most of the time, another effector will also be modified. That is, if 'solidity' is modified, then at least one of the effectors that interacts with it will also be modified, because that effector now interacts with solidity in a different way.

Indeed, it may often be unclear which of the effectors has been modified, or whether both have. After all, the mutors are just as much part of one as part of the other. I suspect that this question is not very important. If a lot of mutors for one effector are modified at once, then we will be inclined to say that that is the effector that has been changed, while if only one mutor has been altered, I am not sure that we would say anything definite if asked which of the effectors had been altered: perhaps we would settle on 'both' as the best answer.

The basic element of all effector-explanations is the provision of a new mutor. This may be simply added to an effector, replace an already-existing mutor, or be part of a completely new effector. However, since I am proposing that effectors are merely unordered lists of mutors, the complications introduced by having to deal with more than one at a time are likely to be minor. Thus, for the remainder of this section I shall concentrate on the way in which a new mutor can be introduced.

The first thing to note is that the recipient of the explanation must do much of the work. A mutor is a structure in the mind which behaves in a certain way, and the only thing that is known to be capable of altering the mind in this way is the mind that is to be altered. Thus, although guidance can be provided, in the end the recipient must learn for themselves.

Further, knowing how a mutor ought to behave, and having a mutor which does behave in that way, are different mental states. Thus, if a mutor can be completely and explicitly characterised, learning that characterisation will still not be sufficient to give the person access to the mutor. It is likely that some practice using the mutor is required.

What, then, can the person giving the explanation do in order to convey this mutor? The most important point is that the counterfactual behaviour of the mutor must be conveyed. A mutor is something which will behave in such-and-such a way in such-and-such a situation, and this must be part of its description. Of course, complete counterfactual information cannot be included, simply because there is too much of it. Thus, the explainer will have to rely on specific examples to define the limits. This, however, will grossly underdetermine the mutor, and while it could be modified later, in response to experience or further explanation, it would be better to minimise the modification required.

One possible strategy is to hijack another mutor for the purpose. That is, describe the mutor as working like another mutor that the person already has, but with certain modifications. The other mutor would then fill in the gaps in the behaviour and, provided that the analogy was well-chosen, the mutor created would be much nearer to the correct version than it would otherwise have been.

This method is probably the basis for explanation by reduction to the familiar. When an unfamiliar process is likened to a familiar one, this allows the recipient of the explanation to copy the mutors governing the familiar process and use them, with appropriate modifications, to simulate the new one.

Another possible strategy is to produce a mathematisation of the behaviour of the mutor. An equation can imply the behaviour of the mutor over a wide range, in full detail. Study of, and use of, the equation can then provide constraints on the mutor, allowing the mutor in the mind to conform closely to the behaviour of the thing in the real world. Of course, this will take time, and experience of the equation, but the explainer can, by providing the equation, give the recipient enough information to build the mutor himself.

Is this the primary purpose of equations in mathematical sciences? I doubt it. I think that it is more likely that the equations are primarily to serve as 'external mutors'. That is, even when they have not been incorporated into a mental model, they can be used to simulate the things in question, by the process of solving the equation. However, I do think that the fact that they allow simulation is important. Perhaps the reason why mathematisations are looked upon favourably can be found here: they specify the full range of behaviour quite precisely, and thus can be used for simulations that the original penner never thought of. Non-mathematical expressions of ideas would suffer from the general problem noted above, that it is difficult to give an accurate impression of the full range of behaviour, and thus difficult to fully specify the mutor.

Another strategy could be described as the 'teaching' strategy. The explainer engages in dialogue with the recipient of the explanation, asking them to use the mutor under a range of circumstances, and correcting them when their simulation goes wrong. While this process does suffer from the 'missing points' problem, it does allow the explainer to check that the mutor is working accurately, at least in the main areas of interest. Although there are an infinite number of possible mathematical functions, the structure of mutors is almost certainly rather more restricted. Thus, a survey at well chosen points could provide extremely good evidence that the mutor was correct: conversely, information at those points could allow the construction of the correct mutor, perhaps all but determining its form.

In this section I have spoken as if people explicitly make use of the ideas of my theory when providing these sorts of explanations. Obviously, I think nothing of the kind. Even if my theory is true, I am sure that it is not widely believed — not yet, anyway. How, then, do I think that people think about these things? I am not sure that we have any terrible choate thoughts at all. Certainly, when I was trying to develop this theory, I had little to go on in my intuitions beyond 'understanding'. Thus, I suspect that people simply try to create understanding in other people, and that, from experience, both theirs and that of others, they know that strategies such as these are prone to producing understanding. What I am aiming to do in this book is provide good theoretical reasons for (most of) our practice in this regard.

To summarise, then, there are three ways in which understanding of a situation can be improved. First, the improvement can be completely specific to the situation. Another simulant can be added to the model of the situation, or the classification of certain simulants already in the model altered, or the values of some of the effectors of the simulants changed. None of these explanations will have any impact beyond the simulation of that particular situation. Second, the improvement can affect the long-term models of particular things. More effectors can be added to the models, one effector substituted for another, or a completely new simulor can be added to the repertoire of models. These explanations have long-term effects, but they are relatively easy to convey, as they only involve the re-arrangement of mental equipment already possessed. Finally, the improvement can consist in the modification or creation of new mutors. This is the most complicated kind of explanation to give, and explanation at this level can hardly be distinguished from teaching. Analogy and mathematical equations can play important roles here, as can prolonged dialogue.

Explanatory Pragmatics

In the previous section, I discussed the ways in which a mental model can be improved: the possible types of explanation, if you like. This is not, however, the whole story. It leaves open the question of which improvement should be made in a given situation. This is clearly not a trivial problem: any given model can be improved in many ways, and a large number of these ways are likely to be relevant to the case at hand. However, not all of these improvements will be acceptable explanations. In this section, I will consider the pragmatic factors which influence the choice of particular explanation.

The Base State

The first, and probably most important, pragmatic factor is also the easiest to handle. Since an explanation is supposed to improve a person's mental model, people with different mental models will require different explanations. While some applications of this principle are easy, others are rather more subtle. In this section, I shall consider a wide range.

If something is already part of a person's mental model, then telling them about it will not bring about an improvement. If someone asks why a window is broken, and they already know about the cricket ball hitting it, then telling them about the cricket ball will not improve their mental model, and thus will not be explanatory. This requirement is often added to other theories of explanation, as a prohibition on 'old news'. It is clearly a good pragmatic requirement, and it arises naturally from the structure of my account.

Another simple pragmatic requirement is that the recipient of the explanation should be able to understand it. If it is given in a language that they do not understand, or is so compressed as to be incomprehensible, then it will not improve their understanding, because they will be completely unable to incorporate it into their mental model. These factors, however, do not really come under the heading of the base state of their model. There are other failures of comprehensibility which do, and I shall deal with those in more detail.

Suppose that someone explains a puzzling phenomenon on your computer by saying that there is an extension conflict. This would, for me, constitute a perfectly good explanation, but might well, for other people, be no use at all. This is because, in order for that statement to provide an increase in understanding, I must be able to model 'extensions' and what happens when they conflict. Similarly, explanations in terms of quantum mechanics are no use to someone who knows no quantum mechanics: he does not have the relevant bits of mental model available, and thus cannot improve his simulation on the basis of what he has been told.

This is similar to the pragmatic requirement of not assuming things that the recipient does not know. However, it is more specific than that. I can assume any number of things in my answer, as long as the recipient can build an improved model from the bits that he does know. A good example of this sort of thing can be constructed in science. If I explain the behaviour of, say, the two slit experiment in quantum mechanics to a novice, I will assume a wide variety of things that he does not know: an interpretation of quantum mechanics, certain limits on the properties of the particles, certain properties of the observation set-up, and so on. For the answer to be accurate, as I am presenting it in good faith to be, all these assumptions must be acknowledged. However, if the explanation allows the recipient to build a model of what is going on, even without these assumptions, then his understanding has been improved. There is still room for further improvement, but that is not the problem immediately at hand.

The pragmatic dependence of the explanation on the recipient's mental model can have more surprising consequences, however. These arise when we consider people who have mental models which differ radically from those which are generally agreed to be accurate. This is best illustrated with an example.

Consider someone who is heavily into New Age 'philosophy'. He is a staunch believer in astrology, and has made a substantial study of the subject. He is also an expert at reading tarot cards, and can tell you more than you ever wanted to know about the mystical auras around crystals. Suppose that he contracts a nasty case of flu, and wants an explanation.

We would want to say that the explanation is that he caught it off someone else. But wait: this person has no mental model of germs and communicable disease. He sees disease as caused by the position of planets, and auric emanations from crystals. Thus, it is no good telling him that he caught it off someone: he simply wouldn't understand. If, however, you were to tell him that it was due to using feldspar crystals while Saturn and Venus were in trine, he would be perfectly happy, and would be able to simulate the situation much more accurately. Does this make the bogus New Age drivel a good explanation of his flu?

It is quite possible that it does. It has improved his understanding of the situation quite significantly, and thus seems to fulfil the requirements on an explanation. It should be noted that his understanding is very poor, but it is better than it was, albeit not a great deal better. If we can convince him of the germ theory of disease, his understanding will be greatly improved, but we cannot do that simply by telling him that he caught the flu off one of his friends. The distinction between understanding and explanation here allows us to say that the drivel is, indeed, an explanation for him, even though it is not connected to a good understanding of the process involved. I suspect that this is an advantage: to see why, we must consider a less extreme case.

There are two scientists, A and B, who have different theories of a certain process. These theories are very different, maybe even incommensurable, but they agree on most of the rest of their world-view, and the scientific community regards both of them as legitimate scientists who disagree about a certain point. Furthermore, they are both recognised as experts on the field of disagreement: the consensus is that the evidence does not, at present, distinguish between the theories.

Suppose that new results come to light concerning the process. A produces an explanation in accord with his theory, B produces one in accordance with hers. Both seem to be good explanations, and it is generally agreed that these experiments have failed to resolve the question. A and B continue being bitingly polite to one another in print.

This seems like a reasonable way of talking. However, for a scientific realist, either A is wrong, or B is wrong (or both are wrong). If the theory is wrong, then the understanding that it provides is not good. At the very least, the understanding provided by the correct theory is substantially better. Despite this, we still want to be able to talk about good explanations produced by both sides. If nothing else, we want to be able to compare the explanatory resources of the two theories as part of the process of deciding which one is better.

My theory easily incorporates this. Both explanations can increase understanding, but one of the mental models is, probably, better than the other, and provides a higher base level of understanding. In the long run, it will probably become inordinately hard to increase understanding in the poorer model, and at that point the fact that the other theory can provide better explanations, and better understanding, will become evidence in its favour. The difference between this case and the New Age drivel example is merely one of degree: the New Ager's theory is extremely poor, whereas the two scientists can be supposed to have fairly good theories at worst. Thus, if we want to allow this case, we must allow that statements about planetary conjunctions are explanatory, if only to a slight degree, from a poor baseline.

We can now turn to the pragmatic influence. In the case of the scientists, an explanation based on A's theory is almost certainly better for him, because he has the necessary mental equipment to handle it. Similarly, one based on B's theory is likely to be better for her. Now, in the extreme, it is possible that an explanation based on New Age drivel is better than a lot of scientifically accurate explanations for the New Ager. It could, perhaps, be argued that a better explanation for the New Ager would be a complete scientific education, giving him the mental equipment to understand the viral transmission explanation. However, it is not clear that such an involved process could really be called an 'explanation': there does seem to be a limit on how big an explanation can be, and that limit is lower than 'several years of schooling'. Thus, it might be the case that the best explanation available for the New Ager is one involving planets: it is still the case that his understanding is woefully poor.

At least some of the explanations that I have been considering have been false: A's and B's explanations are incompatible, so at least one of them is false. However, I have claimed that both explanations are actual explanations, and, in fact, the true explanation may be worse than the false one. After all, it may be that the false explanation pulls large amounts of the false theory together, and gives it wide simulatory power, while the true explanation is very specific to this situation and, in fact, not brilliant for this situation, because it fails to be the whole truth.

There is a very good reason why I do not make truth a requirement on a good explanation: truth is not accessible. Clearly, someone must believe that an explanation is true in order to accept it. The discussion, above, of the factors contributing to the quality of models made it clear that a model which is believed to be false will not be preferred to one which is believed to be true. However, as should also have been clear, a false model may be preferred to a true one, simply by mistaking the false for the true, and vice versa. The criteria on which an explanation or a model is assessed must be accessible to the assessor. It is a feature of human life that accessible criteria may come apart from truth. As a result, a good explanation, and a good understanding, may be false.

To summarise this section, the base state of someone receiving an explanation can affect the explanation to be given in a number of ways. First, anything that they already have in their mental model will not improve it, and thus cannot be given as an explanation. Second, they must have the necessary bits of mental model to apply whatever they are told. Third, the explanation must fit in with their current beliefs to a certain extent, otherwise they will be completely incapable of using it.

Particular Improvements

While the considerations outlined in the previous section will certainly restrict the number of available explanations, they are unlikely to bring the number of candidates down to one. Now, while in some cases there may, in fact, be a couple of possible explanations which seem equally suitable, this is not generally the case. Thus, there must be other factors to be considered. In this section I shall set some of them out.

First, there is a consideration which is not particularly pragmatic. Some of the candidate explanations will improve understanding more than others. All else being equal, it is clearly better to give the explanation which provides the greatest increase in understanding. Indeed, it might even be possible to get away with the simple rule that the best of the possible explanations should be given.

I think that this rule will not quite work, however. This is not because there is anything intrinsically wrong with it, but because of the difficulties involved in assessing the quality of explanations. Recall my discussion of the quality of understanding: understanding could be improved along two or more axes, and I was not sure that these were commensurable. The case for explanation is even worse. Even if the improvement in understanding given could be measured simply, the length of time which it takes to give the explanation is still a factor. Since different sorts of improvement in understanding are likely to be available, even this level of simplicity is not attainable. Thus, it is likely that pragmatic rules will be required to select the explanation to give.

These rules are likely to be based on the picture that the explainer forms of the questioner's current mental model. I will not even try to give an exhaustive list here, as I am sure that I would fail, but I will give some plausible candidates. First, if the questioner's mental model contains a major error which will cause problems in many contexts, then explanations which correct that error are to be preferred. Even if the error is small, if it is wide-ranging, then correcting it may be a priority.

Second, if there is a simple omission from the model, which is leading to a wildly inaccurate simulation, then repairing that omission is probably sufficient, even if there are a number of minor errors in other factors of the model. It will be quick and easy to supply the bit of additional information, and there will be a big improvement in understanding of the current situation.

Third, explanations which do not require the construction or modification of mutors are to be preferred to those which do, and explanations which do not require the creation or modification of simulors are to be preferred to those which do. If understanding can be improved without getting into the long and complex job of completely rebuilding the questioner's mental model, then it should be. This may seem a little odd: surely, if we are aware of deep errors, we have some sort of obligation to correct them. However, practice seems to bear out the contention that there is not. After all, scientists do not launch into detailed expositions of molecular biology or quantum physics when asked to explain things which impinge on their field. There seems to be a convention that simulations need only be good enough in most cases.

Of course, if you are teaching someone a field, things are different. In that case, you should aim to correct as many deep misunderstandings as possible in your explanations, because the mental models built will serve them well in the future. However, this is a different pragmatic situation, and not really one in which you are simply providing an explanation: an acknowledged teaching situation is bound by very different conventions from normal conversation. After all, you do not argue if your teacher tells you that you have made an error, on the whole, but you would probably dispute with one of your friends who did so.

These three requirements are in tension to a certain extent. The latter two suggest that an explanation should be a quick patch on the understanding, rendering it better in the current situation, while the first suggests that we should try to correct things as broadly as possible. I think that this tension is probably real, and that details of the pragmatic situation determine which way the balance swings.

Are these considerations likely to be enough to limit the field of candidate explanations to one? I think that they are capable of doing so, but it is very difficult to argue clearly for such a position. One cannot present the complete list of explanations available in a particular case and show how these rules eliminate all but one, much less provide a general argument that they will do so. Further, some of the pragmatic rules which apply in a given situation will have nothing at all to do with my theory. For example, if you are in a hurry, the length of the explanation may become an overriding consideration. Similarly, there will be contexts in which the explanation should not even be true — see the discussion above. For example, if someone is a known thief, there are strong pragmatic reasons for not explaining your security procedures to them, and even for lying about them. Such considerations are obviously outside the immediate scope of this book: to do justice to all of them would require a complete theory of conversation and I do not feel that I am able to provide one here.

Asking Questions

At this point, I should like to consider the pragmatics of asking why-questions. According to my theory, these should be provoked by a perceived failure of understanding or, perhaps, by a worry about the adequacy of an understanding that has not yet failed. Roughly speaking, since explanations are supposed to improve understanding, we should request one when we feel that our understanding is in need of improvement. In this section, I shall attempt a broad taxonomy of such situations. I shall endeavour to be exhaustive, but I shall not characterise the individual cases very closely.

The first, and simplest, case is when a simulation fails to give the right result. If our simulation has the window breaking, and instead the brick just bounces off, then we are likely to ask for an explanation. It is obvious that there must be something wrong with our simulation, because it came up with the wrong result, and so it is reasonable to ask for an explanation, in order to improve the simulation.

The second case is also quite simple. If we encounter a situation that we are simply unable to simulate, then we may ask for an explanation. This is different from the previous case, since we cannot simulate it at all. This problem can arise if, for example, we have no mental models of the things involved in the situation, or if the properties that interact in the situation have no maxim governing their interactions. It is obvious that there must be further considerations influencing the decision to ask a question, however. If we were to look around us with the right frame of mind, we would see lots of situations which we were unable to simulate, and yet we do not ask for explanations of all of them. For example, looking out of my window I can see a number of people, and I cannot simulate the results of meetings between them. I do not, however, feel an overwhelming need to rush out and try to get mental models of all of them. These further considerations are unlikely, however, to be directly related to our understanding: they will depend on our interests, and our perceived needs.

The third case is slightly more complex. If our simulation gives the right answer, but we suspect that this may have been more by luck than from the intrinsic quality of the model, then we may ask for an explanation. For example, if we are trying to simulate a complex situation, in which we are not sure of our understanding of some of the participants, then we might well ask for an explanation afterwards, even if our simulation produces the right result, just to make sure that our model is on the right lines.

A fourth case is a variant on the third. If we simulate a situation accurately, but not very precisely, then we may ask for an explanation in order to increase the precision of our model. Thus, if something gets hotter, as predicted, when connected into an electrical circuit, we may still ask for an explanation if we would like to know how much hotter it would get in similar circumstances.

The fifth case is a variant of the fourth. We may be able to simulate a situation accurately and precisely, but be unhappy about the length of time that the simulation takes. In this case, we may ask for an explanation in the hopes of producing a model which will allow quicker simulations.

The final case, I think, is when we have not even performed a simulation, but think that our model of a thing may be incomplete or incorrect. For example, if my models of people normally include their preference in ice cream (because I sell it, for instance), then I may ask for someone's preference in ice cream, when I do not know it, even if no simulation has been involved.

In the last case, however, the question is unlikely to be phrased as 'why...?', because I know which part of the mental model I want to have improved. Thus, I can simply ask what their preference in ice cream is, and save the answerer the effort of figuring out what I want to know. In some cases, of course, I may not know quite what I want to know. In this case, I may well explicitly ask for an explanation. 'Explain the rules of chess to me', or 'explain this computer, please' are examples of such requests for explanation. It is clear that, on my theory, the responses are likely to be explanations, in that they improve the mental model of a situation, so that there is no need for a special sense of explanation to cover these cases.

I suspect that these six cases cover all the possibilities. If the simulation goes wrong, then we are in either the first or second case: either the simulation has produced the wrong answer, or we were not able to run the simulation at all. If the simulation goes right, then we are in either the third, fourth or fifth, since the simulation must be unsatisfactory in some way if we want to improve it: either we must be unhappy with its precision, or we must be unsure that it produced the right answer in the right way, or we must think that it is too slow. If there is no immediately relevant simulation, then the sixth case covers it: we want to improve our model for future reference.

An Example

An example may help to make the issues involved in explanation clearer. Consider someone trying to explain the earth's magnetic field. The simplest way to do this is to say that there is something like a big bar magnet in the earth, with its south pole in the north. This takes over mental models that the recipient already has, and thus allows quick building of the model: he simply adds something to his model of the earth.

You might then have to explain why the magnetic north pole moves around relative to the earth's axis of rotation, and you can do that by saying that the bar magnet moves around within the liquid core of the earth. The model can handle this perfectly well. At this point, however, you have a problem: when you are asked why the bar magnet doesn't melt (as the model suggests that it should — everything else is liquid, after all, and the centre of the earth is hot), you have to confess that there isn't, in fact, a bar magnet at all.

You have to move to a different analogy. Rotating electric currents produce magnetic fields, and if the recipient doesn't know this, you will have to explain rather more about electromagnetism before you can go any further, helping them to develop new mutors. Once they can handle currents in wires, you can talk about the core of the earth. It is liquid, and largely iron. This means that it is capable of carrying electric currents, and being magnetised. It is also heated by the decay of radioactive elements, and so it is moving due to convection (thus borrowing mutors from yet another model). The moving iron generates an electric current, which in turn generates the magnetic field. The earth's rotation biases the movement of the liquid iron in a certain way, and thus the axis of the magnetic field is close to the axis of rotation. This works in the same way as spinning a bucket makes the water within it start to move: so, again, mutors can be borrowed from a different field.

If you are then asked to explain the variations in the earth's field, you find yourself at the edges of scientific knowledge. However, the best current theory is that they depend on variations on flow in the mantle. This is another layer of semi-liquid rock, outside the core. This feature can be added to the model fairly easily — it's rather like another core outside the old one. It doesn't contain as much iron (altering one of the values of one of its effectors), so it only modifies the field produced by the core. However, its motion is much more complex, because it has the core in the middle, and thus isn't a nice sphere. These complex motions give rise to complex modifications to the earth's magnetic field. This last point requires the introduction of a new mutor, and will thus take a lot of effort if the model is to be at all accurate. Indeed, I don't understand the details, so I can't give them in this example.

Features of Explanation

In this section, I shall discuss two features of explanations which have been remarked upon in the literature, and show how they arise in my model. The first is the possibility of the why-regress: the fact that, after receiving an answer to one why-question, it is usually possible to ask why again. The second is the possibility of self-evidencing explanations. These are explanations in which the only evidence for the things doing the explaining is the thing to be explained.

The Why-Regress

The why-regress is a phenomenon observed particularly often with five year-olds. No matter what the answer to one why-question, one can always ask 'why?' again, and there is normally the possibility of an answer. However, this fact does not mean that the answer given to the first why-question was not a good explanation. Even if the why-regress eventually comes to an end, this does not mean that only those things which admit of no further explanation are truly explanatory.

On my account of explanation, this feature is easy to explain. An explanation increases our understanding of something. However, it does not make our understanding perfect. It may well be that, as the world is far larger and more complex than our minds (our minds being a proper part of the world, after all), our understanding, even of a particular thing, can never be perfect. In this case, no matter how many explanations you have received, your understanding could always be improved still further, and thus another explanation could be reasonably requested. The possibility of further improvement in no way suggests that earlier explanations have failed to improve understanding, and thus in no way impugns their status as explanations.

It is worth noting that the why-regress often involves a change of subject matter. 'Why is the window broken' 'Because it was hit by a cricket ball?' 'Why was it hit?' 'Because Bob threw the ball at it' 'Why did Bob throw the ball?' 'Because he was trying to bowl.' Thus, the improvement in understanding is gained in different places. In this case, my account can even explain why the why-regress is likely to arise. Each explanation given will set up a new situation for consideration. In many cases, you will not be able to simulate this situation, partly because you have never thought about it before. Thus, you will be inclined to ask for another explanation, and so the why-regress gets going.

Self-Evidencing Explanations

A self-evidencing explanation is one in which the only evidence for the fact doing the explaining, or an essential part of the evidence, is the fact being explained. A good example is the red shift of a distant galaxy. The light is red shifted because the galaxy is receding from us, and the galaxy is receding from us because the universe is expanding. However, the only evidence that the galaxy is receding is the red shift, and the only evidence that the universe is expanding is the recession of all the galaxies. On some accounts of explanation, this is a problem, since the explanation is supposed to give evidential support for the explanandum, or to make it more familiar. On my account, however, it is no problem at all.

Let us take a simpler example. Suppose I see a car with darkly tinted windows driving around the streets. I can improve my mental model of the car if I assume that there is a driver in the car, despite the fact that my only evidence for the existence of this driver is the intelligent behaviour of the car. Similarly, unobserved or unobservable things generally can be used to improve my mental models. They could be simple computational short-cuts, in which case I would have no need to believe that they were true, or they could be included because I thought that they were real, and thus their behaviour ought to be simulated. Either way, things for which there is no direct evidence can improve understanding.

The case of self-evidencing explanations is a bit more specific, however: the only evidence for the explanatory hypothesis is the thing that it is to explain. Does this pose a problem? Not for explanation, on my account. The degree of evidence that there is for a thing does not affect the improvement that it makes to the mental model. There may be good, inferential, reasons to reject the explanatory hypothesis, although I think that it will often be acceptable, but these must be derived from a good theory of inference. My theory of understanding is silent on the subject. In summary, then, the improvement that an hypothesis makes in a mental model is independent of its prior evidential support, so there is no reason why self-evidencing explanations cannot be explanatory.

Problem Cases

In this section, I shall consider some of the classic problem cases in the theory of explanation, and show how my theory handles them. These cases do not all provide problems for all other theories of explanation: however, between them they provide at least one problem for each of them. They are not, strictly speaking, counter-examples to the theories, since it is always possible that our intuitive conception of explanation is incoherent, and that any theory will have to alter it somewhat. They do, however, indicate problems, and in some cases, such as the Deductive-Nomological model, they are so numerous that it seems clear that the theory is really not capturing anything very close to our notion of explanation.

I shall first consider cases of explanatory asymmetries, which are problematic for the Deductive-Nomological model, and then problems of explanatory irrelevance, which also pose problems for that theory. I shall then consider non-causal explanations, which are tricky for causal models, and finally discuss functional explanations, which seem to pose problems for most accounts.

Explanatory Asymmetries

The classic example of an explanatory asymmetry is the flagpole. If we ask why the shadow of a flagpole is a certain length, we can explain that by citing the height of the flagpole. The height of the flagpole, however, cannot be explained by citing the length of the shadow. The problem for the Deductive-Nomological model is that both can be deduced from the other, in conjunction with the laws of optics and the position of the sun. Thus, it seems that some asymmetry must be introduced here.

van Fraassen, however, has argued that there is no asymmetry:[2] which explains which is purely a matter of pragmatics. Had the flagpole been erected in order to cast a shadow of a certain length, then the length of the shadow would explain the height of the flagpole. There seems to be something right about both contentions: there does seem to be an asymmetry, while it also seems that the length of the shadow could, in some circumstances, explain the height of the flagpole. I think that my theory can capture this quite neatly.

Let us consider the asymmetry first. Why should one answer be better than the other? Consider the situation which is being modelled: we have the flagpole, the sun, and its shadow. Now, this situation will, like any other, be governed by certain mutors, and these mutors, like all others, will be unidirectional. Thus, if we wish to simulate the result of changes in that situation, it will be necessary to know the values of those effectors which serve as inputs to the mutors. It seems to be a matter of fact that the mutors governing this situation go from the height of the flagpole to the length of the shadow. Thus, if the model is to be improved, the height of the flagpole must be specified. This explanation gives the value of one of the effectors in the model, and thus falls into one of the categories set out earlier. Further, it allows simulation of the situation. If, on the other hand, the length of the shadow is supplied, no simulation is possible. The relevant mutors do not take the length of the shadow as an input, and so this piece of information is useless in our modelling.

---

[2]   van Fraassen 1980, p 132–4.

This argument does rely on the existence of the asymmetry in our mutors. However, I argued earlier that there would be such an asymmetry, and that it would be an asymmetry such that prior things explain later things. Further, when we give an explanation we try, on the whole, to make the recipient's mental model closer to our own. Thus, if our own model goes from the flagpole to the shadow, we will try to make the recipient's model go the same way. I do not think that we can demonstrate that this direction is a necessary feature of the models, but that is not necessary: I need only argue that it is an actual feature and that, given this actual feature, these results are expected.

If we now turn to van Fraassen's case, there is a very clear reason why the asymmetry should appear different. We are talking about the mental model of a different situation, in this case the construction of the flagpole. This model is driven by different mutors, and so it is not too surprising that the length of the shadow can be an input into certain of those mutors. If the builder wants a shadow of a certain length, then he will build a flagpole of a certain height. Under these circumstances, the length of the shadow is an input into the mutors: change it, and you change the height of flagpole that the builder wants.

Explanatory asymmetries, then, reflect asymmetries in the way that our mutors are set up. If the model under consideration is changed, then different properties and things may serve as inputs to the mutors, and the asymmetry may, apparently, be reversed.

Explanatory Irrelevance

The possibility of explanatory irrelevance underpins some more cases which pose problems for the Deductive-Nomological model. The basis of the problem is the fact of logic that you cannot render a valid deduction invalid by adding premises, or by adding detail to the premises. However, the addition of irrelevant information does seem to hurt the quality of an explanation. The classic example here is hexed salt. You hex salt by waving your hands over it while saying 'Abracadabra'. Now, if a sample is placed in water, it dissolves, and the explanation offered is that all hexed salt dissolves in water. This is clearly true, and the explanandum can be deduced from the explanans, but the explanation seems to have major problems.

How does my theory handle this case? Here, we are dealing with quality of explanation. We would not want to say that 'all hexed salt dissolves in water' is completely unexplanatory: the relevant factor is cited, and the statement is true. What we do want to say is that it is significantly inferior, as an explanation, to the explanation 'all salt dissolves in water'. And this follows quite naturally from my model. If we build a model of hexed salt, saying that it all dissolves in water, then this is inferior in two ways to a model of all salt. First, it does not cover as wide a range of instances: it has nothing to say about unhexed salt. Second, it is more complex. Another property of the substance must be kept track of, thus adding to the load of the model. This complexity is completely unnecessary, since whether the salt is hexed or not is irrelevant to its dissolution in water. Thus, while the explanation with hexed salt is not completely useless, it is much worse than the explanation that simply cites the solubility of all salt.

There are, however, other cases that pose greater problems for my theory. These are cases of fail-safe overdetermination. As an example, consider a hospital. Its power is normally supplied by the national grid, but, as it is important that it has a continuous power supply, there is also a back-up generator, which kicks in if the national grid ceases to supply power. Now, suppose that the national grid is functioning normally, and someone asks 'why are the lights on?' It seems wrong to say that they are on because of the back-up generator, and right to say that they are on because of the national grid.

However, both of these pieces of information could improve the mental model of the situation. Information about the national grid allows you to simulate the flow of power, but information about the backup generator allows you to simulate what would happen if the grid were cut off: the lights would continue to be on, because the generator would kick in. Thus, both pieces of information seem to improve the mental model and thus, on my theory both seem to count as explanatory.

How can I resolve this problem within my theory? Consider the following solution. When I am told that the generator explains the lights being on, the model that I am invited to build is one in which the generator is currently supplying the energy. According to this model, if the generator runs out of fuel, the lights will go out, while a power surge on the national grid would have no effect at all. Both of these simulations are inaccurate, because the power is actually being supplied by the national grid. Although the information about the generator can improve my general mental model of the situation, it would make my model of the current, specific, situation considerably worse. Thus, if explanations are required to improve my mental model of the situation being explained, as they are, citing the generator as an explanation of the lights is not acceptable, or, at the very least, a far inferior explanation to the national grid.

Does this solution also work for other examples of this type? The other classic example is that of Jo, who is on the pill and a virgin. If we are asked why she is not pregnant, it seems that the fact that she is on the pill is irrelevant: as she is a virgin, she is not going to be pregnant. Both pieces of information will, however, contribute to our mental model of Jo, so the apparent situation is the same as before. Can we apply the same solution?

Unfortunately, it seems that we cannot, at least not in a simple way. If we are told only that she is on the pill, then we might suppose that, were she to stop taking the pill, or if the pill were, in fact, ineffective, then she would be likely to get pregnant. However, since she is a virgin, this is not likely even under those circumstances. On the other hand, if we are told that she is a virgin, then we might suppose that, were she to lose her virginity, she would be at risk of becoming pregnant. Since she is on the pill, this is not the case.

Perhaps the problem here is that the event to be explained is a non-event. We are to run our simulations, and this event is not to happen. There are many ways in which something can not happen, even if there is only one way in which it can. The relevant process can never get started, or it can be interrupted at some point. If Jo is a virgin, the process leading to pregnancy never gets started in one way, and if she is on the pill, it never gets started in another. Given this way of looking at it, is it clear that the fact that she is on the pill is actually unexplanatory? It is, in fact, possible to become pregnant without losing one's virginity, even without divine intervention, although I shall leave the details to the reader's imagination. Thus, it might well be that, although Jo is a virgin, she would almost certainly have become pregnant had she not been on the pill. Even if that is not the case, if she was on the pill, then she almost certainly would not have become pregnant even had she lost her virginity.

In this case, then, I am inclined to say that, if our intuitions state that Jo's being on the pill is not explanatory, then our intuitions are wrong. The details of the situation might make her virginity more explanatory, but the information that she is on the pill will still, I think, provide a significant increase in the quality of the relevant mental model.

Can I make a more general claim about explanatory relevance? I think that I can. Something is explanatorily relevant if it is relevant to simulating the situation at hand. Thus, hexing the salt is not explanatorily relevant at all. The back-up generator is relevant to the simulation of the lights in the hospital, but, given that they are actually being powered by the national grid, the grid is more relevant. In the case of Jo and the pill, it is not even clear which is more relevant, since that will depend on the other details of the situation. However, just because something is explanatorily relevant does not mean that it can be given as the explanation. When an explanation is requested, there will usually be a specific problem with the model that needs fixing: the explanation proffered must fix that problem, not just be relevant somewhere else in the model. This is why information about the generator will not answer the question 'why are the lights on?'

Non-Causal Explanations

Non-causal explanations are a problem for causal models, unsurprisingly. While some of the problems can be avoided by restricting the scope of the theory — Lewis only claims to provide a theory of the explanation of particular events — this strategy has problems of its own. In particular, it provides no account of why we call these non-causal explanations explanations. In this section I will consider some examples of non-causal explanations, and argue that they are easily accounted for by my theory.

Mathematical Explanations   Explanations in mathematics are a good example of non-causal explanation. Since there are no causes in mathematics, explanations in that field cannot cite them. However, the idea of a mathematical explanation seems perfectly coherent, so it would be useful to give some account of what is happening. I think that mathematical explanations can be characterised as improving mental models of mathematical situations, and thus improving the ability to simulate them.

It might not, however, be clear exactly what simulation of a mathematical situation involves, and thus I shall work with an example in an attempt to explain it. It is a mathematical fact that the digits of any multiple of three sum to a multiple of three. Knowledge of this fact is useful, as it allows faster checking of whether some integer will divide exactly by three. This is not understanding, however.

Understanding would involve being able to simulate the behaviour under different circumstances. Now, since mathematical truths are necessary truths, it might not be clear what different circumstances could be. In this particular case, however, there is a possible example of different circumstances. Suppose that we wrote our numbers in base twelve. In this case, the digits of multiples of three would not sum to three: the digits of 12, in base twelve, are 10, and sum to 1. If we understood why three had the property it does, however, we could simulate this situation, and work out which number holds the same position: eleven, as it happens.

However, simulation can take place under logically impossible antecedent conditions. A simulation does not fail or give meaningless results simply because there is a contradiction implied by the conjunction of two of the mutors or effectors involved. Thus, we could see that if 4 was the square root of nine, then all multiples of 4 would have digits that sum to a multiple of four in base 10, as they do in base 17.

Presumably, a similar notion of understanding can be applied to more complex mathematical constructs. My mathematics, however, is not really up to the task, so I will not give examples here. The possibility of simulating impossible situations will be particularly useful here, as there is unlikely to be an analogy in topology to changing the base in which our numbers are written down. If the notion can be extended, then it may help to explain why some varieties of mathematical proof are more satisfying than others.

Consider a constructive proof of a theorem. In this case, the theorem is shown to be true by deriving it from other things known to be true. With such a proof, a skilled mathematician could simulate the behaviour of the theorem if the axioms were slightly different. Thus, such proofs could be said to give understanding of the theorem. On the other hand, consider proofs by *reductio ad absurdum*. These demonstrate that the contradictory of the theorem is incompatible with something known to be true. Possession of such a proof tells you that the theorem is true, but tells you nothing about the form of the theorem under different mathematical conditions. Even if the thing that the contradictory is incompatible with was known to be false, the theorem might still be true: true theorems can have contradictories that are incompatible with falsehoods. Hence, such a proof provides no understanding of the theorem.

Thus, it seems that explanations and understanding can be had of mathematical things in just the same way as of physical things, according to my theory. Further, the theory gives an account of why some kinds of mathematical proof are less satisfying than others.

Physical non-causal explanations   In his paper on causal explanation[3] David Lewis gives three putative examples of non-causal explanation of singular events and purports to deal with them. His responses are not always very convincing, but need not concern us to a great extent here. Instead, I will show that the examples pose no problems at all for my account.

The first example concerns a light ray passing through a block of glass. It enters at A, leaves at B, and passes through C on the way, because C is on the shortest path between A and B. It passes through C because light rays obey Fermat's principle, and always take the path of least action.[4] This seems non-causal, since the length of time that it takes light to travel the whole path cannot, in the absence of backwards causation, have an influence on the route of light part way along the path.

However, this is no problem for my theory. Fermat's principle is a useful addition to our mental model of the behaviour of light, as it will be very helpful in simulating the behaviour of light rays, allowing us to skip detailed causal analysis at every stage. Thus, the proffered explanation increases our understanding of the situation, and thus counts as an explanation. Perhaps there is a better causal explanation, but perhaps such a model would be so complex as to lose out to one based on Fermat's principle in terms of speed.

Note that none of the mutors involved in the simulation run backwards in time. Instead there are mutors which say that a light ray entering the glass will take the path of least action. Given the point and angle of entry, and the structure of the glass, this path is specified. If we are told that the glass is homogeneous, we know that the path will be a straight line, again by simulation — the homogeneity of the glass is causally and temporally prior to the path of the light. Given both the entry and exit points, then, we can infer the path without simulating it in detail: we need merely simulate that it is straight, and then we can jump to make an inference from the known exit point. However, the exit point is strictly unnecessary: simulation by the principle of least action will give us the whole route. Further, in a simulation the light would pass through that point because of the principle of least action: that is the mutor responsible for producing the path. The exit point does not explain why the ray passes through C, because it would not be involved in simulating the situation.

The second example concerns the collapse of a neutron star.[5] The collapse eventually stops, not because there is some force which opposes gravity and holds the star up, but because there are no remaining states for

---

3   Lewis 1986a.
4   Lewis 1986a, pp 221–2.
5   Lewis 1986a, pp 222–3.

the neutrons to pass into. That is, the neutrons have run out of space to collapse in, in a sense, rather than actually being caused to stop.

Lewis's answer here is particularly unsatisfactory: he claims that this is information about the causal history, albeit negative information. However, if negative information is allowed, then it is hard to see why 'It wasn't because the universe is a steady state system' is not a candidate explanation for everything. It is possible that pragmatic features could determine things more closely: however, if you are allowed to cite anything that is in the causal history, or anything that isn't, then it is not clear in what sense you have a theory of causal explanation at all.

On my account, this explanation is easily accommodated. You may not have been told a cause: you have, however, certainly been told something very important to an accurate simulation of the collapse of a neutron star. You need to know that it runs out of state space if you are to accurately simulate the process. Thus, this is an explanation, for exactly the same reason that other explanations are.

Functional Explanation

Functional explanations pose problems for many theories of explanation, for several reasons. First, they often seem to cite an effect of the explanandum, rather than a cause, making them hard for causal theories to cover. Second, one functional explanans is often capable of explaining several incompatible explananda equally well, rather stymieing any attempts to put it into a deductive system which implies the explanandum. In this section I shall argue that my theory can accommodate them very easily.

First, let us consider functional explanations in biology. For example, a plant had chlorophyll because that enables it to perform photosynthesis. How can this information be applied to improve our simulations? In a number of ways, as it happens. If we simulate the evolutionary history of the plant, then we can say what alternatives to chlorophyll might have been accepted, and what changes there could have been in the structure of chlorophyll, given the limits that its function places on it. If we are simulating the behaviour of the plant now, then we are in a good position to say what will happen if all the chlorophyll is removed. We can even explain why plants that live in dark conditions tend to lose their chlorophyll: without light, it cannot serve its function, so there is no particular reason to keep it. Thus, the functional information serves to greatly improve our simulation.

Similar considerations apply to motive explanations of human behaviour. If I say that someone is working overtime in order to get enough money to buy a Porsche, this gives me significant ability to simulate the behaviour of this person. I know that, if the overtime is unpaid, he will stop doing it. Further, once he has enough for the Porsche, he will probably stop, as he will then want the spare time in which he can drive around and pose.

However, the desire for the Porsche could also explain other behaviour: taking out a large loan, robbing a bank, or trying to find someone willing to trade a Porsche for sexual favours. This does not reduce the usefulness of the information in the simulation. Indeed, it could be taken to demonstrate it, as these options are all things that the simulation suggests as behaviour if overtime is no longer available. Of course, the information that he wants a Porsche does not suffice, by itself, to simulate all of his behaviour in detail, but then no explanation suffices for that, in any context. It does, however, significantly improve the quality of the simulation.

It may seem that these mutors would point the wrong way in time, and thus could not be part of the model. This is not the case, however. In the case of the Porsche, the mutor is more nearly expressed as 'he wants a Porsche, so he will ...'. In this case, a causal model could help. The assimilation in the case of evolutionary theory, however, is something like 'Because evolution wants to retain photosynthesis ...'. This is not a cause in the standard sense, because evolution does not have desires.

It does, however, help us to model things at a certain level. We might have no idea how evolutionary forces will act to ensure that photosynthesis is retained, but we do know that, under a wide range of circumstances, they will do so. Thus, adding the mutor to our model will allow us to simulate better. There is a penalty to pay, however. Since we have a real mutor, there will be a strong tendency to think of a real cause where there is none. Even a most cursory acquaintance with the literature of evolutionary science will show that this tendency is very real: people often talk about what evolution wants, and promptly say that this is, of course, just a way of speaking. This model suggests that this is not quite right: it is a way of thinking.

On this account, then, something serves a function if knowledge of that function helps you to simulate its actions and development. Consider a race of mice with white fur. Suppose that they live in a bright, hot desert with white sand. The white fur has two effects: first, it makes the mice difficult to see, and second, it reduces the amount of heat they absorb from the sun, thus helping with thermoregulation. Both of these may well be functions of the colour, but one is likely to be the main function. If the mice move to a hot, black area (a basalt desert), or a cold, white one (the arctic) the two will come apart, and the function of the colour is determined by which one allows accurate simulation. If the mice in the desert turn black and grow big ears to dissipate heat, then the function of the fur was to ward off predators. If, on the other hand, they stay white but develop poisonous sweat, then its function was to reflect heat.

This account is, of course, precisely the opposite of the conventional one, where the function is defined by evolutionary origin. It has the advantage of being concerned with what the functional thing is for *now*, rather than in the past, but it can also incorporate the other account. We can try to simulate the history of the mice just as well as their future. In this case, the colour's function is to reduce predation if it evolved in response to those pressures — if, for example, they used to live on basalt, where they were black, and only turned white on moving to the white desert.

Thus, seeing functional explanations as providing mutors which help in simulation explains why there is such a strong tendency to see evolution as an active force, and why there is a strong urge to say that something's function is what it does *now*, but also what it did that gave it a selective advantage.

In this section, I have argued that my theory can handle the problem cases of explanation easily, and without straining the definition. I hope that this has strengthened my case that the correct way to look at explanation is, indeed, in terms of understanding.

Error Theory

My account of explanation is obviously different from earlier ones, even if it often gives the same answers as to what is an explanation. In this section I will assume that my theory is basically correct, and suggest how other theories could have come to seem plausible.

Covering Law Models

There are two aspects of Hempel's Covering Law model of explanation which are particularly interesting. The first is Hempel's insistence on the structural identity[6] between explanation and prediction. If an explanation is an attempt to convey part of a mental model, and the primary use of mental models is simulation, then it is clear that there is a close link between explanation and prediction. Since the model is no good unless it can be used for simulation (and thus prediction), there is a sense in which the explanation could be said to be no good unless it would be a prediction in the right circumstances. Certainly, if there is no connection between the explanation and possible prediction, the explanation will not be a good one. This connection may be purely theoretical, however. Consider self-evidencing explanations, where the explanandum is the only evidence we have for the truth of the explanans. An example is the Doppler shift in receding stars. This shift towards the red end of the spectrum is explained by the star's velocity of recession, but the shift in the spectrum is the only evidence for that recession. This model cannot be used to predict the shift, because we must know the shift to be able to apply the model. However, it does allow us to simulate the system, and to know that the red shift will change if the star's velocity changes. We can, therefore, predict what would happen, were the velocity to change, despite the fact that we would only become aware of such a change through the very effect we predict.

---

6   Hempel 1965, §2.4.

However, the explanation itself need be not be a potential prediction. For a start, the explanation need not include a lot of information that is already in the mental model, but which is essential to the possibility of prediction. Further, we can improve poor models of a situation quite substantially, without getting to the stage where we can actually predict what will happen. This can even apply to fairly good models in particularly complex cases: very few people can consistently predict the behaviour even of people whom they understand well. Thus, we would expect there to be many objections made to the structural identity thesis, as indeed there were.

The second point concerns the deductive nature of the explanations, and the presence of the law. A good model must cover more than one case, which could easily be seen as requiring a law. Certainly, it needs a generalisation of some sort, and the search for things that are unequivocally explanatory might push us towards the position that this generalisation must be one of the ultimate ones, one of the laws of nature. The requirement of deductive entailment stems from the perceived need to get the explanandum out of the explanation. The model must, when run, simulate the explanandum if the explanation is to be good, and deduction is an appealing way to capture this process, especially if you are a logical empiricist.

The mental model theory of understanding, however, reveals that we do not need ultimately general laws, or, indeed, anything that is without exceptions. Mutors can work against one another, and produce certain results *ceteris paribus*. This does not harm the ability to simulate, but it does prevent the mutors from expressing exceptionless generalisations. They are not laws of nature. Further, the simulation process does not, in fact, run by logical deduction, and this is a strength, as the many problems that this mechanism raised for Covering Law models demonstrate.

Familiarity Models

The theory that explanation is reduction to the familiar seems to be cited only to be dismissed, to the extent that I have found no recent work that supports it. Despite this, it can be seen to arise naturally in the context of my account. In the first place, when explaining something it is best if you can relate it to familiar things. They will already by modelled by the questioner, and thus it will be easy for him to improve his model by using them. Thus, telling someone that an apparently surprising event was, in fact, just a new perspective on something familiar will often serve to explain it. He can now model the effect of this perspective, and he could already model the event itself.

Similarly, when explaining something completely new it is a great advantage if you can describe it in terms of the familiar. Relativistic space-time is not much like a rubber sheet, but the model of that relatively familiar thing can be used to model space-time, with some alterations. Since it is difficult to describe how mutors should work, starting by taking them over from a different model is a good technique. Although, in this particular case, the model is analogical, most mental models are not, on my account, in contrast to Hesse's position.[7] Nevertheless, it should be possible to give an account of analogical reasoning in terms of my theory: roughly, a good analogy allows you to use established mutors to model a new field. I cannot, however, develop such an account here.

These are, however, only guidelines, as far as my account is concerned. There is no reason to mention familiar things unless they give you a boost in explanation, and in some cases it may be easier to explain the familiar by recourse to the unfamiliar. There may simply be no familiar models that are at all close to the correct model of the colour of the sky.

Causal Models

Causal models are about the easiest to fit into my theory. In many cases, we model something by setting up its causes, or the causes of the causes, and then letting the model proceed. Under these circumstances, it is clear that we will often improve the model by giving information about the causal history of the event.

It is equally clear that not just any information about this history will do: go back too far, and the mental model will not be able to handle the intervening space, mention something that is always around, and the model will not be altered. Thus, we would expect causal models to be hedged around with accounts of just which causes are explanatory, as indeed we find in Lewis's account.

Similarly, we model many things that are not causal: mathematics and purposes among others. In these cases, explanation will not refer to the causal history of the event, and so the causal model will not apply to all explanations.

Unification Models

Unification models, such as that of Kitcher,[8] are the closest in spirit to the account presented here. Indeed, rather than offering an account of why, given my theory, we would expect people to think that this is a good theory, I would claim that my theory could be seen as an account of what it means to unify phenomena. They are unified when they are all part of a single mental model. The more comprehensive and connected our model of the world, the more unified the phenomena we experience, the better our understanding. The main weakness of previous unification theories is that they have failed to advance beyond the programmatic. I hope that my theory, while still lacking fine detail, is rather more detailed than that.

I have argued that a theory of explanation can be derived from my theory of understanding, and that this theory can handle the standard

---

[7]   Hesse 1966.
[8]   Kitcher 1981.

problems that are raised for other theories. I have also argued that the competing theories of explanation have arisen from consideration of one feature of mental models, to the exclusion of others. This means that my account should be able to take over all the best features of such theories, while avoiding their weaknesses.

Chapter 7

Metaphysical Matters

As this is the final chapter of my book, I intend to take advantage of the conventional licence afforded to final chapters, and speculate on some of the wider implications of my theory. Indeed, I will finish by suggesting that space, time, and objects do not really exist. This should be taken with a grain of salt — I think these speculations are interesting, thought provoking, and probably true, but I do not think that the arguments supporting them are even close to watertight. Indeed, I'm not sure whether such arguments could be given.

There are some obvious analogies between features of mental models, as described by this theory, and standard metaphysical things. Mutors seem remarkably similar to causal glue, effectors and simulors to universals, and simulants to particulars. Indeed, I think that these analogies are genuine: that, at least, these features of models will, in a good model, correspond to those metaphysical things, if they actually exist. Moreover, I think the goodness of match is cause for concern over the grounds of metaphysics: is it possible that, when we suppose we are considering the most basic structure of the world, we are actually thinking about how we think?

Models and Metaphysics

Although there are obvious analogies between features of models and metaphysical creations, it is not immediately clear that these analogies are anything more than superficial resemblances. It is necessary to provide some argument for the depth of the analogy.

Causation

Starting at the deepest level of mental models, mutors have much in common with causation. Most important, they provide a necessary connection between two events: the mutor makes the antecedent condition give rise to the consequent. This is not simply co-occurrence: one state brings about the other. This match is, however, with the feature of causation which has proved hardest to explicate. Do they match up equally well with features that are better understood?

There are two ways in which it seems likely that maxims would fail to match up with the properties of causation. First, causation is asymmetric, while simulation by mutors seems not to be: we can simulate causes based on their effects just as well as *vice versa*. Second, mutors might be able to simulate a given situation without matching the causal structure. In this section I will address these problems in turn.

The direction of causation   Causation, and explanation, seem to be asymmetric: the cause explains the effect, but the effect does not explain the cause. Simulation, on the other hand, seems to be symmetric: causes predict their effects, effects retrodict their causes. In this section, I will argue that the asymmetry will arise naturally on my model, given only the resources of simulation. The asymmetry of mutors is central to this argument: because mutors only go from the input to the output, and not the other way, they are suitable units with which to build an asymmetric system. However, I have so far given no reason to suppose that systems do not contain mutors in pairs: a§b always being coupled with b§a. If this were the case, the system would be symmetrical, no matter how asymmetric the mutors were. Thus, I need to argue that our models will consist of mutors in only one direction.

This argument falls into two parts. First, I will argue that the model must contain mutors that point in only one direction, or else it will automatically fail to simulate accurately. Second, I will argue that, given the choice, we will want mutors that go from the past to the future.

Suppose that mutors did point in both directions. Suppose, further, that a gives rise to b, which gives rise to c, and suppose that these are all different objects, but that the producing object is destroyed when it produces its successor (that is, the lower case letters refer to simulors rather than effectors: the mutors would obviously be organised in effectors within the simulors, but that is not relevant here). The simulor b would then contain the mutors b§c, b§-b (pointing forward in time) and b§a (pointing back). a would contain a§b and a§-a, pointing forwards, while c contains c§b, pointing back.

If we start with an object of type a, we will get, in sequence, an object of type b and an object of type c. In no case will there be more than one object. If we run the model, however, we get a very different result. a§b produces b, while a§-a destroys a. So far, so good. On the next cycle, however, b§c produces c, b§a produces a, and b§-b destroys b. On the third cycle c§b produces b, a§b produces b, and a§-a destroys a. We now have one c and two bs in the model, and the number of simulants will keep increasing.

There is no way to avoid such a result if the models are set up as described: the backward mutors do not know that they point backwards, and so they will simply activate. Thus, models using mutors that point in different directions in time would have to be kept completely, and carefully, separate.

A different problem arises if a, b and c represent incompatible properties of the same object. In this case, our model will tell us impossible things (that an object is both red and green all over, for example). The solution is the same: keep the mutors separate.

Now, there is a clear reason for a preference for the forward direction. It is a fact about people that they remember the past and act in the future, and that they are unable to change the past. As long as this fact preceded the development of mental models and simulation, the simulations would be preferentially developed to go from the present to the future. If you are a hunter-gatherer armed with a club, you do not want to know where the tiger came from, you want to know what it will do next, and how you can make sure that it will not eat you. All of these decisions require the ability to simulate the future on the basis of the present. Thus most mutors will be designed to permit such simulation: those mutors provide better possibilities of survival.

Note that I have not even pretended to explain the origin of the basic asymmetry: it may arise from the fundamental nature of time itself, from real causal asymmetry, or simply from the direction of entropy. However, given that asymmetry, which no-one can sanely deny, the model which simulates the future, based on the past, is much more use than that which simulates the past based on the present.

So, if we have two sets of mutors, one facing forwards and one facing back, then the forward ones will get more use than the others. Not only that, but it is easier to test and refine them: we can bring about their antecedent conditions, and see if the right thing happens. This cannot be done with backward facing mutors: we can only look at the world and decide whether the mutor was accurate. As philosophers have noted since Mill, we can be much more certain of our beliefs about the world if we can manipulate the world and see what happens.

If, then, we have two models, one facing forwards and facing backwards, the one facing forwards has all the advantages. It is used most often, it is the most accurate, and the world behaves that way: the direction of time in the model reflects the direction of time in the world. Thus, if we were to draw conclusions about the structure of the world, we would draw them from that model, and so that model would underwrite our understanding. However, not every feature of the past explains or causes that which it allows you to predict. In the next section, I will argue that only those which do will be linked by mutors to their results.

Causes and mere correlation   Hume famously noted that the causal structure of the world is not directly observable. However, it is generally regarded as desirable that our model of the world distinguish between things that are causally related and things that are merely correlated: for example, as effects of a common cause. In this section, I will argue that the requirement to simulate the observable drives a model towards reflecting the causal structure of the world.

I will not argue that our model-building will necessarily pick out the causal structure of the world. That would both assume that causation is an objective feature of reality, and that our inferential processes are perfect. The latter is probably false, and the former raises metaphysical questions which I do not wish to discuss just yet. What I will argue is that model-building will yield models of the world that match its apparent causal structure.

I believe that the causal structure we see in the world is, immediately, a feature of our models. Specifically, we see a causal link when we have a mutor that takes us from one state to another. The automatic operation of the mutor leads to the perception of some sort of necessity, and the fact that mutors are unidirectional gives rise to the asymmetry of causation. This is not, however, to claim that causation is not an objective feature of the world. We should hope that our models reflect real structure, and thus that the mutors reflect some real thing that is causation in the world. I am claiming that if we would form certain mutors under certain circumstances, then we would form similar beliefs about the causes in such a case.

This may seem to beg the question: if I stipulate that belief in a causal link is evidence for the existence of a mutor, it seems obvious that our mental models must follow what we believe about the causal structure of the world. I think that this is right, and that it is obvious — within my theory it is little more than the statement that we believe the causal structure of the world to be the way we believe it to be. Accordingly, my argument will aim to show that the causal structure that we would expect to arise from matching the simulation to the observed is similar to that which we have actually constructed.

The limitation to match with the observed does, in practice, oversimplify our methods for refining models. I think that we also take into account consistency with the other models that we already have. Part of this derives from simplicity constraints: if we can re-use the same mutors, we reduce the load on the mind. Another part comes from the possibility of avoiding errors. If we know that in one case prolonged investigation led to a certain type of conclusion, then we may assume that, in a similar case, we would, eventually, get a similar result, and thus start out by assuming that the final model will be of a certain form. For example, many problems in solid state physics have been solved by treating the behaviour of each atom as influenced by its immediate neighbours, and so this technique is used for new problems. However, the use of such a technique influences the structure of the model: in this case, only the influence of immediate neighbours is thought to be relevant. Sometimes, this is wrong, and then the disagreement with observation over-rules the assumption, and a different model is constructed. In the specific discussion which follows, I shall avoid reference to these shortcuts, as I think that they are nothing more than that.

Let us consider one of the classic cases of mere correlation, in this case due to common cause. A barometer falls before a storm comes, but the fall in the barometer does not cause the storm. The actual causal structure, let us suppose, is that a fall in air pressure causes the barometer to fall and, somewhat later, causes the storm. (This is simplified from the actual picture, of course.) Thus, the barometer and the storm are merely correlated, and a good mental model should not regard them as causally linked. Can this be derived by purely observed constraints?

If we are considering a single incident, the only one ever to be observed of a barometer being correlated with a coming storm, then it cannot. The storm was preceded by two events, and its arrival can be simulated by linking the mutor to either of them. However, if only one instance ever were observed, it is likely that any understanding of that situation would be defective, no matter what theory of understanding is adopted. Thus, we must consider wider cases: the model must be able to preserve accuracy of simulation in more cases than this.

So, suppose that we do, initially, set up a mental model in which the mutor links the fall of the barometer to the storm. Often, this will allow accurate simulation. However, sometimes the barometer will be broken, and then the simulation will fail. In looking for a way to cover those instances, we must discover the low air pressure (there are no alternatives in the simplified example), and once we have discovered that, the barometer becomes redundant. Even when the barometer is working, the air pressure falls before the storm, and so the pressures on simplicity of the model will eliminate the mutor leading from the barometer.

However, it will be objected that I am assuming that one of the correlations is not perfect, and so the situation is not truly symmetrical. Thus, let us suppose that the barometer never breaks: it always falls before a storm occurs near it. In this case, the necessary push comes from other places. It is not possible to simulate storms in other places by reference to the barometer, as it is not present. Again, air pressure will enter the scheme, and again the barometer will be eliminated even in the original case.

Of course, the correlation between the barometer and the storm is now imperfect over space. Let us, then, assume that there are perfect barometers all over the world, so that no matter where we go, we can simulate the approach of the storm by reference to the barometers. Now, let us unpack the notion of perfect barometers a bit. If it is possible to grab the needle and move it — i.e., to make the barometer imperfect — then we can learn about air pressure as noted above: the barometer does not predict the storm when we move the needle, but the air pressure does. Thus, the barometer must be untouchable in order for the correlation to deceive us.

But I may have conceded too much to my opponent: the argument assumes that there is no relevant knowledge about atmospheric physics or the functioning of barometers. The existence of perfect barometers does not prevent us from finding the correlation between air pressure and storms, and building that model. If we have lots of models of other atmospheric phenomena, and they all depend on air pressure and the like, then simplicity will probably drive us towards rejecting the barometer correlation. Similarly, if barometers have no apparent means of causing storms, the existence of such a singular maxim would be militated against by simplicity considerations.

Suppose that the background knowledge does not make any distinction. Still it seems that we may be able to make the distinction. We can learn about the air pressure, and we can simulate the behaviour of the barometer in terms of the fall of air pressure. Since we can also simulate the storm in terms of such a fall, a mutor linking the barometer to the storm would be redundant, and might well be excluded by simplicity considerations.

This consideration will also apply in cases in which low pressure is not perfectly correlated with storms. If a fall on a barometer never precedes a storm unless low pressure also does (which will be the case under the hypothesis as to the working of the barometer), then we can discover this double correlation, and eliminate the redundant mutor from the barometer to the storm. Of course, in this case the low pressure is also better correlated with the storms than the barometer. If the two are equally correlated (so that the air pressure and barometer are perfectly correlated), then the above consideration applies in almost exactly the same form. If the barometer is better correlated, or the correlations are equal, but the air pressure and barometer are not perfectly correlated, then the data strongly suggests that there is a causal link between the barometer and the storm, and we should not be surprised that people make mistakes.

This raises a general point about counter-examples to this model. In the most difficult cases it has been assumed that there is a sort of cosmic conspiracy to make the causal correlation obscure to us, and under such circumstances it is not unlikely that we would make mistakes. Since I am not trying to give an analysis of the metaphysics of causation, but merely of its epistemology, I can admit the possibility of error, even undetectable error, with no qualms. I think it is clear that a mutor which does not reflect a genuine causal link will, almost always, result in a false simulation under some circumstances. Since I am concerned with epistemology, any proffered counter-examples must be such that modelling could not discover the correct causal pattern, but some other technique could, and I believe that this would be impossible.

The above discussion has rested heavily on simplicity considerations, and it might be thought that these would not often be strong enough to force out isolated pseudo-causes like the barometer. However, we must suppose that the link between air pressure and storms is known, because otherwise there is no other known cause of the storm, and the perfect barometer would be a very good guess: remember, it is everywhere, always functions, and is never wrong. If it fails in any of these, we can exclude it on other grounds.

Once we know about the air pressure drop, however, we have a good reason to exclude the barometer. The pressure drop is just as well correlated with the barometer as the storm, but it is earlier. As argued above, mutors in a model can only point one way, so there cannot be a mutor from the barometer to the pressure drop. Thus, there must be a mutor from the pressure drop to the barometer. We therefore get the result that the pressure drop causes the barometer reading. We may now choose whether to link from the pressure drop to the storm, or from the barometer to the storm. In this case, simplicity considerations seem strongly in favour of linking from the pressure drop, because we can use all our knowledge about the behaviour of water vapour and air masses under conditions of lowered pressure. If the barometer is slightly short of perfect, these considerations become even stronger.

A potential problem does remain, however. The barometer does predict the storm to a certain extent, even in the simplest case. Why, then, can't we keep the mutor in our model, since it helps us with our predictions? It won't be a large loss of simplicity, after all, and it might help. We can't appeal to causality to rule it out, because we want causality to drop out of the account.

However, if there is a mutor from the barometer reading to the storm, our models will predict that if we bring the barometer reading about (grab the needle and pull), we will bring about a storm. That is simply how mutors work. If there is a mutor from the reading to the storm, then whenever we have the reading, we have the storm, or at least a fixed chance of it. The mutor is blind: it doesn't know that the reading was obtained in the wrong way. Indeed, unless we import notions of causality, it can't know, because we have no way to define 'the wrong way'. Since the simulation would obviously fail in this case, we cannot have a mutor representing the link from the barometer to the storm. It is a useful indicator, but it must be accommodated in some other way — perhaps as a 'non-causal pseudo-mutor'. It doesn't matter how we accommodate it, because we have discovered that it can't be a real mutor by examining failures of simulation, as required by the theory.

We can push the example further, however. Suppose that, whenever we move the needle to 'storm' we do, indeed, get a storm. By coincidence, the air pressure has fallen, so we get a storm, but the barometer still doesn't cause it. In this case, the mutor will not give false predictions.

At this point I, and just about anyone else, would believe that barometers cause storms. Whenever the needle points to 'storm', you get a storm. If you want a storm, you can make one by moving the needle so that it points there. If you don't want one, you keep the needle away from that point. My evidence for my belief that the light switch in my room operates the light is no better than this. It is a sad fact that the world could be so perverse that we were deceived about its true causal structure. Even in this case, of course, we would want to have the correct model. The coincidental correlation fails in many nomically possible worlds, one of which might be the future of our world. The evidence is such, however, that we will not be able to learn the true correlation. This is true on *any* model of causal inference, and thus not a problem for my account — it is an inevitable result of the way that the world is.

Thus, there are basic theoretical reasons for supposing that the mutors in a model will all point in the same temporal direction. Given this, and the other constraints, reliance on simulation is fully as capable of letting us discover the causal structure of the world as any other process of inference. Mutors and causation therefore seem to be deeply analogous.

Universals

Effectors and universals have many features in common. An effector can be shared by many things, and yet it does not become more than one effector, just as a universal can be one thing in many particulars. Furthermore, effectors are the same sorts of things as universals: colours, masses, and the like. Simulors account for such universals as dog and house, and their slots for certain types of effector account for the fact that the universal house has a number of windows, but no particular number.

Suppose that there are real universals. In that case, those dispositions bound together in the real universals will always occur together, while those which are not, will not. Thus, if our models are to accurately reflect the world, we want our effectors and simulors to correspond to the actual universals, as that is the only way to guarantee that the dispositions we suppose to be present are, in fact, present. So, just as mutors should match the real causal structure of the world, effectors and simulors should match the real structure of universals.

It could be argued that effectors and simulors need not match up with the genuine universals, just as was argued for causation above. However, I think that a very similar argument can be given in response. Suppose that a particular group of dispositions are not really linked by a universal. It then seems likely that they will, on at least some occasions, occur apart. Once it has been determined that the presence of one of the dispositions is not generally connected with, and thus is no evidence for, the presence of the others, the effector in the model loses its utility. Instead of organising mutors to match the organisation of dispositions, it introduces errors as often as not. Of course, there will be some particularly difficult cases which we will still get wrong, but that is inevitable, just as was argued for causation.

Ersatz effectors are not as obviously pernicious as false mutors, however. Suppose that a group of dispositions occur together often, but not always. It might seem to be useful to group the corresponding mutors in an effector, and simply assign the mutors separately when they do not occur together. We would make mistakes, of course, and assign the effector when it was not warranted, but we do not expect to be infallible.

This, however, is not how mental models work. Bare mutors cannot be attached to simulants: they are all organised through effectors, even if the effector has only a single mutor. There may be a higher level effector grouping several other effectors, so that if something has the higher level effector, it has all the mutors in question, while other objects can possess the lower level effectors piecemeal. Such a higher level effector may be useful in organising someone's mental models, but only if the lower effectors really do cluster reliably. If they do, then it is not clear that the modeller is wrong in supposing that there is a real universal involved. Once again, evidence that he was wrong would also constitute a reason to change the model so as not to include that effector.

Particulars

Simulants are very similar to particulars. Each one is different from every other, even if they have exactly the same properties. Further, we want the simulants in our models to correspond one for one with the particulars that are actually present in the situation at hand. If they do not, we may find that the real particulars diverge, while our model, representing them by one simulant, forces them to remain together. The arguments in this case are, once again, closely parallel to those given above, and so I will not repeat them here. While we may be wrong about which particulars there are, we want our models to include only the real particulars, and simulation will allow us to discover what those are, if anything will.

Metaphysical Methodology

Suppose that our minds do work this way, and that someone sits down to consider the way in which the world works. First, all tokens of a type have their type in common, even if they differ in the values of all properties. Thus, there are grounds in our models for thinking about universals that refer to things, like 'man' and 'horse'.

Further, every simulant, as well as being a collection of effector instances, is also an instance of the simulor. This latter instance is, in a deep sense, what the simulant is: it was brought into the model by instantiating that type, not by assembling the effectors. The values of all the effectors within the instance can be changed as the simulation is run, but the simulant remains the same, unless it is broken up and replaced by simulants of another type. Thus, consideration might suggest that there is a substance, in which all the properties inhere, and which determines the individuality of the object.

The simulant, however, has no maxims, and does nothing: all activity takes place through the medium of its effectors. Thus, it may seem that

> if any one will examine himself concerning his *Notion of pure Substance in general*, he will find he has no other *Idea* of it at all, but only a Supposition of he knows not what support of such Qualities, which are capable of producing simple *Ideas* in us; which Qualities are commonly called Accidents.[1]

The model account makes both of these conclusions very natural: the model cannot work without the notion of substance, so we cannot easily imagine a world without it, but on the other hand it seems to be purely a feature of the model, and need not mark anything in the real world.

Further, effectors behave in much the same way. Every red simulant makes use of the effector red, quite possibly using identically the same

---

[1]   Locke 1975, p 295 §2.

mutors every time. However, there is absolutely no way to introduce a bare effector into a simulation: everything comes tied to simulants. Thus, there are strange property universals, equally present in all their instances but unable to exist by themselves.

What is more, human beings have properties, such as emotions and thoughts, that are not properties of any of their parts. The hand has no emotions: if you examine the model of the hand, there are no emotions attached. The same applies to the brain: lots of grey, squishy properties, but no emotions. Thus, there is some total thing that is the human being, which has these properties. The body is exhausted by the parts, hence there must be an immaterial soul.

Thus, if metaphysicians spent their time thinking about the structure of mental models, they would come up with the conclusions which they have, in fact, proposed. What is more, we would expect many of the actual metaphysical problems. Consider the problems over individuals: if I take all the planks out of a ship one at a time, replacing them as I go, and build those planks into a second ship, which one is the original ship? At no point will the simulant representing the first ship have been removed from the model, so the first ship is still that ship. On the other hand, all its parts are now in a second ship, and it isn't clear that there is anything in the world corresponding to the simulant of the first ship. So maybe the second ship is that ship. Intuitions could, and do, go either way.

This strongly suggests, at least to me, that metaphysics proceeds by thinking about the way we think, and has nothing directly to do with the world. Indeed, it is a little hard to see how it could be otherwise: the problem of epistemic access to metaphysical matters is also an ancient one. The *a priori* would simply be that which was essential to thought. Thus, the structure of universals and particulars would be *a priori,* while the universals and particulars which actually existed would have to be discovered *a posteriori.*

There are two ways of looking at this situation. One is to note that we have evolved to live in this world, and that it would be helpful if our mental equipment tallied with the structure of the world. Evolution then provides good reason for believing in causation and universals. Evolutionary metaphysics fits nicely with evolutionary epistemology.

The second way is rather Kantian, and the way that I lean. We cannot think about the world without dividing it into objects with properties connected by causal links in space and time, but this does not mean that the universe actually has anything resembling these features. This takes one of the standard arguments against evolutionary epistemology, and uses it in the new context. Evolution need not produce an ideal system, it need only produce one which is good enough. Space, time, and objects are good enough for survival in the world with which human beings interact: the world of medium sized dry goods. They might well fail horribly in other contexts.

One reason I incline towards this view is that there seems to be a good deal of evidence for it. General relativity paints a picture of the universe in which space and time are very different from our naive intuitions, and quantum mechanics does the same for objects. Indeed, the discoveries of quantum mechanics have stubbornly resisted incorporation into our mental models — the formalism is well understood, and works well, but the interpretation, the mapping from mathematics to mental models, has progressed in numerous contradictory and unsatisfactory directions over the last seventy years. What is more, two and a half thousand years of inconclusive debate in metaphysics tends to suggest that our mental models are not entirely coherent. Even at the most basic level, elements seem to be in conflict.

This evidence is hardly conclusive, of course, and there are problems with this view. One is that I have described the mental models in terms of causal links and individual neurons evolving over time. If causation, objects, and time are all products of the model, they cannot maintain the model. I don't think that this is a very serious problem. There is a real world out there (*pace* extreme scepticism), and it can, quite clearly, be described fairly well in terms of mental models. Thus, it is not surprising that mental models can do a fairly good job of describing their own basis.

The nature of this real world poses a difficult question. It might be possible to discover it, and perhaps the formalisms of quantum mechanics and of general relativity have made progress here, but we could never understand it, because we understand things by building mental models, and those are fundamentally inadequate for the task. Maybe our mental structure is now holding scientific progress back, by making the correct solutions look ridiculous, rather as non-Euclidean space once seemed absurd.

However, I don't have any strong arguments for this position, so it is time to return to earth. The interpretation of quantum mechanics may simply be a very hard task in which no-one has yet succeeded. Nevertheless, my inclination is to believe that, at the very least, we have no good reason to believe in space, time, or objects.

Conclusions

In this book I have argued that the conventional approach to the philosophy of explanation is fundamentally flawed. Explanation is too diverse a beast to be captured by one unified concept, if that concept is required to refer only to things internal to explanation. I argued that this suggested that a better theory might be one that treated explanation in terms of what it was supposed to provide: understanding.

I then argued that understanding was the ability to simulate, and that we simulated by means of mental models, so that to understand is to possess a mental model. The better our simulation, the better our understanding. I then discussed how one could build a theory of explanation on the foundation of this theory of understanding, and argued that such a theory could avoid the problems that arise for the theories already available.

This does not end the work to be done on this theory, however. There remain, of course, many points of detail to be tidied up. Most importantly, the theory of mental models is still, in many ways, merely a sketch. It is not clear to me whether much further work can be done within philosophy, and I suspect that we must look to cognitive psychology for more answers.

Similarly, the theory of explanation could be developed in more detail for particular cases. For example, explanation in biology should follow this pattern, and so the application of the theory should shed light on debates over whether natural selection can explain the complex features seen in living creatures. Similarly, it should be possible to show whether a fundamentally indeterministic view of quantum mechanics can explain the world.

The implications of the theory stretch beyond here, however. My brief remarks on inference and induction are very far from exhausting that topic. At the very least, this theory seems to lend itself naturally to elucidations of inference to the best explanation, and I am hopeful that a good descriptive, although not justificatory, account of induction could be drawn from it.

Further, the brief account I gave of understanding words could, I think, be extended to give a theory of meaning and reference. The link between the models built on account of words and those built as a result of perception may even allow some account to be given of what referring actually involves.

The theory I have presented is less a conceptual analysis than an hypothesis about the way that the mind works. If I am right, and understanding, inference, language, and counterfactuals are all closely linked, then it might be possible to predict what talents or deficiencies would tend to go together. Such predictions could provide a useful empirical test of the theory, and may be more accessible than questions concerning the basis of mental models.

All this, however, requires further work. In this book I have claimed that we understand things by building mental models that allow us to simulate them. I have argued that the capacity and desire to build these models would have been useful at earlier stages of our evolution, and that they could have been refined by natural selection to their current pitch. I argued that, when we have a good mental model, we have everything that we could want from understanding: we can simulate the mechanism, structure, and purpose behind any event, say what would happen under different circumstances, and successfully plan future actions.

This account of understanding seems to lead naturally to a good account of explanation and sheds light, in passing, on many other areas of philosophy. It fits our beliefs about understanding, and allows us to account for its origin and current use. In short, I believe that this theory gives us a true understanding of understanding.

Bibliography

Achinstein, P. 1981. 'Can There be a Model of Explanation?' in Ruben 1993.

Achinstein, P. 1983. *The Nature of Explanation* (Oxford: Oxford University Press).

Achinstein, P. 1985. 'The Pragmatic Character of Explanation' in Ruben 1993.

Anderson, J. R. 1983. *The Architecture of Cognition* (Cambridge, MA: Harvard University Press).

Aristotle. *Posterior Analytics.*

Aristotle. *Physics* (1996, Oxford: Oxford University Press).

Bailer-Jones, D. M. 1998 *Scientific Models: a cognitive approach with an application in astrophysics* (Ph.D. dissertation, University of Cambridge).

Bailer-Jones, D. M. 2000 'Modelling Extended Extragalactic Radio Sources' *Studies in History and Philosophy of Modern Physics* **31B** 49–74.

Barnes, E. 1993. 'Why P rather than Q? The Curiosities of Fact and Foil' *Philosophical Studies* **71.**

Boyd, R. 1985. 'Observations, Explanatory Power, and Simplicity: Toward a Non-Humean Account' in Boyd *et al.* 1991.

Boyd, R., Gasper, P., & Trout, J. D., eds. 1991 *The Philosophy of Science* (Cambridge, MA: MIT Press).

Braithwaite, R. B. 1953. *Scientific Explanation* (Cambridge: Cambridge University Press).

Brody, B. 1970. ed. *Readings in the Philosophy of Science* (Englewood Cliffs, NJ: Prentice Hall).

Brody, B. 1972. 'Towards an Aristotelian Theory of Scientific Explanation' in Ruben 1993.

Bromberger, S. 1966. 'Why-Questions' in Brody 1970.

Bundy, A. & Byrd, L. 'Using the Method of Fibres in Mecho to Calculate Radii of Gyration' in Gentner & Stevens 1983.

Butler, R. J. (ed.). 1966 *Analytical Philosophy* 1st series (Oxford).

McCarthy, T. 1977. 'On an Aristotelian Model of Scientific Explanation' in Ruben 1993.

Carroll, L. 1895 [1995]. 'What the Tortoise Said to Achilles' Mind **104** 691–3.

Cartwright, N. 1989. 'Capacities and Abstractions' in Kitcher & Salmon 1989.

Chisholm. 1955. 'Law Statements and Counterfactual Inference' in Sosa 1975.

Churchland, P. 1981. 'Eliminative Materialism and the Propositional Attitudes' in Boyd *et al.* 1991.

Churchland, P. M. 1995. *The Engine of Reason, the Seat of the Soul* (Cambridge, MA: The MIT Press).

Clark, P. 1990. 'Explanation in Physical Theory' in Knowles 1990.

Clark, S. R. L. 1990. 'Limited Explanations' in Knowles 1990.

Clement, J. 1983 'A Conceptual Model Discussed by Galileo and Used Intuitively by Physics Students' in Gentner & Stevens 1983.

Coffa, J. A. 1974. 'Hempel's Ambiguity' in Ruben, 1993.

Cohen, G. A. 1978. 'Functional Explanation: In General' in *Karl Marx's Theory of History: A Defence* (Oxford: Clarendon Press).

Craik, K. 1943. *The Nature of Explanation* (Cambridge: Cambridge University Press).

Cummins, R. 1983. *The Nature of Psychological Explanation* (Cambridge, MA: The MIT Press).

Dennett, D. 1991. *Consciousness Explained* (Harmondsworth: Penguin).

diSessa, A. A. 1983 'Phenomenology and the Evolution of Intuition' in Gentner & Stevens 1983.

Edwards, J. 1990. 'Functional Support for Anomalous Monism' in Knowles 1990.

Forbus, K. D. 'Qualitative Reasoning about Space and Motion' in Gentner & Stevens 1983.

van Fraassen, B. C. 1977. 'The Pragmatics of Explanation' in Boyd *et al.* 1991.

van Fraassen, B. C. 1980. *The Scientific Image* (Oxford: Clarendon Press).

Friedman, M. 1971. 'Explanation and Scientific Understanding' in Pitt 1988.

Garfinkel, A. 1981. *Forms of Explanation* (New Haven, CT: Yale University Press).

Gasper, P. 1990. 'Explanation and Scientific Realism' in Knowles 1990.

Gasper, P. 1991. 'Causation and Explanation' in Boyd *et al.* 1991.

Gentner, D., & Gentner D. R. 1983 'Flowing Waters or Teeming Crowds: Mental Models of Electricity' in Gentner & Stevens 1983.

Gentner, D. & Stevens, A. L. eds. 1983. *Mental Models* (Hillsdale, NJ: Lawrence Erlbaum Associates).

Giere, R. N. 1988. *Explaining Science* (Chicago: University of Chicago Press).

Ginet, C. 1989. 'Reasons Explanation of Action: An Incompatibilist Account' in Mele (1997), *The Philosophy of Action* (Oxford: Oxford University Press).

Goodman, N. 1954. *Fact, Fiction, and Forecast* (London: The Athlone Press).

Greeno, J. G. 1983 'Conceptual Entities' in Gentner & Stevens 1983.

Grimes, T. R. 1993. 'Explanatory Understanding and Contrastive Facts' *Philosophica* **51.**

Harman, G. 1973. *Thought* (Princeton, NJ: Princeton University Press).

Harman, G. 1986. *Change in View* (Cambridge, MA: The MIT Press).

Hegarty, M, Just, M. A., & Morrison, I. R. 1988. 'Mental Models of Mechanical Systems: Individual Differences in Qualitative and Quantitative Reasoning' *Cognitive Psychology* **20**, 191–236.

Hempel, C. G. 1942 'The Function of General Laws in History' in Hempel 1965a.

Hempel, C. G. & Oppenheim, P. 1948 'Studies in the Logic of Explanation' in Hempel 1965a.

Hempel, C. G. 1959. 'The Logic of Functional Analysis' in Hempel 1965a.

Hempel, C. G. 1965a. *Aspects of Scientific Explanation* (New York: Macmillan).

Hempel, C. G. 1965b. 'Aspects of Scientific Explanation' in Hempel 1965a.

Hesse, M. B. 1966 *Models and Analogies in Science* (Notre Dame, IN: University of Notre Dame Press).

Humphreys, P. W. 1989a. 'Scientific Explanation: The Causes, Some of the Causes, and Nothing But the Causes' in Kitcher & Salmon 1989.

Humphreys, P. W. 1989b. *The Chances of Explanation* (Princeton, NJ: Princeton University Press).

Hutchins, E. 'Understanding Micronesian Navigation' in Gentner & Stevens 1983.

Johnson-Laird, P. N. 1983. *Mental Models* (Cambridge: Cambridge University Press).

Johnson-Laird, P. N. 1989 'Mental Models' in Posner 1989.

Johnson-Laird, P. N. 1993. *Human and Machine Thinking* (Hillsdale, NJ: Lawrence Erlbaum Associates).

Kim, J. 1987. 'Explanatory Realism, Causal Realism, and Explanatory Exclusion' in Ruben 1993.

Kinoshita, J. 1990 'How do Scientific Explanations Explain?' in Knowles 1990.

Kitcher, P. 1976. 'Explanation, Causation, and Unification', *Journal of Philosophy* 1976.

Kitcher, P. 1981. 'Explanatory Unification' in Pitt, 1988.

Kitcher, P. & Salmon, W. C. 1987. 'Van Fraassen on Explanation' in Ruben 1993.

Kitcher, P. & Salmon, W. C. 1989. *Scientific Explanation* (Minnesota Studies in the Philosophy of Science, Volume XIII) (Minneapolis, MN: University of Minnesota Press).

Kitcher, P. 1989 'Explanatory Unification and the Causal Structure of the World' in Kitcher & Salmon 1989.

de Kleer, J. & Brown, J. S. 1983 'Assumptions and Ambiguities in Mechanistic Mental Models' in Gentner & Stevens 1983.

Knowles, D. ed. 1990. *Explanation and its Limits* (Cambridge: Cambridge University Press).

Larkin, J. H. 1983 'The Role of Problem Representation in Physics' in Gentner & Stevens 1983.

Lewis, D. 1986a. 'Causal Explanation' in Ruben 1993.

Lewis, D. 1986b. *Counterfactuals* (Oxford: Blackwell).

Lewis, D. 1986c. 'Causation' in *Philosophical Papers, Volume II* (Oxford: Oxford University Press).

Lipton, P. 1990. 'Contrastive Explanation' in Knowles 1990.

Lipton, P. 1991. *Inference to the Best Explanation* (London: Routledge).

Lipton, P. 1992. 'The Seductive-Nomological Model' in *Stud. Hist. Phil. Sci.*, **23**, 4, 691–698.

Lipton, P. 1993. Review of Humphreys 1989 in *International Studies in the Philosophy of Science*, **7**, 2.

Locke, J. 1975. *An Essay Concerning Human Understanding* ed. P. H. Nidditch (Oxford: Clarendon Press).

Lucas, J. R. 1993. 'The Nature of Things' (Presidential Address to the British Society for the Philosophy of Science).

Mackie, J.L. 1966. 'Counterfactuals and Causal Laws' in Butler 1966.

Mackie, J.L. 1973. *Truth, Probability and Paradox* (Oxford: Clarendon Press).

Marder, M. 1998. 'Unlocking dislocation secrets', *Nature* **391** 637–8.

Matthews, R.J. 1981. 'Explaining and Explanations' in Ruben 1993.

McCloskey, M. 'Naive Theories of Motion' in Gentner & Stevens 1983.

McMullin, E. 1978. 'Structural Explanation' in *American Philosophical Quarterley*, **15**, 2.

Medema, J.P. 1999. 'Life and Death in a FLASH' in *Nature* **398** 756–7.

Medin, D.L. & Ross, B.H. 1997 *Cognitive Psychology*, 2nd ed. (Fort Worth, TX: Harcourt Brace College Publishers).

Mill, J. S. 1843. *A System of Logic* (1973 edition, vol VII of *The Collected Works of John Stuart Mill* (University of Toronto Press)).

Minsky, M. 1985 *The Society of Mind* (London: Heinemann).

Moore, G. E. 1966. *Lectures on Philosophy* (London: George Allen & Unwin Ltd).

Newell, A. 1990 *Unified Theories of Cognition* (Cambridge, MA: Harvard University Press).

Norman, D. A. 1983 'Some Observations on Mental Models' in Gentner & Stevens 1983.

Papineau, D. 1990. 'Truth and Teleology' in Knowles 1990.

van Parijs, P. 1981. *Evolutionary Explanation in the Social Sciences* (London: Tavistock Publications).

Pitt, J. C. ed. 1988. *Theories of Explanation* (Oxford: Oxford University Press).

Plotkin, H. C. 1994. *The Nature of Knowledge* (Harmondsworth: Penguin).

Popper, K. 1957. 'The Aim of Science' in his *Objective Knowledge* (1972. Oxford: Clarendon Press).

Porphyry [1994] *Isagoge* in Spade, P. V. ed, *Five Texts on the Mediaeval Problem of Universals* (Indianapolis, IN: Hackett).

Posner, M. I., ed. 1989 *Foundations of Cognitive Science* (Cambridge, MA: The MIT Press).

Pylyshyn, Z. W. 1989 'Computing in Cognitive Science' in Posner 1989.

Railton, P. 1978. 'A Deductive-Nomological Model of Probabilistic Explanation' in Pitt, 1988.

Railton, P. 1980. *Explaining Explanation* (Ph.D. Thesis: Princeton University).

Railton, P. 1981. 'Probability, Explanation, and Information' in Ruben 1993.

Railton, P. 1989. 'Explanation and Metaphysical Controversy' in Kitcher & Salmon 1989.

Rawls, J. 1972. *A Theory of Justice* (Oxford: Clarendon Press).

Redhead, M. 1990. 'Explanation' in Knowles 1990.

Rescher. 1961. 'Belief-Contravening Suppositions and the Problem of Contrary-to-Fact Conditionals' in Sosa 1975.

Ruben, D.-H. 1990a. 'Singular Explanation and the Social Sciences' in Knowles 1990.

Ruben, D.-H. 1990b. *Explaining Explanation* (London: Routledge).

Ruben, D.-H. 1993. *Explanation* (Oxford: Oxford University Press).

Rumelhart, D. E. 1989 'The Architecture of Mind: A Connectionist Approach' in Posner 1989.

Salmon, M. H. 1989. 'Explanation in the Social Sciences' in Kitcher & Salmon, 1989.

Salmon, W. C. 1971. 'Statistical Explanation and Causality' in Pitt, 1988.

Salmon, W. C. 1984. *Scientific Explanation and the Causal Structure of the World* (Princeton, NJ: Princeton University Press).

Salmon, W. C. 1989. 'Four Decades of Scientific Explanation' in Kitcher & Salmon, 1989.

Scheffler, I. 1964. *The Anatomy of Inquiry* (London: Routledge & Kegan Paul).

Schwartz, D. L. & Black, J. B. 1996 'Shuttling Between Depictive Models and Abstract Rules: Induction and Fallback' *Cognitive Science* **20** 457–97.

Scriven, M. 1962. 'Explanations, Predictions and Laws.' in Pitt, 1988.

Sellars, W. 1958. 'Counterfactuals' in Sosa 1975.

Sellars, W. 1963. 'Theoretical Explanations' in Pitt, 1988.

Simon, H. A. & Kaplan, C. A. 1989 'Foundations of Cognitive Science' in Posner 1989.

Sintonen, M. 1989. 'Explanation: In Search of the Rationale' in Kitcher & Salmon, 1989.

Sintonen, M. 1990. 'How to Put Questions to Nature.' in Knowles 1990.

Skorupski, J. 1990. 'Explanation and Understanding in Social Science' in Knowles 1990.

Smart, J. J. C. 1990. 'Explanation-Opening Address' in Knowles 1990.

Smith, E. E. 1989 'Concepts and Induction' in Posner 1989.

Smith, J. M. 1990. 'Explanation in Biology' in Knowles 1990.

Sober, E. 1986. 'Explanatory Presupposition' *Australasian Journal of Philosophy* **64**, 2, 143–9.

Sober, E. 1990. 'Let's Razor Occam's Razor' in Knowles 1990.

Sosa, E. (ed.) 1975. *Causation and Conditionals* (Oxford: Oxford University Press).

Stalnaker, R. C. 1972. 'Pragmatics' in Martinich, A. P. (ed.) 1990. *The Philosophy of Language* (Oxford: Oxford University Press).

Stalnaker, R. C. 1968. 'A Theory of Conditionals' in Sosa 1975.

Swinburne, R. 1990. 'The Limits of Explanation' in Knowles 1990.

Thagard, P. 1996. *Mind* (Cambridge, MA: The MIT Press).

VanLehn, K. 1989 'Problem Solving and Cognitive Skill Acquisition' in Posner 1989.

Williams, M. D., Hollan, J. D., & Stevens, A. L. 1983 'Human Reasoning About a Simple Physical System' in Gentner & Stevens 1983.

Wiser, M. & Carey, S. 'When Heat and Temperature Were One' in Gentner & Stevens 1983.

Wolfson, P. R. 1994. *Geometric Explanation* (M.Phil. Thesis: Department of History and Philosophy of Science, University of Cambridge).

Woodfield, A. 1976. *Teleology* (Cambridge: Cambridge University Press).

Woodward, J. 1984. 'A Theory of Singular Causal Explanation' in Ruben 1993.

Woodward, J. 1989. 'The Causal Mechanical Model of Explanation' in Kitcher & Salmon, 1989.

Woodward, J. 1990. 'Supervenience and Singular Causal Claims' in Knowles 1990.

Woodward, J. 1994. Review of Humphreys 1989 in *Brit. J. Phil. Sci.* **45** (1994), 353–74.

von Wright, G. H. 1971 *Explanation and Understanding* (London: Routledge and Kegan Paul).

Wright, L. 1976. *Teleological Explanations* (Berkeley, California: California University Press).

Yi, Byeong-uk. 1994. 'Glymour on Explanation' in *Brit. J. Phil. Sci.* **45** (1994), 914–17.

Young, R. M. 1983 'Surrogates and Mappings: Two Kinds of Conceptual Models for Interactive Devices' in Gentner & Stevens 1983.

Index